BY BARNABY CONRAD

Fiction
DANGERFIELD
MATADOR
THE INNOCENT VILLA

Translations
THE WOUNDS OF HUNGER (Spota)
THE SECOND LIFE OF CAPTAIN CONTRERAS (Luca de Tena)

Non-Fiction
HOW TO FIGHT A BULL
ENCYCLOPEDIA OF BULLFIGHTING
TAHITI
FAMOUS LAST WORDS
SAN FRANCISCO—PROFILE IN WORDS AND PICTURES
DEATH OF MANOLETE
GATES OF FEAR
MY LIFE AS A MATADOR (Autobiography of Arruza)
LA FIESTA BRAVA
FUN WHILE IT LASTED

Fun While It Lasted

FUN

Barnaby Conrad

WHILE

IT LASTED

Illustrations by the Author

 Random House · New York

For H. H. C.

Fun While It Lasted

FOREWORD

In 1958 I WAS BADLY GORED IN EL ESCORIAL, Spain, while performing in a festival fight; the animal's horn went in nine inches, traversing the upper part of my left leg.

As I lay in critical condition in the hospital, the following dialogue took place in Sardi's restaurant in New York. It was recorded by columnist Leonard Lyons:

Eva Gabor (as she enters and sees Noel Coward at a table): "Noel dahling, have you heard the news about poor Bahnaby? He vass terribly gored in Spain!"

Noel (genuinely alarmed): "He was *what?*"

Eva: "He vass gored!"

Noel (genuinely relieved): "Thank heavens—I thought you said bored."

In spite of the name-dropping, "Gored but never bored" would not be the worst epitaph in the world; it might even serve as a subtitle for this book, wherein I recount some events of my life. It is not a real autobiography, not the whole story, just a baker's dozen of years that were good years, fun, frenetic and rewarding; as Toad of *Wind in the Willows* says, full of "Travel! Change! Excitement."

Whenever I ask myself how dare I presume to write an autobiography, I fall back on the opening paragraph of Benvenuto Cellini's:

All men of every sort, who have done anything that is meritorious, or that indeed resembles merit, ought, if they be truthful persons and of good report, to set forth their lives with their own hand: but they should not commence so noble an undertaking before they have passed the age of forty.

Now I am forty-six—it is, perhaps, high time.

These years began one sultry summer day in Mexico City in 1941 when I was nineteen—

CHAPTER 1

ON JULY 10TH OF THAT YEAR, AT FOUR-
thirty in the afternoon, a trumpet blew, the heavy
red gate banged open and into the arena pounded
an animal that was to change my life. He weighed half a
ton and he was ugly and he had horns on his head that
looked like a pair of sabers from Heidelberg. The plaque
they hung over the *toril* gate said his name was Pretty Boy.
Although I'd only seen two second-rate, dreary bullfights in
my four weeks in Mexico City, I knew that Pretty Boy was
the closest thing to the monsters I'd seen pictured in Hemingway's *Death in the Afternoon*.

The fifteen thousand people in the stands knew it too
and they applauded appreciatively. Nacho Suárez, the *novillero* who had the bad luck of having drawn this animal,
hesitantly stepped out from behind the wooden shield in
front of the opening in the fence, which is called, I had

learned, the *burladero*. The novice's face was as pale as his Aztec ancestry would permit. In a weak voice he quavered, "*Ah-hah, toro!*" He shook the big magenta cape. The animal charged across the ocher sand. Nacho flopped his cape out in a spastic parody of a verónica, his legs jittering him back out of range of the horns.

"*Fuera*," booed the crowd. Even I, untutored as I was, knew it was very bad.

Adrian Spies passed the bottle of tequila to me.

"Now," he stated solemnly.

Adrian was, like me, a summer student at the University of Mexico. Unlike me, he was fat and curly-haired and highly literate and from Brooklyn. We were studying Mexican history, painting and Spanish. I was nineteen, he was twenty-one. We had known each other at the University of North Carolina where he was editor of the literary magazine.

I took a swig of the powerful fermented juice of the maguey cactus. "Now *what?*"

"Now you go down there," he said. "You said it looked easy—you said the animal's so dumb it always goes at the cape."

"So did you."

"You swore you could do it."

I enjoyed the colorful spectacle the two times we had seen it and was not overwhelmed by the cruelty; after all, the horses were protected by padding and the bull died almost as quickly as he would have in the stockyards. It was no crueler than deer hunting, fox hunting, or the barbaric trapping of fur-bearing animals for the vanity of the women of the world. But I was also not particularly impressed with either the inherent danger or the skill that would be required to do what we'd seen toreros do.

For several days we had been talking of what fun it would be to *have* fought a bull.

"What a wonderful pose!" Adrian had said. He always talked like the characters in his current literary enthusiasm and now it was Evelyn Waugh.

"Why don't you go down if it's so easy?"

"I've got a bad ankle."

"I've got a bad knee."

"Sure, this bug is big, sure," said Adrian, "But it's a nun, a sweet pear, and it charges on rails." He'd only seen two bullfights also but he'd read everything about bullfighting, knew all the terms, and fancied himself as the classic bullfight manager ("I, Curro, say that when Juan Gallardo was born, there was salt in the air!"). He had the actor Laird Creagar's figure to go with the role, too, straight from Twentieth Century Fox's *Blood and Sand.*

Down in the arena Nacho was having serious problems coping with Pretty Boy. It seemed to me, little as I knew about it, that Adrian was right. It was a good bull; it charged straight without hooking. Nacho was not standing up to it, and by stepping back on each pass, he was encouraging the animal to swerve into his body. He could not possibly execute a decent cape pass, crouched and humped over like a cautious accountant.

The audiece was booing and throwing cushions. "*Cobarde!*" "*Sinverguenza!*" they screamed. "Coward, shameless." The bleachers' inhabitants began urinating in wine bottles and flinging them toward the matador in the arena. Some filled women's stockings with talcum powder, swung them around their heads and sailed the missiles through the air to explode on the sand or on blue serge suits in lower seats. Several piled cushions together and set fire to them, meanwhile screaming epithets at Nacho, the bullfight authorities and the President of the Republic.

"The climate is right for your presentation," said Adrian pontifically. "Descend."

"Screw you," I explained.

Yet I was trembling. I knew I might, if—if what—if I could conquer that huge hunk of fear that hung there like a stone just below the V of my rib cage. I realized then, for the first (but not the last) time that the thing about being a Hemingway hero is that it's tough, really tough, unless you're one, a hero or two, Hemingway.

"Many would be Cowards, if they had Courage enough," wrote Thomas Fuller back in 1732. I was beginning to feel my heart pound in that terrible way that meant I might not be ʾble to summon up the courage to be a coward.

I had always thought of myself as a physical coward, especially where bovines were concerned, ever since I was ten and was the only one of a dozen kids to weasel out of riding a calf at a dude ranch rodeo in Montana. How my fearless sixteen-year-old brother scoffed. (The next year he lost a leg riding in a rodeo which only confirmed my fears.) I had always been afraid of body-contact sports yet because I was tall and reasonably well-coordinated I was pressured at prep school to go out for football and felt the coach's scorn when I refused. At college I went out for freshman boxing, mainly to prove to somebody—probably my brother—that I wasn't really as scared as I was. Although elected captain of the team, I was relieved when a knee injury kept me from competing. Strangely enough, once a bout was started, my fears would diminish and I would comport myself well enough. But oh, the pre and post trembling and imaginings!

Now here I was, full of youth and tequila, sixteen rows up

in the stands of a bull ring, actually considering the ludicrous idea of going down and confronting this lethal animal with its rapier horns. If only I were to do it—boy, nobody could ever call me a coward again! The crowd cheering, the cameras clicking, the newsreels recording it all to be shown to everyone back home in San Francisco—it was a heartwarming thought. Wait till my brother hears about this! Wait till my girl, Betty, reads the papers!

Yet, arguing against this lovely fictional dream was the chilling sight of that murderous bull down there. Now he was crashing into the side of the picador's padded horse. His back legs drove hard; a horn clanged against the metal stirrup; the horse and rider were slammed back against the fence. Only the heavy leather *peto* mattress around the horse's body prevented one of those horns from disemboweling it instantly.

Could I possibly bring myself to be an *espontáneo*? I knew that aspirants sometimes jumped down into the ring in the hopes that if they performed a few good passes an impresario might give them a chance on the program of a regular bill. But, as I understood it, these were experienced youths, trained since about the age of twelve. My only taurine experience was caping a couple of cars with my raincoat. (A favorite sport of bull-conscious Mexico was simulating cape passes at the automobiles in the city streets, so much so that some cars wore stickers saying, "Please don't bullfight this car.")

And now as I watched the ring action I thought of the depressing statistics in *Death in the Afternoon*, the fatalities, the fact that something like a fourth of all major matadors since 1700 have been killed, that every professional matador expects to be gored at least once a season.

Another matador had lured the bull away from the horse

and was caping it. He was little better than Nacho and obviously terrified of the animal, too. The crowd continued to boo. Then they began yelling, "Guzmán! Guzmán!" Felix Guzmán was billed as the star of the show.

Adrian took a big pull on the bottle and passed it to me.

"Lots of toreros have jumped down and fought for the first time this way," he said encouragingly.

"And for the last, too," I muttered. I pushed the bottle away.

"Tha's right," said Adrian, "one of the first rules of bull-fighting—never fight a bull when drunk. Drunken bulls are the worst kind of all."

Liquor certainly wasn't going to help me now. As I was to hear from a great torero years later, "No hay borracho que coma lumbre"—no one gets so drunk that he eats a hot piece of coal. If I was going to do it I wanted no further handicaps than my own cowardice and ignorance.

"If you only had a cape," said Adrian.

And suddenly I knew I was going to do it.

"I've got one," I said as calmly as I could. The decision was made, I felt dizzy, the heart going, the adrenaline pumping in. I clutched my raincoat and, crouching, I went down the aisle fast. People I passed said, "Look—an espontáneo!" They could tell by the way I hid my raincoat from the ushers what I was up to. Some patted my back as I went by, much the way it is when a Death Row inhabitant makes the long last walk.

I clambered over the rail in front of the first row and dropped what seemed a long way down to the alleyway. I just missed landing on a fat banderillero. Before the startled man could grab me I had sprawled myself over the barrera fence.

I was in the ring. Oh Lord, I was in the ring! The bull was

about thirty feet away from me, about to charge another picador. It looked like the biggest animal I had ever seen, far larger than the almost aerial view I had had of it from the sixteenth row. Anyone who has ever scoffed at bullfighting should attend one from this viewpoint and watch the creature grow.

The crowd buzzed with excitement and later I learned that the announcer lost all aplomb and shouted into the microphone, "*Madre de Dios*—there's a gringo in the ring! A gringo!" (My height, Ivy League clothes and brown hair instantly revealed my nationality to the Mexicans.)

I opened my tan raincoat. Brooks Brothers had never designed the garment for this purpose; it was half the size of a real cape, and half the weight. A small breeze would have made it useless, but there was no wind this day. I wasn't worried about its not being red—I had noticed that on certain passes when the matadors flipped the cape behind their backs, the bulls charged just as hard at the yellow lining as they did the magenta side. Also the horse that the bull was now charging so enthusiastically was not red.

A brace of banderilleros were quickly sidling over toward me. I was tempted to simply let them catch me—hell, I'd tried, hadn't I? But I was too involved now; I had to give it one pass at least. I dodged the banderilleros and ran up behind the animal, yelling as I'd heard the pros do—"*Toro, ah-hah!*"—to get its attention.

The bull wheeled, and saw me. And then, incredibly, its head went down and I could hear the angry bite of its hooves in the sand. The great horns, ivory and black-tipped in the sunlight, were aimed straight at me. At *me!*

I couldn't quite believe the nightmare—like Pierre in *War and Peace* who sees the enemy forces aiming at him and thinks: "Can they be shooting at me? And why? To kill me? Me—of whom everyone is so fond?"

My first thought was that since he obviously was charging at the coat if I hid the damn thing behind me maybe he'd go away and leave me alone. I fought off that fatal impulse and offered the coat, holding it away from my body with both hands, and giving it a shake. The bull covered the ten feet separating us with unbelievable speed. I held my ground and tried to swing the cape smoothly in front of its snout. I hadn't calculated on that speed, though. The bull's right horn ripped the raincoat and almost tore it from my hands. But the horns missed me, and I felt the great bulk of its shoulders brush by me and saw the corral dust blowing off its greenish black hide.

I was still too petrified to feel any elation and too busy getting ready for the next charge. The bull had wheeled and stopped momentarily to study this new adversary in the seersucker coat and strange cape. My instinct again was to retreat, but the fence was fifteen feet away and I knew I could never outrun the bull. Remembering how Nacho had always taken steps back and given down to the bull, I screwed up all my remaining courage and took a step forward, not *toward* the bull but parallel to it, across the line of its intended charge.

It was the best thing I could have done. The bull charged hard at the lure and not at me. I swung the coat in front of its head, gauging the speed better this time. I dimly heard a cheer from the crowd as I executed something that vaguely resembled a verónica. The animal's momentum carried it six feet past me and when it wheeled around I again took a step forward. The great head dropped and it lunged forward. I swung the coat. But this time I did not follow through properly, and the bull skidded to a stop in mid-pass. It tossed its head, impaled my raincoat on its horns, and tore it from my grasp. I was defenseless. The coat hung over the animal's eyes blinding it as it tossed its head trying to rip it apart. I seized the moment to bolt for the fence on shaky legs. I slid through the *burladero* opening and took a breath for the first time in what seemed like eons. I might have collapsed had not two hard-looking uniformed policemen grabbed me roughly by the arms.

"A *la carcel*," said one, "ten days in the shade!"

I'd forgotten that there was another punishment other than the bull for *espontáneos*. Pushing, pummeling and jerking, they started me down the passageway. Then I saw one of the matadors, the one dressed in a handsome green and gold "suit of lights," take off his hat. He held it up imploringly to the *presidente* of the arena and gestured towards me. The cops stopped and looked up also. I could see the *Presidente* way up there. He waved his handkerchief and the cops let me go.

I went up to the matador. "*Gracias*," I managed to say. "*Mil gracias*."

He was a Nordic looking seventeen-year-old with brown curly hair. He was named Felix Guzmán and he was on his way to becoming the *novillero de moda*. I'd read that though born in Mexico his parents were German and Italian and his real name was Felix Beglio Schopenhauer and, it was claimed, he was a descendant of the philosopher. He looked older than seventeen, older than I, and he had a good face and a sad smile.

"You ver' brave," he said, with a slight stammer. "Consider you don' know wha' the hell you do."

I didn't feel brave. I felt faint. I hid my trembling hands behind me and hoped my face wasn't chalk white.

"Why you not come study? Learn something. Here, to-morrow morning."

His sword boy handed him his big cape. He smiled, "Well, back to work."

I returned to the stands and as I made my way to my seat there was much patting of my back, laughter, and "Muy bien, muchacho!" from the amused crowd.

Silently Adrian passed me the bottle. I noticed his hand was trembling almost as much as mine.

"I was scared," I said as I drank.

"Me, too."

"You can't imagine what it's like out there."

"As my old father used to say: 'Fly an airplane when you're not scared, it's nothing, and not fly an airplane when you're scared, it's nothing.'" He was a little drunk now. "'But to fly an airplane when you're scared—that's something.'"

Nacho somehow managed to dispatch Pretty Boy, and I felt a pang when the big bull keeled over; we had shared some special moments out there, he and I. And he'd been nice and not killed me as I deserved.

But now another bull skidded into the arena, and Felix Guzmán was ready for it. Without even waiting to see how it charged he ran into the ring, slid to his knees, and flung the cape out in front of him.

"A larga cambiada!" Adrian exclaimed.

Holding the cape by one corner Felix stayed motionless as the animal bore down on him. When the bull was six feet away Felix swung the cape from right to left over his head in one languid, unruffled, fluid, sure movement, the yellow side flipping over, the cloth sailing gracefully around his body and guiding the hurtling bull past his shoulder. A kinetic painting in yellow and black and magenta and green and gold, it was breathtakingly beautiful—at once death-defying and as aesthetic as any ballet maneuver. Involuntarily, a roar was wrenched from me along with fifteen thousand other people. I had immediately been struck by the color and pageantry of *"la fiesta brava,"* as Adrian insisted on calling it, but I had never until that moment appreciated just how profoundly it could move one, simply because I had never seen an artist in the arena before. Berenson's yardstick for any work of art was "Is it life-enhancing?" Strange as it sounds applied to such a lethal spectacle, what I had just witnessed was life-enhancing.

Now he was on his feet executing verónicas, and I was glad I had seen Nacho do them badly for now we were seeing how the basic pass should be done. Where Nacho leaned over at the waist and bent at the knees, Felix stood straight, back arched, knees locked. Where Nacho flopped the cape in front of the bull, Felix floated it—offering it casually and swinging it elegantly, almost gently, just in front of the great head of the charging animal. The bull followed the folds of the cloth as though its nose were sewed to the hem. Where Nacho preened and postured and acted independently of the bull, Felix seemed to be saying, "Look at us—look what a beautiful thing *we* are doing out here!"

He ended the series with a half verónica that turned the bull in its tracks, left it "fixed" in place, and was as lyrical as a poem by Lorca. The crowd cheered him as loudly as they had booed Nacho. Adrian thumped me on the back—this was a little more like it, a little closer to the bill of goods Hemingway had sold us.

With the banderillas he was a gold and green bird. He loped and serpentined in close to the bull, planted the barbed sticks in the withers, and easily spun away to safety. With the muleta, the red serge cloth draped over a stick and spread with the sword, he worked in so close to the horns that it seemed impossible that he wouldn't get hooked. And, after a dozen hair-raising passes, it happened. The horn ripped up his gold pants and flung him into the air as the crowd screamed; they had come to see a man risk his life, to see him *almost*, but not actually, gored. He fell to the sand and lay there inert. His banderilleros were there in a flash, dazzling and distracting the bull. Felix scrambled to his feet. He looked down at the rip down his thigh—we could see the torn braid, the white long underwear, the bare flesh of one buttock and a red scratch. His mouth went down at the corners scornfully to signify that it was nothing, and he went back to the bull. He gave it five more thrilling passes. Then he lifted the sword, sighted down the blade and flung himself over the bull's horns. The sword went into the withers up to the hilt. The bull hesitated at the end of the charge, coughed twice, and crashed over on its side, its dead eyes crossed and one back leg twitching.

"Fantastic," I said, too stunned by this performance and too weary from my own exploit to applaud.

"I told you!" shrieked Adrian, as though he had seen hundreds of corridas of this caliber.

Felix was awarded both ears and the tail of the animal and happily circled the arena with the trophies in his hands as the crowd went wild. He threw an ear up to someone and Adrian kept signaling for him to throw us the other, but he didn't see us.

"I'm going to learn how to do that," I said.

That night, as I lay in my bed in the drab room of the Mexican family's house where I boarded, I thought about it. I had had a tentative date with Ofelia, a strange but bewitching Mexican girl, but I totally forgot her, caught up as I was with this new obsession. I was a little sore in several parts of my body from spilling over the barrera, from the unaccustomed movements with the bull, from the rough handling of the cops. But I felt good.

I doubt that many firsts can compare with one's first encounter with a bull. From just those few ludicrous moments with the bull I somehow knew I'd already learned more about bullfighting than Adrian ever would with all his reading. I rehashed my every second in the arena. In retrospect, what a thrill it had been when that half a ton of black muscle had been persuaded by a piece of cloth not to hit me! How wonderful it would be to be so technicaly skilled and sure of oneself that the moment could be savored at the time. Was it pure sport and art, or was there an element of what the psychiatrist, Otto Fenichel, called "the counter-phobic attitude"?

"It will generally hold true that the essential joy in sport is that one actively brings about in play certain tensions which were formerly feared, so that one may enjoy the fact that now one can overcome them without fearing them."

It really didn't matter a damn what the reasons were. That which I had feared I no longer feared, or so I thought.

This night I resolved that I would become a torero, a good torero, and I trembled at the resolve. There came to me graphic visions of myself being espaliered across monstrous horns, of the subsequent telegrams to a mourning family, of the small but tasteful funeral, followed by a short but heartfelt paragraph in the Class of '40 notes of the *Taft Alumni Bulletin*. But no matter—I was committed.

How had I arrived at this decision? How came I by the situation in which I now found myself? Little in my background would shed any clues.

Being born (in 1922) in San Francisco and reared in conservative Hillsborough was not the conventional route to the *plaza de toros*. Hillsborough (or Burlingame, as the old-time residents are careful to refer to it in order to show that they are old-time residents) is a state of mind twenty miles down the Peninsula from San Francisco, bordering the authentic little town of Burlingame. Hillsborough was then one of the richest residential districts in the world, a Palm Beach on hills. We were one of the first thirty or so families to build there, and though our house was large and staffed we were not all that rich. The wealth around us, however, was old money and staggering. I attended a small day school created by these families, and of the forty or so children, I can think of only two or three who didn't arrive by a chauffeur-driven car generally accompanied by a governess.

Though normally a trouble-free child, I remember that one rainy day when I was twelve, our chauffeur had to come and take me home in disgrace. I had found a steep bank of delicious molten mud flowing lava-like down its side, and on a dare from my best friend, Nion Tucker, I took a running leap and slid down it. I ended up looking like a creature from the deep lagoon, and as I was led away to the car by the principal, I saw the prettiest little girl in the lower school looking at me with fascination and disapproval in her serious face.

"I'm going to marry that girl someday," Nion had said.

"No you're not," I answered. "I am."

Nion would be killed on Iwo Jima; I would live to fulfill my boyhood boast.

Those years were easy for us, considering nearly everyone else in America was racked by the Depression. My father's investment banking firm suffered big losses, and his partner committed suicide, but it seemed to affect our way of life very little. Our activities centered around the elegant Burlingame Country Club and the pools and tennis courts of our friends. Occasionally we would venture down to Burlingame Avenue, pick up girls at Ladd's drugstore and "buzz the Ave." in an older boy's Terraplane or Model A.

It was the innocent era of cherry phosphates, "Arf says Sandy" on the Atwater-Kent, "and now, Mrs. Pettibone, if you *please!*," mah-jongg, Captain Billy's Whiz-Bang, Ouija boards, croquet and white flannels with blue blazers.

On weekends there were always guests of various ages, mint juleps and welsh rarebit on the patio overlooking the oak trees in the canyon, paddle-tennis games on the lawn and swimming races in the pool. A ukulele and/or piano was always being played—if not by me, by my mother or a guest —and the music carried through the French doors out across the hundred yards of lawn to the swimming pool. One day my brother brought home a charming brash young Armenian named William Saroyan who was quite willing to tell everyone he had just written a great story called *The Man on the Flying Trapeze* and that he would soon be acclaimed one of America's finest writers. At one point, full of exuberance and beer, I jumped into the swimming pool with all my clothes on.

"Look at that crazy kid," my brother said angrily, looking back at the porch to see if our parents had observed it.

"Not at all," said Saroyan, "he did exactly what he wanted to do exactly at the moment he wanted to do it!" And with a joyous shout he followed me into the pool dressed in his one suit and the ski boots he used to affect in those days.

In spite of my exploits my mother claimed I was not wild —just impulsive. One day, for example, when I was fifteen, my pretty cousin Joan and I went down to the pier in San

Francisco to see some friends off to Honolulu on a Matson liner. At noon the "All ashore" was called but I said let's stowaway; and we did. We danced most of that night, then found an empty stateroom. The next afternoon we were discovered and kicked off the ship at Los Angeles. Her father, Admiral Wilkinson, was not amused and her mother less so when the escapade hit the San Francisco papers.

Every summer we would go for three months to a ranch in Big Timber, Montana, which was run by childhood friends of my parents and which accepted thirty guests. All of us were good horsemen but my brother Hunt was the best and when he was seventeen he was hired by the ranch as a wrangler. That summer he entered the big annual Fourth of July rodeo at Livingston and in one race his horse slammed into another and his left leg was crushed. He developed osteomylitis and almost died. He was too sick to be moved for several months. I attended a rural school in Big Timber where there were only two other students. I would ride bareback five miles over the snowy ground to the typical little schoolhouse, be taught by one of the cowboys' wives, and play with the pet coyote that slept in front of the potbellied stove. Finally, Hunt was able to be moved by train back to Burlingame, but he was forced to spend some fourteen months in the hospital. When he was able to get around on crutches, his first thought was to get in some fishing in British Columbia. One evening as he made his way to a lake, he tripped and fell and broke his leg again. He lay there for nine hours before help came. This time the doctors amputated.

He was fitted with an artificial leg and to raise his spirits my father gave us two thousand dollars and told us to take a trip to Honolulu. Hunt was nineteen and I was fourteen and we rented a grand suite at the Royal Hawaiian. We took

Jack Morgan, the prototype of wranglers,
taught me how to ride anything
and everything.

a couple of Oahu's most attractive debutantes in tow and between the deep-sea fishing and the elaborate parties we gave, the money lasted almost ten days before we had to wire our father for more.

But I was not essentially a playboy. I was too busy painting or sculpting or raising racing pigeons or taxiderming or playing the piano or guitar or reading. I took lessons in art and became a good enough artist to earn a gabardine suit from the fanciest apparel shop in Burlingame, Gates Brothers, in exchange for a Hawaiian motif mural. When I was sixteen I did the murals in San Francisco's most popular night club at the time, the Tahitian Hut.

Our life in that sequestered world was highly privileged, and it has gone forever, for better or for worse. Now the chauffeurs in Hillsborough are few and far between, the great estates broken up into tracts, and the Country School is a Catholic seminary. Our beautiful Normandy-style house at 1049 San Raymundo has new owners. It looks today almost as it did then, but now it is on two acres, not six. The rest of the land has been parceled off; now two small houses occupy the space that used to be reserved for my brother's kennels and the fifteen dogs he raised.

Across the wooded canyon one can still see where Stewart Edward White lived. He was a best-selling author and adventurer, having been a pioneer in Alaska and one of the first men to go big-game hunting in Africa armed only with bow and arrow. He and his wife were my parents' best friends, and when I was about fifteen I used to take advantage of their friendship by calling on him in "The Ark." This was his studio, a building separate from the house which contained his trophies. He had a full-sized giraffe and an entire pride of lions installed there among other fascinating memorabilia from Africa. By the door was a leaping leopard which had attacked one of his bearers. Though quiet and reticent, Stewart one day told me about it—how he had pulled the big cat off the man and strangled it. And he showed me the marks on his neck where the claws had ripped his flesh and sent him to the hospital for six weeks.

His house and his profession and his mind were an endless fascination to me. I remember that one year he had ten huge live rattlesnakes in a herpetarium. Once, for my birthday, Stewart gave me a pair of two-foot-long alligators which subsequently got away; six years later his wife came across one in the canyon, by then six feet long, and she fed it regularly until some boys stoned it to death.

My friend Mike Macauley from the estate next to ours used to accompany me on my forays up the canyon when we hunted deer and rabbits with bow and arrow, pretending to be on safari. (To our relief, we never hit either a deer or a rabbit.)

Perhaps Stewart kindled in me the desire to be a writer and to try some paths other than those leading to the country club and the commuter's train. The summer I was fourteen I worked in my father's office as an office boy while he and my mother went to Alaska in the Whites' yacht. I didn't like it. The following two summers I went to art school at the California School of Fine Arts in San Francisco, which I did like.

Although we usually ate with the servants in a separate dining room as was the custom then, my mother and father were concerned, tolerant and understanding parents. Whatever I took up they encouraged, offering me lessons. I was given lessons in puppetry, guitar, boat building, wood carving, skeet shooting and calf roping, to name a few. My father must have had a solid streak of adventure in him. I remember his coming home from the office one afternoon when I was eleven and saying, "Let's go to Panama tomorrow—just you and I!" And off we went the next day on a wonderful two-week cruise on a United Fruit banana boat. Born to a Rhode Island woman of wealthy merchant antecedents and a father who left the family for his mining, cattle and political ambitions in Montana, he was brought up in England. But after attending Yale he headed for Montana and the wilds of Saskatchewan where he had various experiences ranching and as a surveyor before marrying my mother. During the last year of World War One he was a flyer in the fledgling U.S. Naval Air Corps. Until he was incapacitated by a horse accident, he was athletic and an outdoorsman. My earliest memories of him are of his carrying me on his back across a roaring trout stream, of his doing a front flip as he ran across the lawn in his bathing suit, of playing polo dressed in an African pith helmet and jodhpurs with the cowboys in Montana. From the time I was eight we would start out every morning before breakfast with a boxing session in his dressing room. He was small, and at twelve I was large for my age; I was horrified when one day I connected with a left hook and knocked him out. He complimented me when he came to, but thereafter the sessions dwindled off.

My mother came from a long line of statesmen—more later of my lineage, which includes a figure in a classic murder case, a pirate and a President of the United States. She was born in Helena, Montana, where her father had been assigned as a federal judge. During his stint as governor of Puerto Rico my mother would spend her summers with the Theodore Roosevelts in the White House. An amateur actress and writer, she was a handsome, vivacious woman who

My father

was active in San Francisco's cultural life, especially music. She played and sang everything, from madrigals to the current "No Matter How Young a Prune May Be, It's Always Full of Wrinkles." She held frequent musicales and string quartet recitals, and after bedtime I would sneak downstairs in my pajamas and listen to them. She played piano duets, worked for charities and won golf tournaments at The Club. (Now over eighty, she can still place a full glass of water on her forehead, lie down on the floor and get up without spilling a drop.) Outgoing, talkative and unfailingly gay, she was always sympathetic to whatever project my brother and I might take an interest in.

But bullfighting? Would they ever understand how I'd gotten myself into this? Would I?

It seemed the morning would never come. I caped a hundred bulls that night and slept little. Had I known what was in store for me—and poor Felix—I wouldn't have slept at all.

CHAPTER 2

SINCE I NO LONGER OWNED A RAINCOAT I could not actually cape the automobiles that I encountered on my way to the bull ring. But I pretended to cape them, swinging my hands in front of the fender, trying for some of that grace and insouciance that Felix had demonstrated the day before.

Adrian came with me, though we both had classes that we should have been attending if we wanted credits for the summer session. Especially I, since I was hoping to transfer to Yale. But somehow, reading *Platero y Yo* ("the lovable little donkey") in beginning Spanish, studying the philosophy of Ortega y Gasset, learning Yucatán folk dances, and painting still lifes seemed very tame stuff and far removed from real living now.

We arrived at the bull ring, called El Toreo, at nine. It was quite a different place than the boisterous setting of yesterday afternoon. Empty of the crowds and the band and the noise and the danger it seemed a quiet, attractive refuge. When we told the gateman that we had an appointment with Felix Guzmán, he touched his cap and quickly opened the iron grill gate. We went down a tunnel and came out in the *callejón* passage that runs around the ring between the stands and the fence. Two boys were practicing capework in the arena. They were Indian brown and dressed in bathing suits. They were about eighteen and one youth had two jagged white scars on his inner leg. He was practicing cape passes while his companion charged him holding a pair of large horns fitted on the ends of a rolling-pin-shaped piece of wood. I learned later that they were Carlos "Cañitas" and Eduardo Liceaga, two promising *novilleros*. (The former would ultimately sacrifice a leg to the bulls, the latter his life.) They paid no attention to us and we wandered down the alleyway. We went through a large archway that led to the corrals. We looked through the big slots of the cement wall and saw the bulls for next Sunday's fight. Some were lying down, some eating, some quietly ambling around the big enclosure. Two lazily locked horns and fenced halfheartedly, good-naturedly. They all acted like ordinary domestic cattle. It was hard to believe that these were the same fierce breed we had seen yesterday. A large sign stenciled on the wall said, "It is prohibited to talk to the bulls or molest them."

Adrian clapped his hands twice. Immediately the scene changed. The animals all looked at us, every fiber suddenly on the alert. The ones lying down got up, the others snorted, some pawing the ground. The hump of tossing muscle behind their horns was suddenly swollen; they were ready to kill anything that came near them. It made me quiver just to look at them and I was grateful for the three-foot-thick walls that separated us.

Had I really confronted such a beast? Yes I had, for it was mentioned—very briefly—in the morning newspaper and I had the clipping to prove it. There was also a fine write-up and many photos of Felix, proclaiming him *"El Nuevo As"*—The New Star. I cut them out for a scrapbook I was going to start.

We remained still, and the animals calmed down and went about their business. Adrian and I moved on and looked in at the garish little chapel where the toreros prayed. Next to it was the infirmary with its modern operating equipment.

"Matadors don't eat the day of a fight," said Adrian, "so they can be operated on right away case something goes wrong."

We walked down the tunnel where the bullfighters gathered before making the parade. I wondered how I'd feel waiting there on a Sunday at four in the afternoon, the band blaring, the crowd expectant. There were some more bullfighters in the arena now, but Felix wasn't among them. We took off our jackets and sat down in the sun on the white *estribo* board—the stirrup board that ran around the inside of the red fence. I had brought my copy of *Death in the Afternoon* with me, in the naïve hope of getting the autographs of some of the Spanish stars mentioned by Hemingway—maybe Cagancho, or Domingo Ortega or even the great Belmonte. I didn't yet know that, first of all, those millionaire stars, Mexican or Spanish, wouldn't be training here with a bunch of aspirant urchins; they'd be on their own great estates working out in their private little bull rings, playing jai alai in their own courts or out in the fields caping some of their own animals. And secondly, it was summer and the top stars were in Spain for the big season there; Mexico's didn't start until November. These toreros we were watching were just *novilleros*, or would-be *novilleros* —not amateurs but professional novices, equivalent to preliminary boxers, waiting for the experience and breaks that would boost them into the front ranks, the main eventers.

Yet they looked very expert to me as they manipulated those big capes with grace and ease; it was hard to see how the stars could do it much better, just the way the local club champion tennis player looks great—until coming up against even a third-rate pro.

Felix finally arrived. He was dressed in a pair of green slacks, two-tone shoes, a sports shirt, and the golf-style cap that many of the other young toreros affected. Out of costume, he seemed so much shorter than yesterday. He wore dark glasses and a cluster of gold religious medallions around his neck. His sword boy—not a boy, but an older man— followed carrying capes. The aspirants all looked up with respect. Some called, "*Mucho, Felix!*" and some patted him on the back; yesterday he had achieved the triumph that everyone of them was yearning and striving for and which some would never see because of ineptitude or lack of courage, or injury or death.

"*Gracias,*" said Felix, and I could see his gold tooth flash in the sunlight as he smiled. He saw us and we were flattered that he left his friends to come over.

"Hola, gringo," he said and held out his hand. "How goes it? I bet you don't sleep much last night."

I introduced him to Adrian, then told him my name.

"You have a ridiculous name for a torero," he said. "Almost as bad as Schopenhauer. I will call you Bernabé."

He had very little English and my Spanish was adequate after a freshman course at college, so we spoke in Spanish.

He saw the book and took it from me. He leafed through, studying those pictures with the marvelous captions, the best captions since Goya's for his *Disasters of War* series of etchings. Every once in a while he would come to a shot of a torero doing something that particularly impressed him and he would show it to me and shake his head over the beauty or the danger of it.

"Belmonte," he would say. "The best! He invented what all of us toreros since do. And look here—Joselito—what grace, eh? He was killed before I was born. But Pepe here"— he pointed to the wizened little man in a beret with a monkey face who stood off at a distance holding Felix's cape—"he's from Madrid. He saw Joselito's last fight in Talavera."

"Ay!" The little man suddenly clutched his abdomen as though he'd been ripped open by a horn—"He tried to push his intestines back in. They were only bulging out a little—" he carefully measured how much, one index finger with the other. "It wasn't really a fatal wound—the doctors said he died of the shock of seeing himself wounded. He had begun to believe he was immortal, the way we all had."

Pepe smiled a simian smile, pleased with his graphic narrative. Felix listened seriously. When would this happen to *him*? Where was *his* Bailador right now? A calf on some ranch—or over there in the corral of this bull ring?

He turned to me. "You still want to do this thing, Gringo?"

"I'd like to give it a try."

"Lots of work," he said.

I nodded.

He said in English, "You be sorry!"

"Tell me what mistakes I made yesterday."

"Well," he said with his good grin, "the first mistake was going in the ring at all."

"Besides that?"

"Everything. Except when you crossed with him. How did you know to do that?"

"Lucky guess."

"Maybe you have instincts." He sat down on the estribo board. He took a pencil from his shirt pocket and with the eraser end drew a circle in the sand.

"What you don't know is placement. If the bull is going to pass, well, everything depends on where you place yourself in relationship to him. You know why you got in trouble on that last pass? First, you stopped your cape halfway through the pass—"

"No follow through," I said, thinking of golf and tennis.

"Right. This game is just like jai alai, any sport. You got to run that cloth. As long as your arms can reach. But the other reason"—he drew an X in the circle—"You are here, the bull is here, the fence is here. When he charged he was heading straight for the fence—too close. He's not dumb— he doesn't want to hit a solid fence; he would have pulled up short even if you had followed through."

"What about my capework?"

He grinned. "You ever see my grandmother hang out shirts on the wash line?"

He stood up, extended his arm, snapped his fingers and Pepe instantly had a cape in his hand. Felix went through a few frightful passes with the cape.

"I am sorry—that is how you looked. First learn how to hold it."

He handed me the cape, showed me how to grab it, about a foot and a half on each side of the collar. It was so heavy! He stood in back of me, his hands grasping my wrists, like a golf pro.

"Stand profiled—hold the left high and out in front like a boxer. Now, here comes the bull—drop your left— no, no—don't move your right yet—drop your left down until it gets even with your right. Now! Move both hands together—together!—waist high—as far as you can reach— lead that bull by!"

I tried it alone.

"No, no! You're jerking the cape. Smooth, smooth! Your knees are bent. Your back isn't arched. Your chin's way up in the air; drop your chin down on your chest as you follow through with your upper body."

He pushed me back against the fence. "Try it without ungluing your back from the boards."

I swung the cape.

"Again," Felix commanded. "And again."

After I had swung the cape a dozen times he let me rest. Strange that such a simple maneuver proved to be so exhausting on forearms, back muscles and even thighs and calves. But that was it—it wasn't so simple; it merely looked simple when Felix did it. He made every maneuver, with or without a bull, look easy.

"Now do it away from the fence," he ordered.

I did better. But I still had a tendency to insert a funny sort of sway and dip that had no place in a verónica. Felix sat on the sand behind me and held my knees rigid for several passes. Little by little, I corrected it. After an hour's practice he called: "Hey, Chucho—over here!"

A sober-faced boy of about thirteen interrupted his charge against the cape of another aspirant.

"Si, Matador?" he said, trotting over.

"Be a good bull," Felix said. "No tricks today."

The boy gave a little salute of understanding. He crouched over and held up the horns in front of his head. He positioned himself ten feet away.

He pawed the ground and shook the horns menacingly. I waited with the cape held in readiness, my hands like a boxer's, the left high and extended, the right as though protecting my chin.

"He won't charge," I said.

"Talk to it," Felix said. "He is paid to behave at all times like a real bull."

"Ah-hah, toro!" I said.

The "bull" pawed again.

"Shake the cape when you talk to it—get it to associate the annoyance of your voice with the movement."

"Ah-hah toro!"

The boy charged, and I swung the cape. I was so busy gauging the speed of the charge that the dip came back in my legs. Felix turned to Adrian in exasperation. "Am I going to have to tie splints on his legs?"

I swore to myself I wouldn't do it again. The boy wheeled at the end of the charge, giving a remarkably accurate imitation of the way a real bull would try to correct the impetus of its momentum to get back at its adversary, tossing its horns and skidding on the sand. I cited the boy for another charge. Again he was reluctant to charge.

"Cross with him, hombre," called Felix. "Cross, talk, and shake at the same time!"

I took a big step forward—parallel to the boy—at the same time shaking the cloth and shouting "Toro!"

This time I concentrated on style and started an acceptable verónica.

"Olé!" Felix cheered.

But he spoke too soon, for I hadn't gauged the speed right. I swung the cape too slowly, the "bull" overran it, deliberately stepping on it and thus jerking it from my hands. I was defenseless. Felix, with a cape in one hand, ran between me and the boy before he could charge. Flopping it in front of the horns, Felix lured him away so I could pick up my cape.

"Your speed was right for later in the fight," Felix said. "But when the bull first comes in the ring he's faster than a race horse. The boy did right."

I cited again. This time I took special care to start my swing long before the horns got to the cloth. I thought I was doing everything perfectly. Halfway through the pass I suddenly felt something crash into my legs. I was knocked back to the sand. The horns were jabbing at my body. I tried to roll away from the sharp points. The boy kept following me and jabbing me hard each time I rolled. Finally, Felix's cape lured the torment away, and I got to my feet shakily.

"I thought you said he was supposed to be a good bull," I muttered as I wiped my face with my sleeve.

Felix helped dust me off. "He is acting as any normal bull would. That is what we pay him for. We want to make our mistakes with him—he only weighs one hundred pounds, not a thousand."

"So what did I do wrong this time?"

"First, you swung the cape so fast, so far in front of its horns, that it ran out of target. There was suddenly nothing for a bull to charge at near him."

"Except my legs."

"That is what a bull would go for if it didn't have a tantalizing cape just out of reach in front of its head. You must swing the cape neither too fast nor too slow. Like driving in traffic—you've got to gear yourself to the speed of the car in front or there will be an accident. Only here one of the two parties very much desires the accident. Another thing—" he lay down on the sand—"when you get knocked down and the bull is near, don't try to roll the way you did. You'd never make it. A bull will go at anything that moves. So don't move. Lie on your face, lie *dead*, with your face buried in your arms to protect your eyes. He will smell you, maybe try a jab or two, but by that time the banderilleros will be there to attract him away. You have enough for today?"

"Whatever you say," I said, but I was relieved when Felix flipped Chucho a fifty centavo piece.

"*Gracias*," the boy said, as he caught it. "*Hasta mañana!*" and trotted off to practice his unique profession with another aspirant.

"Maybe I am too hard on you the first day," Felix said. "Come—I buy you a beer at The Tupi."

I was tired and sweaty and sore. The only reason the horns hadn't punctured my skin was the lack of weight of the wielder. It was harder than I had ever expected, this torero business. And it would get a lot harder.

"A beer sounds good," I said, as I put on my jacket and picked up my copy of *Death in the Afternoon*.

I had heard of The Tupinamba. James M. Cain wrote about it in his novel *Serenade*: "The place was pretty full, with bullfight managers, agents, newspaper men, pimps, cops and almost everybody you can think of, except somebody you would trust with your watch . . ."

It was a good description. The Tupinamba was actually a cold, dirty cafeteria at 44 Bolívar Street; people were its only attraction, its only decoration. There were no bulls' heads or even posters. It was then I made a mental note to someday create a place that looked the way a bullfighter's hangout ought to look. (It would be some eight years before I could carry out the idea.) But in 1941 in Mexico City, the Tupinamba was where all the toreros went to have a *bizcocho* and coffee and to talk about how great they'd been in the provinces or needle their managers for not getting them a fight in the capital all season or boast what they would do in Spain next year or show off after a successful fight.

Felix, his star in ascendance, was a good guide for us. People came over to his table rather than the other way around, which is the way toreros like it. He made a point of introducing us to everyone with much protocol. I was very appreciative of Felix's friendship and wondered why he was being so kind. Perhaps, aside from our obvious admiration for him and his profession, we were a novelty for him. Although already a hero to every Mexican urchin, we were probably his first international fans.

Throughout lunch various newspaper men, promoters, would-be managers, and veteran banderilleros looking for jobs, came up to him. It was amazing to see how these much older men deferred to a youth, barely turned seventeen, simply because he had on two or three occasions publicly manipulated a piece of cloth in the face of a bull with grace and courage. This, of course, is one of the great attractions of bullfighting; virtually overnight a poor and unknown youth can become a star. Even I, in a ridiculous way, had become somebody: Felix could introduce me as "the *espontáneo* of yesterday" and that would produce a laugh and a warm handshake. It was Adrian, not I, who finally asked him in his bad Spanish how he thought I had done in today's practice session.

Felix shrugged and said bluntly but not unkindly, "What can I say? He learned today what every *chamaco* over ten in Mexico can do better. We will wait and see. Meanwhile, you should buy some equipment."

Above Felix's protestations, I paid for lunch. It was obvious that although he was on his way to big money, he was still quite a distance from it. He also had a mother and siblings to support. I, with an allowance of one hundred American dollars per month from my parents, and my board paid, was in a far more secure economic condition.

We followed Felix out of the restaurant. After walking for blocks, we went through a huge market place—it seemed a mile long—with tents and awnings and hundreds of costumed Indians and their naked children selling every conceivable kind of food and ware. It was like a vast primitive jungle world. (In such a market I had accidentally bumped into Adrian three weeks before without even knowing he was in Mexico. He had feigned no surprise at seeing me, merely extending his hand as he Doctor Livingstoned me.)

We finally came to an adobe hovel in an appallingly grubby part of town near where Felix lived. The dirt floor was crowded with half-dressed children of various ages but all with runny noses and big black eyes and solemn stares. Carlitos welcomed us. He was a *novillero*, badly gored twice, and at twenty-six too old with no chance of taking the alternative, of graduating to full matador; he was selling his things. It was touching the way the prematurely balding young man fondled the capes and muleta and one costume.

One of the gorings had been in his right eye, and he wore a black octagonal patch over it, crudely made of coarse cloth.

The fact that even a patch for a blind eye had to be made at home impressed me with his poverty even more than the squalid surroundings he lived in. And he was no poorer than many, or even most of the Mexican youths who strive to become bullfighters.

As Carlitos handled the tools of his trade that he loved and had to give up, a tear seeped out obscenely from under the black patch. (Or was it merely sweat from the sauna-like heat?) His wrinkled mother was crying with relief and joy that her son was getting out of this dangerous profession. She was the cliché bullfighter's mother, pitiful in the corner, a black rebozo over her head, fingering the silver cross that hung from her neck, alternately saying prayers, smiling and crying as we bargained over the capes that her family had scrimped and saved to buy for her son, he who such a short time ago had sworn to lift them out of this miserable poverty with these artifacts.

I bought a *capote*, the big cape, for thirty-five dollars, which seemed expensive to me, but which Felix said was a bargain. Ten dollars bought a muleta cape and the wooden practice sword which is used to spread the small cape until the time to kill. It is used rather than the heavy steel sword because of the strain of holding the latter. Carlitos had a real sword but Felix assured me it would be a long time before I would be ready to use one.

Felix showed me how to fold the *capote*; holding it up by the *esclavina* collar with his left hand, he took a corner of the heavy cape with his right, and giving a sudden snap brought the opposite corner also into his right fingers. Then the two corners were snapped to the collar, the cape was dropped on the floor and one more fold made it a compact flat rectangle. More and more I was beginning to see that there was a right way and a stylish way to do everything connected with *la fiesta brava,* no matter how minor a maneuver it might appear to be.

Carlitos held up his sparkling silver and blue suit of lights by its hanger. Any rips had been mended, and any bloodstains removed and the sequins polished (with bread, I was to learn later) so that they shone even in the dim light of the hovel. "What about this, Felix?" he mumbled. "What will you give me for it?"

Felix shook his head.

"It was made by Manfredi in Sevilla," Carlitos urged.

Felix snorted, fingered the costume, and examined the lining. "Manfredi never even saw that suit. Maybe your sister copied it from a Manfredi suit."

Carlitos hung his head. I thought Felix was being strangely cruel and unsympathetic to a fellow *novillero.* But this was a dog-eat-dog world that I could not possibly comprehend with my soft background. I was tempted to buy the suit.

"What for?" Felix asked sharply, "a costume party? Wait till you earn the right to wear it. Then get a good one."

I soon learned that while usually kind and gentle, Felix was hard and uncompromising wherever it concerned his profession.

When we left, Adrian said, "Hemingway could have made something out of that scene."

"Do all toreros come from that sort of background?" I asked Felix tactlessly.

He gave a rueful smile. "You should see where I came from."

He said he had to visit his manager, so we shook hands with him.

"See you same time tomorrow at the workshop," said

Felix, "And do your homework. Tomorrow we will really sweat."

"When do I try what I've learned?"

"With a bull?"

"Yes."

He laughed. "You are impatient. It is not so easy to find bulls. Not like learning to be a boxer where it's easy to find opponents, where you just go out and punch someone in the nose. Bulls are expensive. But we will see."

We said good-by. Adrian offered to buy a beer at Sanborn's, the tourists' mecca; we were not so Mexicanfied as we had thought, and it would be good to wash away the poverty with a Carta Blanca in more familiar and hygienic surroundings. To get there we had to go through a red light district. Some streets were five-peso streets, others twenty, and the quality of the girls on the sidewalks varied accordingly. We came to one section where the girls were comparatively pretty and persuasive. Some bold ones actually made low grabs at us and then laughed brassily.

At Sanborn's we ordered beer and looked around the attractive blue-tiled room at the pretty, scrubbed, tweedy tourist women writing their postcards home. But the girls we'd seen on the streets were still on our minds, as was the knowledge that we could have any one of them for little more than the price of the beers we were drinking. Perhaps I would have checked the action on that street if I had not met Ofelia.

CHAPTER 3

I HAD MET HER UNDER SOMEWHAT ROMANTIC circumstances and being an incurable romanticist, I imbued her with all manner of attributes which, now, I'm not at all sure she possessed.

I had hitchhiked into Mexico City four weeks earlier from San Francisco. It had taken me a week and I arrived in this unfamiliar city at ten o'clock at night in a ferocious downpour. My last ride from Guadalajara had dropped me and my suitcase off at a corner where it suited him. I dashed for the first shelter I saw, which was a drug store. I had two dollars in my pocket. But I knew that money was waiting for me at the University of Mexico, where I was expected for the opening of the summer session in the morning. I asked the druggist where I could find a decent inexpensive hotel and he told me of one a few blocks away. But the rain was flooding down, so I waited for a cab. Also waiting under the awning was a small, pert American-looking woman of about thirty. She was well dressed in a blue suit with a little mink hat on her blond head. A cab pulled up and I gestured to it. "Yours," I said.

"Were you not here before me?" she asked in her soft Spanish.

"No," I said.

She smiled gratefully and got in. Then she leaned out and said, "*Libres* are hard to get—he can drop you where you are going after me."

I got in. She spoke not a word of English. She asked me where I was from. I understood everything she said but classroom Spanish and conversational Spanish are two different things, and I found I wasn't as fluent as I thought. But I did all right, and when we got to her house I screwed up my courage and told her I was hungry and would she do me the honor of joining me for dinner. She hesitated. Then she gave her tinkly laugh, and said, "*Porqué no?*"

She suggested El Coconut Grove nearby. It was a penthouse night club affair and not exactly the local color I was expecting or seeking. There was a tired *mariachi* show, a magician, and a dance floor. I held Ofelia tight as we danced and she seemed to respond.

She asked me how old I was. "Twenty-five," I lied. I asked her how old she was and she said, "Guess," and I said, "About thirty," and she looked shocked and said, "No, only twenty-six."

The check came for ten dollars and I only had two. But I assured her I would pay her back in the morning and she cheerily paid the check. She invited me into her flat for a drink and told me something about herself. Her name was Ofelia Escobar Booth—and she said she had been married a couple of years to an American named Bunny Booth. She owned and operated a chain of doggie diners like the Pam-Pams in Paris, all called Bunny after her divorced husband. She had a Bunny in Monterrey, Morelia, Guadalajara, Acapulco and three Bunnys in Mexico City.

Somehow I had hoped for a more exotic romance when I had set out for Mexico; a dark-eyed señorita with a mantilla, long black hair, a fan, and the daughter of a marqués would have done. I hadn't figured on getting tied up with the Queen of Mexican hot dogs.

She said it was late and I could sleep on her couch. I accepted. Several times during the night I tried to invade her bedroom but she artfully put me off every time. I also was requested to leave early the next morning for some reason that was unexplained. I was pushed out the door at seven.

Four weeks later I was still no closer to garnering the favors of *"la reina de los perros calientes,"* as I called her. Nevertheless, the promise was always there. I saw a great deal of her, she was a pleasant companion, and I learned Spanish fast.

She appeared to know a lot about bullfighting, knew exactly what part of the bull ring to take me to for practice sessions, and I accused her of having had a torero for a lover. She denied it but was evasive as to how she came by her knowledge. It was a long time before I found out.

After a while Adrian didn't come to the bull ring with me; he had other interests—he was involved in Mexican history, Aztec ruins, and cathedrals. I was interested in just two things now: bullfighting and art, and the latter only when it concerned the former.

Ofelia gave me a commuter-type kiss as she delivered me with my cape and muleta to the bull ring for my next lesson and drove off to a Bunny's to count the hot dogs, or whatever she did there. The gate man knew me now and gave me a cheery "*Buenos días.*" I went down the tunnel and saw Felix already in the arena. He was running backwards. He ran around the entire ring backwards as fast as most people run forwards. Then he practiced vaulting the fence. How gracefully he did even that! He would run at the fence as though being pursued by a bull, place one hand on the top of the high fence and sail over easily with his feet together.

He saw me and came over panting.

"Remember this, Bernabé," he said solemnly, "A matador must never, never run." He winked. "But he knows *how* to run."

Felix whistled for Chucho and the boy trotted over dutifully. He touched his finger to his forehead in greeting to me. Then he bent over, wagged the horns, pawed the ground and prepared to charge.

I executed a verónica.

"Not bad," said Felix, "but arch that body *into* the horns, not away from them. People go to the *plaza de toros* to see a man behave exactly the opposite of the way they'd behave if they were down in the ring."

I did another, and another.

"That's it—maximize the danger, don't minimize it. Let the horn come closer to your leg on each pass. It shouldn't be more than three or four inches away on the last one."

I began to realize that bullfighting is like going off a thirty-foot diving platform. To go off it at all takes some courage. But a person could do a cannonball and thus survive, if that's all he cared about. But a cannonball is neither aesthetic nor much fun to watch. If a person dove straight in with feet and hands together, that would take more courage and be prettier to see. And if a master did a flip, a layout and then entered the water like a knife blade, that could be a thrilling experience to watch. The verónica, I realized, was similar to a swan dive; anyone can simulate the basic maneuver off the side of a swimming pool. But to do it from a high platform with perfect form requires skill, training and courage. The other cape passes were equivalent in complexity and danger to the more intricate dives such as a jackknife, triple flip and so forth.

Felix called: "Try a half-verónica."

I gathered the cloth up on my hip, and the "bull" followed it around my body and pulled up short.

"Now look at it over your off shoulder and stride away."

"With my back turned?" I protested. I didn't trust that little devil with the horns.

"The bull won't charge if you walk slowly away. He's winded, he's been jerked up short and he feels he's won the battle for a little while when he sees you retreat."

I walked ten feet away and stood with my back to the bull.

"Just don't make any sudden movement with the cape and he won't charge."

Then he began to show me the basics of the muleta, saying, "No matter how great a man is with the cape he will never get anywhere if he can't work this thing."

It was just a red serge rag, really, with a two-foot stick screw-eyed into it for a handle. Yet when Felix spread it wide with the wooden sword and swung it in front of Chucho's horns what a magical thing it became! I thought of Hemingway: "It is impossible to believe the emotional and spiritual intensity, and pure, classic beauty that can be produced by a man, an animal and a piece of scarlet serge draped over a stick."

The techniques were quite different than with the cape,

and in the next hour I was knocked down three times by Chucho for mistakes. But I finally caught on and was performing adequately when the lesson came to an end.

"You have a feel for the muleta that you don't with the cape," said Felix. Then he added casually, "How soon do you think you'll be ready to try what you've learned on a real bull?"

I could feel my heart skip a beat. "When do you think?"

"If you work hard the rest of the week I think I can line up one for you on Saturday."

I was scared the whole time. It was worse than when I jumped in the arena as an *espontáneo*, for now I knew too much about the dangers. Also I was scared of performing badly after all Felix's work and confidence.

On Wednesday we went into a new phase of my training.

"You have been fighting only perfect bulls," Felix said, "bulls which if you did everything right would also do everything right. Unfortunately, they seldom come out like that except in one's dreams. The bull on Saturday will undoubtedly be defective in some way."

He called Chucho over and gave him instructions.

Before the week was over, Chucho had brought forth his whole repertory of defective bulls, some blind in one eye, some shortsighted, some who put on the brakes in the middle of a pass, some who stared only at the man's body and had to be persuaded to go at the muleta by every means possible. It was good training, and I stayed at it for hours every day. Then Felix and I would go to the Tupinamba and sometimes Adrian would join us for lunch. Ofelia always seemed to be unable to come, though I would invite her regularly.

After lunch, I would work on the murals in a little Hungarian restaurant on Insurgentes Boulevard. My pay was limitless free dinners, and I imagine that the paintings—bullfighting scenes, of course—were very bad. But then, so were the dinners.

An unexpected thrill for me was the afternoon when Felix took me to the studio of Ruano Llopis, the artist. Almost every painter of bullfighting has been influenced by his splashy colorful impressionistic action scenes. He started in Spain as a poster artist and created a style that has become traditional for bullfight posters, and is still being aped by lesser artists in Mexico and Spain. Today his paintings command fortunes, but he was far from unappreciated even before his death in 1951. Bullfighting seems to have inspired more bad paintings than any other human activity, but an exception was the work of this gruff, wrinkled Valencian who had come to Mexico after their Civil War. "Spain is my mother," he told me, "but Mexico is my mistress."

Great sun-filled, action-crammed canvases were arrayed around the room. The bulls seemed enormous and exaggerated, but he assured me that was the way they were in Spain. I had brought some paintings of mine for him to criticize, and criticize them he did. He was as merciless as Felix was about my capework. But I learned from him. And he asked me to come back the next day, that he would have something for me. What he gave me were two watercolors, both of the great Mexican matador, Armillita, doing cape passes. They are still prize possessions. And as an extra fillip he had Armillita himself there to autograph them. This was the first full matador I had ever met and I looked upon his brown chinless face with something akin to reverence. He was mentioned in *Death in the Afternoon*, and he signed the book graciously and with a big toothy smile.

He had seen Felix's last performance, congratulated him and said he'd heard of the *mano-a-mano* coming up next Sunday.

"Maestro," said Felix, "I would like to dedicate a bull to you."

"I shall be honored," said Armillita. "But be careful— Cañitas is a spoiler. He has more experience than you—don't let him push you into doing foolish things."

Ofelia was worried about my fighting on Saturday. "It is too soon," she kept saying.

Preying on her sympathy, I asked if I could spend the night—perhaps my last night—with her.

No, she said, her little boy, Nacho, was coming.

I had still not met or seen him. "I've heard the name, Nacho," I said. "Is it common?"

"It is short for Ignacio," she said, evasively.

"Why doesn't he live with you?" I asked.

"I am too busy with the Bunnys," she said, and changed the subject.

But I finally talked her into going away with me to Taxco. We took a balconied room in a little hotel on the side of the mountain in this, the most picturesque town of Mexico. We arrived at six and I ordered a bottle of champagne, the first I'd ever ordered. I twirled it in a bucket of ice on the porch, while she repaired to take a shower. I was nervous. She emerged in fifteen minutes with a towel wrapped around her waist. I had not quite realized what a superb figure she had. Large breasts for a small girl and a body like a teen-ager. I got over my nervousness soon.

It was an hour later that I finally got the bottle of champagne opened. We never did get out to get dinner, and there was no room service, but there were no complaints from either of us. It was all quite blissful and worth the waiting for.

The next morning, however, I was starved. But I couldn't eat breakfast. It was Saturday, and I was to fight this afternoon. If something went wrong and I had to be operated on, it was better not to have a full stomach.

We drove back to Mexico City in contented silence. A strange calm had come over me compared with the nervousness I had felt for the week I had spent thinking about this encounter. Ofelia refused to watch—"I could not stand it, mi amor." But she offered me her car.

Felix was waiting at the bull ring at noon. He was at the entrance with Pepe, the sword boy carrying various capes, including mine. He also had along a young man named Juan, who had a professional looking camera slung from his neck.

"Isn't this Ofelia Booth's car?" Felix asked.

"I didn't know you knew her," I said.

"She's Nacho's mother," he said.

"Nacho?"

Felix pointed down at the arena where Nacho Suárez, the novillero who I had first seen fighting Pretty Boy, was practicing. He was tall, dark and about twenty-three.

"You remember him," said Felix.

"Yes," I answered weakly.

It was almost impossible to believe. But a lot of things suddenly made sense.

I brooded on this revelation as we drove out of the city and for many days afterward. But, to my credit, I never told Ofelia of my startling discovery.

We drove for about an hour in the country and finally came to a series of corrals.

"You mean—we're going to fight *here?*" I said, as we got out.

"Why not?"

I had expected some sort of a bull ring, no matter how small, not a dusty corral.

Felix clapped me on the back. "Make your mistakes with no audience—better that way."

A grizzled foreman greeted us dressed like a charro with the traditional Pancho Villa-type sombrero. He carried a pistol which, Felix told me, he was empowered to use against any aspirants who tried caping any of the bulls on the hacienda. (Since bulls were worth almost a thousand dollars, and a cape-wise bull should not be sent to a bull ring, he was merely protecting valuable property.) I could see herds of the beautiful black animals in the distant field.

The foreman removed his hat as he approached us. "Matador, I am forced to tell you that Don Luis was obliged to sell the bull he was going to let you cape. It was needed for a *pachanga* in Chilpancingo."

I found that I was tenser than I realized when I experienced a great sense of relief at the thought that the thing was called off.

"*Mierda!*" said Felix. "You mean we've come out here for nothing?"

"I have one bull," said the foreman. "In the first corral."

We climbed up the slats of the high fence and looked down in the big corral.

"That's a bull?" snorted Felix.

The foreman shrugged. "It's all I've got, matador. He's got some good blood in him."

"He keeps it well hidden," said Felix.

It was a very strange looking beast. The horns were not large, but they were sharp. It was not black like the beauties in the meadows. It was kind of a dirty gruel beige. It had a very tight small scrotum. This was reassuring.

"Good," I thought, "Perhaps it's a nice calm steer."

I was glad he couldn't see how tight and small mine was.

The creature was not small, but on the other hand it was not bulky like a real bull. It did not have the huge hump of tossing muscle with which Pretty Boy had been endowed. There was a tubercular look about the animal. Weeks—months—years—of green manure caked its stern.

On the whole, it looked like something that would be worshipped in India, and I took heart. I lost heart shortly: "Who's going first," I asked.

Felix shook his head. "I'm not going to fight. I don't like its looks. You understand?"

I wasn't sure I did.

"I can't take a chance of getting hurt—a lot is riding on tomorrow's fight for me. I'll double him for you, though."

Fine, I thought. My second encounter with a live animal is going to be with a bull that one of the top *novilleros* in the world is scared to fight.

"Take the muleta first," Felix instructed. "Leave the cape for later."

Pepe handed him a cape and me my muleta and a wooden sword.

"Ready?" Felix called.

"Any time." I tried to say it casually, the way Gary Cooper might offer his opponent in the village street the first opportunity to draw his pistol.

"Sure you want to do this?" he asked. It was a rhetorical

question, rather like asking a bridegroom at the church door if he wants to go through with it. I was committed. I nodded.

Felix jumped down into the corral.

"*Torito!*" he called. The bull charged instantly. Felix trailed the cape with one hand, crouched over and with bent knees, with no attempt at style, merely performing the functional role of a banderillero so I could see which horn was the most dangerous. As far as I could see, it hooked equally as unfairly on both sides.

After four charges Felix ran to the fence and climbed up the heavy slats.

"The left horn's worse than the right."

Comforting thought. I got the muleta adjusted in my hand and jumped down. I walked towards the animal. It pawed and studied me. Felix had told me that any bull that paws the ground is cowardly, that a truly brave bull charges with no warning theatrics. A cowardly bull is a dangerous bull.

"*Toro!*" I chanted, shaking the muleta.

It wagged its horns and pawed and looked straight at my legs, not the cloth.

"Cross with him!" called Felix.

I took a step out across the line of charge, shaking the muleta and saying "*Toro!*" in as commanding a tone as I could muster.

"Again!" called Felix.

This time the animal dropped its head and charged. I held my ground and moved the muleta at the correct tempo in front of the animal's horns. I kept my knees locked, arched my back, and tried to "run the hand" as smoothly and as far as I could.

Felix and the others called out, "*Olé!*" and it was a sweet sound.

The bull wheeled and I managed to remember that this was his bad side. As the animal charged, I slid my feet back out of the way, holding the muleta far from my body, and it was good that I did because the horn chopped in where my legs had been.

"Good—good," Felix called encouragingly. "Keep it up!"

I did several more passes, trying things that I had done with Chucho in training sessions. Only once did I get in real trouble and that was when I thought the animal was in control enough for me to try to pass it more closely on the left side. It hooked and slammed me back with the side of the horn, its milky hide brushing against my body. I had to retreat hastily, but I went back to it and made a good pass on its right side. Then I withdrew to the fence for a breather.

"I think I'll try the big cape," I said.

"All right," Felix said. "But watch it. You've already had just about all the clear passes this animal owns."

Pepe handed me the big cape. I adjusted it in my hands. I had to take the first pass on the animal's bad side because that's the way he was facing (and I was careful to always keep my back to the fence). But I took him by me wide and there was no problem. On the return pass I let him come in close and swung the cape as smoothly as I could.

Another "Olé!" from the gallery rewarded me.

Three more verónicas and I was gaining confidence with every one.

It worked! If you did what you'd been taught, it worked! And what a thrill it was to control this ugly beast and do it in a graceful and dignified manner. How different this was from my afternoon as an espontáneo when survival was the only factor and style and art was not even attempted.

"La media!" Felix was shouting jubilantly—"finish with a half-verónica!"

The animal charged for a final time, and I started as though for a regular verónica. The moment the horn passed my legs I gathered the cape up on my hip. The bull swerved off its course, wrenching itself around in its pursuit of the folds. Then it pulled up abruptly and stayed there fixed, just as Chucho had done so often.

With my cape folded, I strode away from the animal, my back to it, with the confidence that hours of practice had given to me. I stopped ten feet away from the animal and grinned up at Felix sitting on the fence.

"How was that, Maestro?"

"Not bad," said Felix. "Not bad." Then, ever the perfectionist, he added, "But you're still holding your hands too high. Hold them lower."

Without thinking, I shook open the cape, saying, "How low—this low?"

I saw it in Felix's face.

"*Cuidado!*" he yelled. "Look out!"

I whirled. The bull, attracted by the movement of the cape had lunged forward. It was too late to run. I futilely flared out the cape, but he was on a dead course at my legs and nothing short of a grenade would have made him swerve. I could only stand and watch it happen. The horns went on either side of my right knee and the great skull cracked into my leg with a sound like a popping log in a fireplace. I felt myself flung up into the air, felt the hardness of the horns and tried to grab them to keep them from going into my body. Then I was slammed to the ground. I lay face down, inert, my face in my arms the way I'd been taught, but waiting for a horn to go in me.

I could actually feel the creature's breath on me and then something smacked hard against the fingers of my right hand. I knew the animal had broken them on the hard dirt. I expected the next jab in the back.

But Felix had leaped off the fence with no cape and yelling, "Toro, Toro!," he dashed the ten feet to where I lay. The bull lifted its head, looked at the new antagonist, and then went back to me. Before it could gore, though, Felix had darted between me and the animal, slapping it hard across the snout as he did. The bull veered after Felix as he sprinted toward the other end of the corral.

I started to get up, found I couldn't stand on my right leg, and sat back on the ground. I tried to crawl to the fence. Pepe and the photographer reached me and dragged me to the fence. I rolled to safety under the bottom slat just as the bull came back for me after a fruitless chase of Felix. The horns banged against the fence repeatedly in frustration.

I lay there dazed for a while, trying to assess the damage. Three fingers in my right hand were broken, I had no doubt of that. My leg didn't work right, but I didn't think it could be broken.

They helped me to the car and stretched me out on the back seat and we started back to town.

"Do you know a doctor?" Felix asked.

I didn't.

"We can't take you to the bullfighters' hospital," he said. "They let you bleed to death right on the steps if you're not a member of the association."

Dr. Rojas was a good doctor, but his small clinic did not even have an X-ray. Nevertheless, he gave me a shot of something that killed some of the pain, splinted my fingers expertly, and bandaged my knee firmly between boards, which at least caused it to stop aching so much. He urged me to get my knee X-rayed and refused any pay, saying it was an honor for him "to treat my first *cornada* case."

In an hour I was able to walk out on crutches though every step was a painful and cautious one. I was driven back to Ofelia's place, and there I kept my bruised body in bed and basked in her tender care and ministrations until the next day. The callow youth suddenly had become the venerated, wounded gladiator; scarred, battered, and delighted to be pampered.

It was Sunday, Felix's big fight, and I had to see it. Adrian had been in Acapulco and hence was forced to miss my brief hour of glory, if that's what it was, in the corral. He came by for me and we went to the big arena together.

Negotiating the steep aisles was not easy on crutches, but Felix had given us two good tickets close to the front row.

It started out to be a great corrida.

The senior matador, Cañitas, performed with the first bull. It was not a good animal, skittish and unpredictable and head-tossing. But because of his long experience he knew just how to fight it. It was not the kind of beast to show off one's fanciest capework, but he fought it intelligently and killed well. The crowd booed the dead bull, as it was dragged out (a custom I found bizarre until I realized it was the way to express disapproval to the bull breeder; since he has had a card file on every animal he breeds since birth, he theoretically can assess the kind of performance the animal is likely to offer). The audience applauded Cañitas as he took a lap around the ring.

Felix drew a smallish pinto animal that charged straight and true. He unfurled all his fancy cape passes to a constant ovation. Then he placed three superb pairs of banderillas that were models of how it should be done. He dedicated the death of the bull to Armillita and after a long and varied and brilliant *faena* he prepared to kill. The blade hit the shoulder bone and flew out. The audience groaned with disappointment. But he quickly retrieved the sword, ran straight at the animal, and sunk the sword in. The animal made two more charges, then fell over dead.

He was awarded both ears of the animal and ran happily around the ring. He tossed the ears up to us and we felt we were the envy of the people around us.

Cañitas was out to triumph today. As his slit Indian eyes watched the *toril* gate open, one could almost hear him praying to the Virgin of Guadalupe: "Make it a half decent bull and I'll stand the audience on its ears!"

It was a great bull. Cañitas ran eagerly out from behind the *burladero* and slid to his knees from where he did a series of *verónicas*. From then on, there was pandemonium in the *plaza de toros*. And when Cañitas killed the bull with one clean thrust it was clear that he would be awarded both ears and the tail. The audience insisted that he take three laps around the arena.

Felix congratulated Cañitas. But his jaw was set and his eyes were grim and he kept changing the grip on his cape nervously. It was obvious that he was going to show Cañitas exactly who the new king of the *novilleros* was, even if it killed him. I was wet with perspiration as the trumpet blew.

Even before the *toril* gate was opened Felix was running out into the arena. He ran up in front of the *toril* and fifteen feet from it he slid to his knees. He flipped the cape out in front of him, holding it by one corner for the *larga cambiada*, the same pass he'd done so beautifully that first time we saw him perform.

The rope on the latch of the gate was jerked and the door was pulled open. Nothing happened for several long seconds.

Felix Guzmán

Then a great black shape came hesitantly out of the tunnel. I'd never seen a bull *stroll* into a ring before. It stood there confusedly for a moment.

"*Toro!*" yelled Felix, shaking the cape.

The bull looked around him for the voice. It was obvious that the animal had defective vision, and hence was very dangerous. But Felix was committed to this pass—he could not get off his knees now without losing face.

"*Toro!*" he yelled frantically.

The bull finally saw him. It lowered its head and charged hard. When the horns were about seven feet away, Felix commenced his swing, flipping the cape over his head perfectly. But the animal didn't respond to the cape movement. It kept coming straight on blindly. As the audience screamed, the left horn caught Felix high on the chest. He was slammed back ten feet away and lay there on his back, rigid, completely unconscious, his chest bloody. The banderilleros lured the animal away and Felix was carried from the arena. Head dangling, he was rushed down the alleyway to the infirmary.

Adrian and I left the stands. Because I knew the guards now, we were permitted to go back around the infirmary. We didn't go in but a nurse appeared at the door. She said that Felix had a broken clavicle and a three-inch wound, but was not critically injured.

We caught a cab and headed for Sanborn's and a drink. I was in a deep depression.

"I'm going to get out of this crummy country," I said.

"You can't blame Mexico," Adrian said.

"The hell I can't," I said.

The next day I had a letter from my mother saying that I was accepted at Yale. It was a lucky break; the University had rarely, if ever, accepted transfer students. I suppose the fact that my father, and other forebears had gone there helped my cause. Over the past two dozen months I had received several letters from Charlottesville, Virginia, from my 90-odd-year-old grandfather regarding Yale. He was Judge William H. Hunt, a stately wonderful man who seemed of a generation even older than the one he did belong to. The first Governor of Puerto Rico, he knew every President of the United States personally, except one (and I do not remember which was the omission) from Abraham Lincoln to Truman. Nine when he was hoisted upon Lincoln's knee he subsequently helped hang out crepe on the front door of their Washington residence after Booth killed him. My grandfather used to casually tell me of knowing a man who had known George Washington. This still astounds me; one tends to forget how young this country is. My grandmother's great-great-great-grandmother was Martha Dandridge Custis Washington.*

My mother put great store by her ancestry and never tired of talking about it. She still does. At the table, she would explain repeatedly how we were related to whom, using pieces of the silverware to represent relatives. "Now, this spoon here is my father's father who was Secretary of the Navy under Garfield, that fork over there is Abel P. Upshur, my mother's great-uncle who was both Secretary of the Navy and Secretary of State, and this knife here is Robert E. Lee who . . ."

---

* When Princess Margaret visited San Francisco in 1966, I was invited to a small dinner in her honor. "You have a very English name," she said when we met. "Are you English?"

"No, Ma'm," I replied, "but my sixth great-grandmother was. Then she married a lieutenant colonel and soon after became an American. His name was George Washington."

"Oh," she said, as only the British can say that word.

It was useless for my brother Hunt and me to point out to her just how many direct ancestors one has—four grandparents, eight great-grandparents, sixteen great-great-grandparents and so on. In just the twentieth generation back around 1300 A.D., one would have more than a million grandparents!

Hunt and I were far prouder of a pirate ancestor who operated in the Caribbean, with the wonderful name of Philander Beadle. Or the fact that our great-great-grandmother Eliza Custis, granddaughter of Martha Washington, married Thomas Law, first cousin of the Bounty's mutineer Fletcher Christian. Or the horrendous murder of our great-grandmother, rich old Mrs. Jerothumel Bowers Barnaby, by her lover-physician (with the novelistic name of T. Thatcher Graves) who sent her a bottle of poisoned whiskey. The crime was solved by the clever sleuthing of my father's father, the murdered woman's son-in-law, and the case is frequently rehashed in magazines and compilations of classic American crimes.

Nevertheless, I couldn't completely ignore the more conservative traditions of my family, even far off in Mexico and immersed in pursuits that would be totally un-understandable to my family.

In one letter my grandfather had written in his antique script:

Dear Boy: Remember, your great-grandfather was a Yale man a *hundred* years ago and during the century between 1840 and 1940 there have been many of your forebears enrolled at Yale. When my roommate, President Taft, was a freshman at Yale he showed me a letter from his father in which his father said that it was a great privilege to be able to go to Yale and that he wished his sons to reflect upon that and to show their appreciation by study-

My mother

ing hard so as to profit by their opportunities. Bill Taft did profit by the chance; so did all the Taft boys.

The letters, and the weight of tradition helped me decide to leave Mexico as soon as I could. I made a plane reservation for the next day. I'd had Mexico all of a sudden. I'd had bullfighting. Or bullfighting had had me. I no longer found it life-enhancing.

I went to see Felix in the hospital. He was pale and despondent. The newspapers with photos of the goring were around him.

"Think of how many fights this has cost me," he said, tapping his bandaged shoulder. "And you—look what I did to you by letting you fight that impersonation of a bull."

"My own stupidity," I said.

"This is my first goring," he said morosely. "They say a man sheds his brave blood first. How will I do when I face the horns again, still feeling the clammy rubber gloves of these doctors on me?"

"You will do fine," I said.

I told him I was leaving Mexico. He nodded but said sadly, "Come back. You are my only gringo friend."

I tried to cheer him up but there was no way to do it. I left him staring at the ceiling.*

My love affair with Mexico and my love affair with Ofelia dwindled simultaneously. It was time for us to return to our own very different worlds. Now there was a need of a world of men for me (as Browning said in his poem about the weekend love affair). My thoughts were suddenly on Yale, my peers, a career, my role in the war that inevitably would involve the United States.

* He went back to the ring with some success, married, and had a child. But in 1943 he was killed by the bull "Reventón"; gored through the back.

Adrian and Ofelia saw me off at the airport. (I was on a cane now and getting about reasonably well but I still knew my leg needed X-rays and perhaps an operation.) Ofelia shed an appropriate tear and we kissed good-by. Adrian wished me luck at Yale and we agreed we'd meet again when we were both rich and famous.

The first hint of trouble with the airliner was after we landed at Mazatlán. I felt the right wheel grab as the plane taxied across the field, and said something about it to the stewardess. But we continued to Hermosillo. Again that periodic jerk of braking on the right side as we taxied. The plane was held up for an hour for mechanical repair and when we took off for Burbank it seemed all right.

I had decided to stop at Los Angeles to see Betty Layne for a day instead of going directly home to San Francisco. It would be good to see her after so many months. We had met and fallen in love when I was at prep school at Taft in Watertown, Connecticut, and she was at nearby St. Margaret's. Since then I had had other girls, but I always came back to Betty. For twenty years I would keep coming back to her.

I felt sorry for her waiting at the airport an extra hour and hoped she had checked the arrival time before leaving her father's house to meet me.

The plane started its descent and everything seemed normal as the Burbank runway slid in front of us. But the moment our wheels touched, the right wheel locked rigidly. With a great roar we skidded across the runway, the right wing up and the left wing down, scraping over the concrete. People in the plane screamed as the plane spun, tearing off the wing and catapulting us off the runway.

After what seemed a long time, we came to a bruising, jolting stop with the remaining wing pointed down into a forty-foot gully. The plane hung over it, precariously. Someone jerked open the emergency door but it was a long drop to the bottom of the gully. For the first time the Captain spoke, advising everyone to remain calm and in his seat.

It was hard to remain calm when the threat of fire was in everyone's mind, but the fifty or so passengers did. One little man near me even cracked a joke: "Folks, I'm a lawyer!"

Finally, the fire trucks arrived and ladders were put up from the gully. Firemen climbed up and came down the aisles. First they removed the inert form of the co-pilot whose head had been split open. Then in orderly procession we were helped down the ladder. Before we were all out a fire burst from the tail but the firemen quickly controlled it. None of the passengers was seriously injured though we were all badly shaken. I looked for Betty as we drove up to the terminal in airline cars and buses. She wasn't there. I was limping for the bar on my cane when I saw her come in. Tweedy, tall, long brown hair streaked with sun-blond strands, she was the prettiest thing I had ever seen.

"Darling!" she said as she put her tanned face against mine. "They said they expected you much later."

"Did you see the plane crash?" I asked.

"No," she said, wrinkling her brow exaggeratedly. "I think I'd have remembered if I had." She saw the cane. "You're hurt!"

"I'll tell you about that too," I said. "I need a drink—badly."

"Poor darling," she said, putting her arm through mine. "Did you have a good time otherwise?"

"It was," I said weakly, leaning on my cane and starting for the bar, "quite a summer."

Benito

CHAPTER 4

STRANGE. WHEN I THINK OF YALE MY FIRST thought is of Benito. Even now I get a visceral pang when I think of the loss of my parrot. To understand, one would have to have known Benito Juárez.

The year before, when I was attending the University of North Carolina, I had hitchhiked from Chapel Hill down to Miami, and from there had bummed a ride on a freighter to Havana. I stayed at the first decent hotel I came to, happened to talk to the owner's pretty daughter in the lobby (Chichi is all of her name that I remember), and asked her if she'd walk around and show me the sights. As we wandered we came to a little pet shop and went in to see the monkeys. Past the tropical fish and near the coati-mundi was a cage containing a green parrot. I had not thought much about parrots one way or another in my life, but I was immediately taken by this one. Not at all the typical Polly-want-a-cracker creature, he was small and sleek, with a long tail—smaller than a pigeon but larger than a parakeet. He was a deep green with a bluish head and iridescent red cheeks and when he opened his wings I could see that the undersides were scarlet. He screaked at me several times and fluttered his wings for attention. I started to put my hand up to the cage and the shop owner warned:

"Be careful, those little devils can take a piece out of you!"

But I put my hand up to the bars anyway, and all he did was open his beak and touch my fingers with his little blunt tongue. In a little while I opened the cage and he hopped out on my hand and ran up my arm. On my shoulder he nuzzled my cheek and gently nibbled my ear lobe. Even the owner was amazed. "Never seen one tame up so fast, and he just came from the jungle, too."

I wanted to buy him, but the price was sixteen dollars, and I had only fifteen with which to get back to North Carolina. I played with him for a while longer, then reluctantly put him back in the cage. But for the next few hours I kept thinking about the bird, the way he had chirped (disconsolately, it had seemed to me) when I put him back in the cage. Finally, just before the boat left I ran back to the shop and offered my watch to the owner for the parrot.

"The watch and five dollars," he countered. It was a deal, and I left the shop elatedly with Benito Juárez, as I named him instantly (for no good reason).

I soon found out that Benito didn't need to stay in his cage. Although he could fly like a—well, like a bird—he would sit happily on my shoulder, and if he did take off for a little fluttering flight he would always return to my shoulder (and always the left shoulder for some reason). I jettisoned the cage over the side of the boat and smuggled Benito into Florida in my coat pocket, since I heard that there was a restriction on parrots because of fear of the disease, psittacosis.

Hitchhiking back to Chapel Hill was a lot easier than it had been going down. I would see a car coming down the highway, launch Benito into the air, and as he circled over my head and then returned to my shoulder I would waggle my extended thumb. Intrigued, the driver would stop more often than not.

Back at college I used to take Benito to classes, where he sat quietly on my shoulder throughout. A great favorite with everyone, my botany teacher sighed, "Conrad, if you were only as smart as that bird," and my English teacher said, "Teach him to say 'Hail to thee, Blithe Spirit, bird thou never wert' and I'll give you an automatic A-plus for the year."

But Benito was a lover, not a talker, except for "I love you" and "pretty boy," plus all sorts of affectionate gurgles and whistles which sounded as if they would be complete and intelligent, perhaps even profound, sentences had they not been unintelligible. He had extraordinary hearing. If for some reason I left him at home at the boarding house, I would whistle when more than a hundred yards away and his ecstatic answers would come back immediately.

He had a sense of humor. In the evenings when I would study he would sometimes lie on his back, take my pen in his feet, and chin himself several times, faster and faster. Then he would look over at me and chortle—it was nothing less. Whenever he would bring me my eraser from across the desk I would have to pretend to erase something or he would nudge my fingers until I did. He liked to fly to my bureau, pick up any coins there, drop them over the side and cackle when they hit the floor.

He was unfailingly cheerful (except for the time he drank

too much beer at a fraternity party, passed out, and had a horrendous hangover). He had many tricks but I did not teach them to him; rather he would teach them to me, little by little. He had one where he would lie on his back in my cupped hands with his feet together, his wings folded. He would chirp three times and on the third chirp I would toss him up in the air, his stiff body would do a somersault and he would light back on my hands without having opened his wings. He would also roll over on command and when held by his feet would play "dead bird," wings dangling, eyes closed, limp.

He was my constant companion. Once I was described in a school publication as "a tall, prematurely balding chap identifiable by a bit of bird lime on the left shoulder of his seersucker." (A calumny, since Benito was toilet trained early.)

While he generally rode on my shoulder, he sometimes preferred to ride inside my breast pocket, just his head and shoulders sticking out like a green handkerchief, his feet hooked over the side, his beady bright eyes taking in the passing world delightedly.

Once he gave me a bad scare. I had a part in the campus musical, singing and playing the piano in a comic number, dressed as a coed. The director thought it would be an added absurd touch to have Benito on my shoulder as I walked down the aisle to the stage. The night of the dress rehearsal, however, when the band broke out and the spotlights suddenly stabbed out, Benito gave a frightened screech, leaped off my shoulder and flew out an open window into the night. For hours I searched for him, calling him in the darkness, and finally had to give up. I got up at dawn the next morning and roamed the campus whistling and staring up into every tree, dreading the thought of finding a cat-torn carcass on the grass. I had to go to classes but spent my noon hour in what now seemed a hopeless search. After my last class I walked home sadly calling and whistling half-heartedly, not minding that I probably appeared certifiable to the passers-by. Suddenly, from a distant tall tree I heard an answering whistle, and there he was in the air, a green and scarlet streak gliding down toward me for a landing on my shoulder.

Six months later, in California, he gave me an even worse scare. I used to take him with me to the Burlingame Country Club where he could fly around the golf course to his heart's content. It was perfectly safe there, I thought. But one morning, as I watched him circling happily at a hundred feet, there suddenly appeared a dark brown shape in the sky high above him. It was a huge red-tailed hawk, and it folded its wings and dove down out of the sun like a bomber making a run on a Piper Cub. I yelled in horror, but Benito had already seen death hurtling at him with talons extended. In his fright, he literally tumbled over backwards in the air, and the attacker's momentum caused it to miss the target. The hawk pulled up and wheeled for another dive. Benito was closer to a clump of eucalyptus than he was to me, and he set his sights on that, his wings flapping frantically, zigging and zagging, screeching pathetically and traveling faster than any other Cuban parrot had ever traveled before, the hawk right on his tail. With only inches to spare Benito disappeared into the dark safety of a maze of branches. The hawk veered away and flapped off in search of less exotic fare. But it was an hour before I could entice the badly shaken Benito down to my shoulder, and when he leaned limply against my neck, I swear he said something that sounded like "Phew!"

Transferred to Yale, I didn't know what my living set-up would be and whether birds would be welcome so I went to New Haven leaving Benito in California to be sent on by mother. It turned out that a parrot would not be amiss in my "college," Timothy Dwight, and I immediately wrote my mother to send Benito on. A few days later she wired saying that Benito was on his way.

I awaited him eagerly. It seemed that the Railway Express was taking forever. Then one afternoon a strange man appeared at my room and I was sure he was bringing me my mascot. But instead he showed me his credentials from the Connecticut Board of Health. He was red-faced, smelled of yesterday's bourbon, wore thick glasses and was trying to be very official.

"You own this parrot down at the railway station?"

I nodded and something about the man's manner sent a chill through me.

"Sign here," he said, "we got to confiscate it. No parrots allowed in Connecticut. New York, Massachusetts and so forth okay, but not in this state.

"Why did the express company accept the consignment, then?" I protested.

He shrugged. "Didn't bother to look up the rules, I guess. Got to take him to Hartford, Health Department Extermination Lab."

"But he hasn't any disease," I said, my voice quavering. "I've had him a long time, he's perfectly healthy."

The man shook his head. "Rules say we got to exterminate all parrots in the state."

"How about a short quarantine?" I pleaded.

I couldn't keep the tears from showing and the man was embarrassed. "Just doing my duty," he said.

"But we could send him back where he came from," I said weakly, "not even take him out of the box."

The man shook his head. "Rules is rules," he said, and left.

I cut all my classes the next day and took the long train trip to Hartford. I saw everyone who would see me in the Health Department and begged, pleaded, offered money, anything to release the bird. But they wouldn't do any more than show me the rules, right there, see, it says no psittacine birds allowed in Connecticut in big print, see. Really doesn't matter whose fault, the bird's in Connecticut, right? So it has to be eliminated.

One official, upon seeing me growing increasingly distraught, said, in an attempt at comfort I suppose, "Hell, it's only a bird. You can probably get another one back in California. Come on, fella, take it like a man."

But I was not quite a man yet, either chronologically or emotionally, and instead of taking it like a man I just took it like a youth who was losing a beloved pet. Losing him to a cat, a hawk, I could understand, but this . . . I felt so totally helpless and defeated.

As he escorted me out of his office he said: "And don't worry about the process, totally painless, just gets put to sleep. Matter of fact they've probably disposed of him already."

At that moment I heard it—a faint screak down the hall.

"The hell they have!" I said. "Benito!"

The bird answered and kept it up until I found the right door. He was in a cage in an antiseptic room with some other unfortunate animals, and he burbled and fluttered his wings with joy and I took him out of the cage and he talked to me and pulled my ear lobes gently and affectionately. But I couldn't stand it very long and I put him back in the cage with unseeing eyes, and I pushed someone out of the way who was droning on about the rules and I ran out of the building and ran all the way to the railroad station.

When the V-12 naval officer program was announced at Yale, I signed up. This was to permit undergraduates to graduate, taking certain courses the Navy required, then become officers and go on active duty. I was ordered to report for a physical by the Naval doctor. Upon my return from Mexico I had undergone an operation on my bull-battered knee for lunar cartilage removal and internal lateral ligament strain. It was prescribed that I wear a leather and metal brace from ankle to hip for support, so before going to the examination room I went into the bathroom and removed the cumbersome thing. (After all, I figured, my leg would be well in the year or more before I went on active duty.) Then I shuffled along in line with the other candidates as doctors checked eyes, hearing, blood pressure and so forth. I passed with flying colors. Then I limped carefully back to the bathroom, put on my brace, and left the building. I was in the Navy.

At their suggestion I took courses in Latin American affairs. They implied that I would be going into Naval Intelligence and be sent to South America. I also took Portuguese, advanced Spanish, English, painting courses, artistic composition and history of art.

There was a far different attitude toward study at Yale than there had been at the University of North Carolina. It seemed to me that the emphasis there had been more on campus activities, politics, and athletics. At Yale the studious were not considered freaks. I got good marks and ultimately made the Dean's list.

Painting, playing the piano, writing for the *Record* and the *Daily News*, drawing ads for the Yale Co-op, took up my spare time. I was not very collegiate; I avoided beer busts, had no connection with the fraternities or societies, and attended no dances or football games. It wasn't that I was antisocial—I had many friends—but there were so many other things I preferred to do with my time.

My Mexican episode seemed like another world, and Ofelia quite unreal. My amorous preoccupation was completely with Betty Layne. Although she lived across the continent in Los Angeles with her father, we managed to see each other during vacations.

We had met in the drugstore in Connecticut and for me it was love at first sight; she had huge brown eyes, tanned skin and a quick mocking laugh. She was tall and incredibly built for her young age. But aside from her beauty I was drawn to her by her mature and irrepressible sense of humor. And though she talked a wild and flirty game there was something almost old-fashionedly straight-laced about her.

Even though she lived, at that time, only a few hundred yards from the school, I wrote her Special Delivery letters every day and called her several times a day. Betty and I "went steady" for the remaining three years of high school and she visited my parents during the summer. I also hitch-hiked the long distance from Connecticut to Kentucky one vacation when she went there to visit relatives. Then her mother and father divorced and she and her father moved to Los Angeles. Once when I was seventeen we decided to get married. Betty left a note for her father saying simply, "off to see the Wizard—home tomorrow," and then we drove off in Dog. Dog was Betty's antediluvian Dodge coupe whose radiator insignia had long since lost the second "d" and the

Betty

"e." With Dog clanking and wheezing we somehow made the trip from Los Angeles to Tijuana, exhilarated but fearful. We soon found out that the license and other procedures surrounding a Mexican marriage came to thirty dollars. We only had fifteen. Rather relievedly, we abandoned the idea and went to a bar and had a drink—Cuba Libres being the libation of those years. When Betty went to the bathroom I asked the bartender what was the best place in town. I meant for dinner, but he must have misunderstood my meaning of "place," for he said El Molino Rojo. We drove to the spot, a building off the main part of town with a large neon sign. It *did* seem as if there were a lot of unescorted girls in the place as we sat at the bar. Then the man next to me remarked proudly that "these are the prettiest and mos' expensive girls in Mexico." When I looked blank he added, "Deed you not know you are in the largest whorehouse in the world?"

He swept back a curtain. After a fleeting look past the curtain at a veritable dormitory of cribs with a girl at every doorway, Betty fled the place as I paid for the drinks.

We spent the night in a Coronado hotel, telephoning her father that we were staying with friends of hers. We slept together during all those years—that is to say, we slept in the same bed; much to my frustration, Betty, while endowed with normal sexual desires, was determined to be a virgin when she married.

This "marriage" took place in September of 1943 while I was a senior at Yale. I had just been discharged from the Naval V-12 program, owing to the second physical required before going on active duty. Like the first time, I reported to the Naval examining doctors after first stopping off at the bathroom to remove my brace. There was only one trouble.

The doctor checking my blood pressure before and after exercising, ordered me to stand on a chair sixty times instead of bending over sixty times the way the first doctor had done in the previous examination. "I'll bend over sixty times," I volunteered helpfully.

"You're in the Navy," the doctor growled, "Do what you're told."

"Sir," I finally had to admit, "Conceivably, I could get up on that chair, but I am afraid I would have to be helped down."

They examined my leg. They were a bit amazed as to how I had ever made my way into the Navy in the first place. They were rather upset. I was subsequently ushered from the service with an official naval discharge. I was very dejected, and could not quite understand why I could not at least be of use to the Navy in some noncombative capacity. But they were adamant.

Though we wrote constantly, I had not seen Betty for almost a year due to the fact that the university eliminated vacations on a speed-up program designed to get students graduated and into the war as soon as possible. I met an attractive woman from Connecticut some ten years older than I. She invited me to her country home on weekends and we had an affair. She was wealthy, handsome, and worldly and I was flattered by the love she professed for me. She talked of marriage, although she wasn't even divorced from her estranged husband. (In fact, she eventually returned to him.)

For some reason, for some inexplicable reason, I wrote Betty about this new alliance. In looking back on it, I can only believe that I was trying, in some juvenile way, to make Betty jealous, to make her more mine. Part of her eternal attraction for me was her elusiveness. I could never totally possess her. I could never impress her the way I wanted to. I'm sure it was part of my young ego; I felt deep inside that I was destined to do something or be somebody out of the ordinary, though I hadn't the faintest idea what. Betty simply wasn't as impressed with me as I thought she should be. I wasn't very impressed with me, but I thought *she* should be. She acknowledged the existence of other men, went out with them, kissed them, probably fell in and out of love with them. Was I so callow that I thought that she should just sit at home 3,000 miles away and moon about me and write letters every day? She was gregarious, loved people, parties, and since she fascinated men, she enjoyed their company. I certainly wasn't sitting around leading a celibate existence, so why did I expect her to? Yet deliberately I let her know about this new woman in my life and told her that I was going to marry her, although I knew that nothing of the sort was going to happen. It would take a psychiatrist to figure out why I did this, but I think that maybe it was a plea, a plea for her to say: you and only you matter, please don't marry anyone else, I will run to your side. The only other reason I can think of was that this was a way of saying, look, I love you too much, I am too young and immature (and there's-a-war-on) to get married so I'll cut it off this way.

Whatever reaction I expected I couldn't have anticipated the letter I received the next week.

Barney dear—
I am so sorry about the Navy. I know how much it meant to you and it seems so sad that after going back to school to study for it that all your plans will be upset—I hope it won't make any difference in your plans to marry Louise. I doubt if the draft will have you because of your leg—Why don't you try the dip-

lomatic service? With your tact and intelligence I should think you'd be nothing short of wonderful.

Unfortunately I am not going to keep my date with your brother in Washington. It has taken me a long time to make up my mind what I want—and it is not running all over the country as I have done for the past four years—I am all alone now that Daddy and Dottie are to be married and I haven't the nerve to take care of myself traveling about so tonight I am going out with Doodles Weaver, tomorrow night with Larry Tibett, Friday with a friend of George Crane's and Saturday I am going to Texas and marry a Lt. in the Air Corps. Wonderful guy and so sweet—he will have to have the basic training of a commando to live with me, but he thinks he can take it. I'm sure I will be happy—I'm going to have my farm, my station wagon and a nice home-loving guy who thinks I need caring for.

I will send you my address in Texas after we are settled so please write—'cause I love hearing from you and will be anxious to know when you are married, what you are doing and if you are happy—

Love always,
Bets—

P.S. Somewhere in this merry-go-round—sometime—I'm still going to catch up with you, Fool!

I read the letter on the way to a Portuguese class. My best friend, Dick Young, happened to see me on the street.

"You look sick," he said.

I did feel faint.

"Have a drink," Dick said, his standard prescription for any problem, physical or mental. He guided me to Kasey's Bar. Kasey's was Dick's *querencia*, as they say in bullfighting, for his entire stay as an undergraduate at New Haven. He had been at Taft with me. He then looked, and still does, sixteen years old. He was the prototype of all those blond actors of the thirties who came through French doors saying "tennis anyone?" His looks were deceiving. He was brilliant. At Taft he was a legend, if only for the fact that once he took an English college board, finished it in half an hour, then spent the remaining time on an essay explaining why it was a poor exam, and received "A" on both papers.

Dick immediately recognized that I needed help. He had known Betty at Taft. Over a drink I showed him the letter. I was terribly shaken.

He shook his head.

"What do you think?"

"I believe it was Montaigne who said no guy can tell no other guy about no dame never. Or was it Bogart? But in my humble opinion you've gone and lost yourself the most beautiful and the most attractive girl who ever lived."

I drank my drink mournfully.

"Conrad, the only consistent thing about you has always been your inconsistency." He picked up the letter again. "Look, this letter was written Wednesday. What day's today?"

"Saturday."

"Saturday?"

"Saturday."

He mused, "Phone her."

"She's probably left for Texas. It's noon."

"Not in Los Angeles. There it's nine. Phone her."

"What will I say to her?"

"Just tell her you love her, you jackass. Tell her you're not getting married. You just can't lose that great girl!"

I put in a call. The circuits across the country were busy. We had another drink. Half an hour later the call came through. "Betty?" a woman's voice said, "she just this minute went out the door—wait, I'll see if I can catch her in the driveway." There was a long wait, then, "No, I'm sorry, she's just left for Texas."

I wrote her, though I have no idea what I said in the letter. I didn't hear from her. Four months later I heard from a mutual friend that she was separated from her husband; she had only known him a short time before the marriage. He loved her and opposed a divorce.

I was investigating the possibility of going to Libya in the Ambulance Corps. I wrote Betty about it, telling her I loved her, wanted to marry her, and adding that "the Ambulance Corps permits wives to accompany the men to Libya." Betty wired back simply, "Great—do they mind whose?"

Subsequently I was turned down by the Ambulance Corps; because of my leg they didn't think I'd be able to hold up my end of the litter. I thought of Betty's suggestion about the diplomatic service. My brother, Hunt, was in Washington working for a company that made depth charges and war equipment. Hunt and I had grown closer than most brothers, probably because of his accident and our father's illness.

He was very demanding of me. He expected me to be all things to all people, to try everything, to be good at everything. He pushed me into all manner of endeavors that he was sensible enough not to try himself. If we saw a good-looking girl in a restaurant, for example, he would not have the nerve to pick her up, but he would send me over, trembling in fear of rebuff, with some spiel about how I was a painter, needed a special model for a mural and she was exactly right; then if I brought her back he would take her away from me like a fish from a cormorant. Yet he really took

Hunt

the place of a father to me for many years: when I was about twelve, our father, while horseback riding with my mother, was struck on the head by an overhanging limb. He went into a decline from that time on, suffering nervous breakdowns and deep depressions. Ultimately he was forced to sell his partnership in Conrad, Bruce & Company, the successful investment banking firm he had worked so hard to build up and which had branches in Seattle, Portland and Los Angeles as well as San Francisco. He lived until 1956, a gentle, kind invalid and we always felt affection for him, but he had become too detached really to function as a father for twenty years. Unlike our mother, he had no interest in art, music or books, being the athletic and outdoor type. But in his early years he taught my brother and me to hunt and fish and we admired him greatly.

I decided to go to Washington the next week to stay with my brother, talk things over, and see what I could get into. I went to the State Department and naïvely announced that I would like to be a diplomat. They looked over my record and said that upon graduation they might have an opening for me of some sort; as with all employees they would have to run an extensive security check on me. Because I had good grades I was allowed to take my final exams several months early so I was graduated after less than two years from Yale.

Just before I was graduated Betty came to New Haven and we had a brief but joyous reunion. She said little about her marriage except that she had married someone she'd known only two weeks, had to be dragged down the hall on their wedding night, that she got what she deserved, that the whole thing was hell, that her husband didn't want a divorce and that it was going to be rough "especially since he was such a decent guy." It was made clear to me that none of it would have happened if my phone call had been placed fifteen minutes earlier. Then she disappeared back to Texas. It was understood that sometime, somewhere we would get married and live happily ever after.

Our step-grandfather died and left my brother and me each $1,000. We took this and went to Mexico City after he quit his job and rented an apartment on National Lottery Street. But everything was different. Felix Guzmán had been killed by a bull, Adrian was no longer there, and Ofelia was being kept by a politician. It was no good any more for me. Even the bullfights were no good. Hunt became intrigued with Ofelia's beautiful friend, Snow White, and formed an alliance with her. After two months I finally heard from the State Department and left Mexico gladly.

I went to Washington and was employed as a Code Clerk at a salary of $1,800 a year. (Even in 1943 this was not exactly handsome.) I found a wretched room over a clinic for only fifteen dollars a month and managed to get along. I picked up some added cash in an unexpected manner. I sent a question in to what was then the country's most popular radio quiz show, and it was accepted. When Clifton Fadiman asked the question and the panel of John Kieran, Oscar Levant, and Franklin P. Adams missed it,* I was awarded a very welcome fifty dollar War Bond and a set of the *Encyclopaedia Britannica*. The books are still around, but I cashed the bond immediately and took Roberta Cameron, an attractive young lady in the Code Room, out to dinner.

I was a terrible Code Clerk. In a heavily guarded room in the top of the State Department Building some twenty

---

* The question was: Identify these portraits in literature: The Duchess of Ferrari (Browning's "My Last Duchess"), "Girl in Black" (Robert Nathan's "Portrait of Jennie"), and "Melancholia" (Kipling's "Light That Failed").

people were engaged in sending vital coded telegrams around the world and decoding incoming telegrams. Although occasionally the messages were interesting, the mechanics of codification were childishly simple and boring. If it were not too important, a message would come in the "Brown" or the "Grey" code. The process called for was simply to take a volume of the Brown or Grey code, a volume as large as *The Columbia Encyclopedia*, look up the words in the message which were unintelligible words like "etaoin" or "shrdlu" and write down their meanings. For putting messages into code the reverse procedure was employed. A six-year-old child would have little trouble handling the assignment. The Top Secret messages were sent and received in Strip Code. This might require a seven-year-old mentality. Strips with letters on them, which were changed regularly to add to the code's security, were threaded on a board and according to the chart of that week, by arranging them according to the garbled words of the telegram, the message would appear by reading down the last column.

I stayed out of trouble for the first month, forcing myself to do as careful a job as possible and to turn out as many messages as possible. But then I goofed. One message from the Secretary of State to the Embassy in Brazil was to have read: INFORM LIEUTENANT FREEMAN THAT HE WILL SHORTLY BE SENT TO EISENHOWER'S HEADQUARTERS AS A GENERAL ASSISTANT. I did everything right except I forgot the word "Assistant."

I suppose poor Lieutenant Freeman had a fine time for a while. He probably went out and bought a general's insignia, a General McArthur cap, wired his family the great news of his remarkable promotion and went on a celebrating bender. It was short-lived, however, as some spoil-sport in Brazil wired back for reaffirmation of the Lieutenant's rapid rise in the Service. I was severely chastised by the head of the Code Room, an old maid who was totally lacking in humor.

I minded my P's and Q's after that and promoted no more lieutenants. But one day there was a lull when no messages needed to be sent or decoded and I idly picked up a pencil and began a sketch of Roberta who worked across the table from me. Her's was a fascinating face. Twenty-six years old, she had black hair with a streak of gray in it, spaniel blue eyes, and a beguiling crooked smile. Though petite she reminded me of Betty.

I finished the face and since she was working on a Strip Code message propped in front of her, I showed a corner of the board with two of the strips sticking out. On one of these I jotted some letters at random and on the other I wrote, "You are beautiful." I slid it across the table to her. She smiled, nodded approval of the likeness and slipped it into her purse.

That night she invited me to her little cottage in Alexandria. Her roommate was out and she cooked me a fine spaghetti dinner. After dinner we stretched out in front of the fire and I kissed her for the first time. She was warm and loving. I slipped down her shoulder strap and she didn't protest. But she wouldn't let me go any farther; her roommate would be coming home soon, she said.

I had not yet mastered the art of undoing a girl's bra clasp with one hand and was struggling ineptly with that problem when suddenly the lights went on in the living room. A man in a dark suit had come in the front door, and another one through the kitchen door at the same time. Roberta blushed and fumbled to arrange her dress.

"FBI," said one of the men in a very FBI-ish manner.

He went over to the table where Roberta's purse was and opened it. "Where is it?" he snapped.

"Where's what?"

"You know what," the other one said. "The diagram."

"I sent it to my sister this afternoon."

"Yeah? Where does she live?"

"Texas."

They turned to me: "We know it was a chart of the Strip Code. Exactly what was written on it?"

"You are beautiful," I said, looking him straight in the face.

"Yeah, and what else."

"I really don't remember."

The ludicrous dialogue went on. We were kept under strict surveillance until the next day when the FBI recovered the drawing from Roberta's sister and flew it to Washington. Finally we were able to convince everyone that we weren't Japanese or German agents. But again I was in the dog house in the Code Room.

A week later on my lunch hour I went into an office on the first floor that said "Assistant Secretary of State, Adolf Berle." I told his secretary that I would like to see The Secretary and in a few moments I was in an imposing office. I was surprised at the comparative youth of the raven-haired man at the desk.

"What can I do for you?" he asked pleasantly.

I identified myself, gathered up my courage and said, "Mr. Secretary, I'm a code clerk and I think I'm too good for my job."

Mr. Berle laughed. "Well, come back tomorrow and I'll tell you whether you are or not."

The next day I walked into the office nervously.

"Mr. Conrad," he said, "I agree with you and so does the

Code Room, you are not made of the stuff great code clerks are. How would you like to be a vice-consul in Spain?"

I couldn't believe my ears.

"Course, you're too young," said Mr. Berle. "At twenty-one you'll probably be the youngest vice-consul we've ever had. But I've checked your background and I think you might be an asset in Spain. We'll get you out on the first boat we can."

I thanked him and turned to go. Then at the door I stopped.

"Mr. Berle, if it's a fair question—what does a vice-consul do?"

He laughed. "You'll find out. Don't worry about it."

CHAPTER 5

DUE TO WAR PRIORITIES, IT WAS MORE than ten days before I could get on a ship to the Iberian Peninsula. It was a Portuguese vessel, the *Joao Bello*, and it left from Philadelphia. Roberta came on the train with me for a teary farewell. We had still not solved the problem of the roommate and since no women were allowed in my rented room, we were very frustrated. Neither of us was necessarily in love with the other, but there had developed great camaraderie as well as physical attraction. Now I was off to Spain and she was expecting to be sent to South America at some indefinite time. The chances of our ever seeing each other again were remote, and we clung hungrily to each other on the deck of the freighter. Then the ship's whistle blasted. She would write, she would have a letter waiting for me in Spain and oh, if only we two could have a weekend in New York, someday, darling, somewhere, when this silly war is over . . .

The tugs nudged the ship away from the dock and I saw

her standing there unhappily, in a gray drizzle, both of us convinced we would never meet again, never laugh together again, never make love.

That evening at dinner I met some of the other passengers. They were missionaries, British or American diplomatic personnel and returning Portuguese nationals, about twenty in all. I was introduced to a woman at my table, a striking Britisher intriguingly named Eve Arrowsmith. She was tall and her blonde hair was coiffed elegantly on top of her head in braids. Except for too strong a chin she was beautiful. She looked like a statue of Minerva come to life.

She spoke Portuguese to the waiter, Spanish to the Guatamalan woman on her right. Later, I was astounded to hear her speak perfect French to the Moroccan diplomat, and hold an interesting conversation with the missionary across the table concerning the versatility of the Arab language.

"Yesterday, for example," I remember her saying, "We were at Grand Central on an escalator and this friend of mine who is studying Arabic at Columbia asked me the word for escalator in Arabic. I had to think for a moment, but then I said, 'daraj-lil-nuzul.' That afternoon my friend asked, 'What did you say the word for escalator was?' I replied, 'daraj-lil-tulue.' 'Ah-hah,' said my friend—'I've caught you! You said "daraj-lil-nuzul" this morning!'" She gave a lovely little laugh.

"'But, my dear, we were going *up* this morning,' I said."

I looked at her questioningly.

"It's perfectly true—" she said, "Arabic is such a delicious language that they differentiate between 'moving-staircase-going-up' and 'moving-staircase-going-down.' I was lucky enough to live in Marrakech for three years."

I could not keep my eyes off her. She wore a tight gold evening gown that did disturbingly good justice to her figure.

When she would lean forward for her drink or cigarette one couldn't help noticing that she wore no brassiere. At least this one couldn't. She was thirty-seven, a widow, connected in some vague way with the British Government and, I subsequently discovered, a spy. She had lived, it seemed, everywhere, and she could talk on any subject entrancingly. We continued sipping our brandy at the table long after the others had left. She was interested in art, music and, having spent a year in Spain, even bullfighting. She answered all my guileless questions about Spain and the Consular Service. She was fascinating. I'm afraid Roberta seemed farther away than the hundred miles she was. She urged me to call her Eve, but I kept calling her Mrs. Arrowsmith. We went up on the deck. It was a beautiful evening, America was already beyond the horizon. Eve told me that now, except for the Azores, we would see no land for seventeen days, due to zig-zagging across the Atlantic on special lanes. Portugal was neutral, but the German U-boats were everywhere and the Captain was taking no chances with Teutonic torpedo-happy submariners.

When we said good night at midnight I had a momentary feeling that she would not resent a good-night kiss on the cheek. But quickly I discarded that wild thought.

I went in to my stateroom which was separated from hers by a common bathroom. I got into my pajamas, briefly studied a book of Consular procedure, thought about the alluring woman I had dined with, and resolved to work up my courage and kiss her before the voyage was over, maybe tomorrow, and dozed off with the light still on. I woke up a few moments later. She was sitting on the bed looking at me bemusedly. She was in a light blue nightgown, and the only opaque part of it was the fringe of pink roses around the neck. Her dark taffy hair was unbraided and down around her shoulders. Without a word she leaned forward and kissed me gently. Then less gently. I recovered from the wonder of it all and kissed her back. She stood up and shed the nightgown in one slither. I had never believed the human body could be so beautiful without being a statue in the Louvre. Dazedly, I moved over and she got into bed.

This was where we stayed for the next seventeen days, except for visits to the dining room and a periodic turn on the deck.

It was the most strenuous time of my life. By the time Lisbon's fair harbor hove into view I had lost nine pounds. I was bruised, bitten, blistered, gaunt and hollow-eyed. And during some esoteric bit of eroticism my back became so wrenched that I literally had trouble walking upright to the deck.

I was not ungrateful for a moment, nor did I bemoan my condition; I was merely terribly, terribly relieved when we steamed into that beautiful bay fringed with hills and tied up to the dock. Eve would immediately depart for England and I could immediately collapse in a hotel for a day or so before leaving for Spain.

As I started, bent and shaky, down the gangplank, I saw an apparition on the dock. I blinked and looked again. Incredibly, it was Roberta. She was waving at me. Roberta, whom I had left on a similar dock thousands of miles across the Atlantic!

"Isn't it wonderful, darling!" she said joyously as she threw her arms around me. "I've been assigned to Lisbon—I caught a ride on a flying boat last week!"

I was glad to see her—very glad to see her. I really was. But . . .

"Wonderful," I said weakly.

"I've already got a little apartment—all by myself, no

roommate! We can be together tonight and until you leave for Spain."

"Wonderful," I said, barely audibly.

Roberta went off to get porter and a cab. I went up to Eve to say good-by.

"But dear heart, I find I am not leaving for England till tomorrow morning! We can be together tonight!"

I murmured something about my having official business.

"But you can't be gauche, dearest," she protested, "I mean it's been too terribly sweet to just cut it off like that. This will be our last night. I don't want to sit in Lisbon alone."

Somehow I managed. I took Roberta to dinner; then on the pretext that I had promised to say good-by to some good friends made on the ship, I dropped a bewildered Roberta off at her apartment and hobbled off to the elegant Aviz Hotel where Eve was staying. In one of the only fifteen lavish rooms this great hotel had, we had a tender farewell. By eleven-thirty I was back at Roberta's apartment, but I had only enough strength to get my clothes off and fall asleep ungallantly.

The next day was Saturday and she didn't have to work. We had a fine time roaming the fascinating streets of Lisbon after lunch. Then we had a long nap before dinner and a round of the exotic night spots. The next day in a car she borrowed from a vice-consul we drove to the beach of Estoril (pronounced, I discovered, "Shstreel"). But it was too crowded and we pushed on to the beautiful beach of Caiscais. There we had a picnic and found a little cave. The war was very far away.

CHAPTER 6

VIGO, MY FIRST POST IN SPAIN, WAS A great disappointment. A city of some 45,000 in the northwest tip of Spain, in the province of Galicia, it was gray and bleak, especially in the winter drizzles. A drab fishing and canning center with no idea about bullfights or the flamenco arts, it was the antithesis of what I had expected colorful sunny Spain to be. I had read in the encyclopedia that in 1702 a Franco-Spanish fleet escorting galleons loaded with American gold and precious stones was destroyed in the Bay of Vigo by the British and Dutch and that the treasure still was there. This was the only romantic aspect about industrial Vigo, and I used to muse about it as I looked out of the consulate windows over the bay. At the dock in the foreground, and bringing one back to modern times with a jolt, was a Nazi submarine. It had been impounded by the neutral Spanish when it was driven too close to land by a storm. Every day we would watch the crew go through their on-deck drills, Nazi flag routines, exercises and the hanging out of their laundry. We observed the "monstrous enemy" with great fascination. Sometimes when laughing and playing checkers and tossing a ball back and forth they looked almost human. We ascribed names to them.

With me in the consulate was another vice-consul, a consul, several Spanish clerks and an American secretary. They were all very helpful to the new green recruit and patiently explained what a Foreign Service officer does to earn his keep abroad. There were citizenship cases to be decided, people of Spanish parents who had been born in America, then returned to Spain, who now wanted American citizenship and its attendant benefits. There were applications by Spaniards to go to America on student and other visas. There were "Americans" who never had lived in the United States, didn't speak English, yet demanded help when they were arrested for drunkenness or whatever. There were countless bills of lading to be signed for Spanish merchandise being shipped out of Spain to America. There were Spanish businessmen who had been placed on our blacklist for having dealt with the Nazis who pleaded innocence and wanted to get off the list. There was the constant sleuthing to find out which Spaniards were dealing with the Germans and in what quantity. Occasionally there would be a downed American flyer, rescued by Spanish fishing boats from the cold Atlantic, to retrieve from other coastal ports in Galicia.

But mostly it was deadly dull paper work, the bulk of which appeared completely unnecessary to me.

Then one day, after barely six weeks in Vigo, the consul,

Leon Cowles, called me into his office. There was a twinkle in his eye. "I understand that you like bullfighting and flamenco music and gypsies and that sort of business," he said. "How would you like to go where they invented it all? You've been transferred clear across Spain to Sevilla—their vice-consul has been moved to Italy."

I was ecstatic. I packed immediately and left by train the next day. The consulate secretary, who had recently come over on the same boat with the matador Sidney Franklin, gave me a letter of introduction to him and told me to look him up in Madrid on my way to Sevilla. This I did on my first day in Madrid, after first checking in with an officer at the embassy with the marvelously Dickensian name of Outerbridge Horsey III (now a distinguished ambassador). Sidney's deep voice was extremely cordial on the phone— said he'd heard of me in Mexico, wasn't I a friend of the late Felix Guzmán, and wouldn't I meet him for a drink at the outdoor café on the Gran Vía?

As I walked from my hotel to the café, taking in the grand fountains, the beautiful Retiro park, the prestigious Prado museum, the big boulevards, the laughing girls, the well-dressed men, I thought that this was a bit more like what Spain should be. I was excited at the prospect of meeting Sidney Franklin. Since he was the only American to achieve fame in Spain as a matador, I liked to identify myself with him in a miniscule way. I knew his biographical chapter in *Death in the Afternoon* by heart. In fact I had the book tucked in my raincoat pocket for his autograph. Hemingway had written glowingly of Sidney: ". . . But I can tell you truly, all question of race and nationality aside, that with the cape he is a great and fine artist and no history of bullfighting that is ever written can be complete unless it gives him the space he is entitled to."

Sidney Franklin

Since one couldn't get a good look at his face in the action photos in the book, I wondered what he would look like. I assumed the man would be small, lithe, swarthy and with patent leather hair. I was amazed when a tall, husky balding redhead with a big grin and an empty cigarette holder jutting out of it came up to me at the entrance to the café.

"Since you're the only gimpy-legged gringo I've seen all day," he said pleasantly in a deep baritone, "you've got to be Conrad."

We sat down and he ordered drinks. Sidney's Spanish was pure Castilian, perfect. And his English was pure New York.

"You sure timed it right," he said. "Arriving in Madrid today—got to hand it to you."

I looked blank.

"Sunday!" he said. "And Manolete! First of the season!"

I looked blanker.

"You must have heard of Manolete! He's the hottest thing in bullfighting in ten years! Fifteen years! Since Belmonte!"

"I've been out of touch with the bulls for a long time."

"I've been away from Spain six years myself, but I've sure heard of Manolete. And I managed to wangle two tickets for us to see him. We'll walk over to the hotel and get them."

He paid and as we left the café he gracefully swung his raincoat around over his head as though going into an *afarolado* pass, letting the coat settle neatly on his shoulders. It was a totally taurine maneuver and I made a mental note to learn that little conceit.

We leisurely strolled down the bustling thoroughfare of the Gran Vía until we reached the hotel. The pretty clerk was from Barcelona and she spoke Catalan as she handed

Sidney the tickets: "Señor Frahng-cleen, these were left off for you by Manolete's sword boy. Please take me with you—tickets are impossible to get!"

Sidney joked with her in the difficult Catalan language. Then he turned and spoke fluent gypsy to the dark-skinned Andaluz bellboy who got us a taxi. I was impressed.

As we drove through the beautiful city Sidney said: "Not a great hotel, but I always stay there. So'd Hemingway. Lost a lot of respect for old Ernie when the shelling got pretty hot around the hotel. During the last year of the Civil War, I had to pull him out from underneath the bed, babbling with fright, actually babbling."

"What's he like?"

"Hem? Never knew who he was at first. Still don't. I wrote a lot of *Death in the Afternoon* for him. He attached himself to me, wanted to know all about bullfighting. I either didn't catch his name or it didn't register. This was way back in 1929. I was in a whirl, I was the big shot then. I let him travel along with me, he was good company. It was weeks before I found out he was a famous writer. Hell, I'd never read his stuff. What's he like? I don't know." He looked momentarily uncomfortable. "He's changed, something's changed. See that street over there? He and I were walking down it one day and we see a Nancy-boy walking along on the other sidewalk—a real hair-dyed, limp-wristed type, but just minding his business. 'Watch this,' says Ernie. He crosses the street and knocks the poor *maricón* down, hurts him, with no warning. That sort of tells one something about Ernie, doesn't it? 'Course, his big problem all his life, I've always thought, was he was always worried about his *picha*. The size of it, that is."

"Large?" I inquired dutifully.

He shook his head.

"Small?"

Sidney solemnly held up the little finger of his left hand with his thumbnail at the base. He appraised it with a critical eye; then he raised his thumbnail up a fraction of an inch in reevaluation. " 'Bout the size of a thirty-thirty shell," he said.* "But he had one, all right. Isn't true the way people will try to tell you he lost it at Caporetto, had it shot off, and that he was the model for Jake Barnes in *The Sun Also Rises*. That certainly isn't true. I can sure tell you that isn't true."

When we arrived at the big bull ring, I was very keyed up. I had thought I had long ago lost most of my interest in *la fiesta brava* but seeing the crowds, hearing the band blaring out a paso doble, and attending the corrida with the legendary Sidney Franklin all got my heart pounding with expectation. It was like having seen and played baseball only with Little Leaguers and then suddenly being taken to one's first World Series by Joe Di Maggio. Sidney seemed to know everyone, and he introduced me to several matadors who were attending the performance today as spectators. I met such celebrated toreros as the Bienvenida brothers and Marcial Lalanda and even the colorful emerald-eyed gypsy Cagancho, recognizing them from the pored over photos in *Death in the Afternoon*.

They were all real! Hemingway hadn't made them up after all. It was somewhat like having read and re-read *Robinson Crusoe* and then meeting the real Alexander Selkirk. Sidney

---

* I bother to pass on this unresearched bit of calumny mainly in retaliation for the cavalier treatment Hemingway himself showed in discussing F. Scott Fitzgerald's supposed preoccupation with the size of his honorables in *A Moveable Feast*.

introduced me as "a *compadre*, a fellow torero," and pointed out my cane as a badge of having tried their dangerous profession. When Sidney told Cagancho that I was to be the new vice-consul in Sevilla the handsome gypsy smiled and said charmingly: "Señor Vice,"—he pronounced it "then-yoh bee-thay"—"that is my home town and I shall see that you get all the bullfighting you want, your leg permitting, that is."

We moved into the stands which were already almost filled and found our seats in the first row. How different the atmosphere was in this ring from Mexico City. How chic and sophisticated the audience appeared. Many of the men wore the old-fashion flat *cordobés* sombrero tipped rakishly over one eye and some of the women wore mantillas. The men smoked thin cigars and some passed wine-skins back and forth.

"You think this is colorful," said Sidney, "wait till you get to Servalavarí."

"Where?"

"That's what the gypsies call Sevilla."

At exactly four o'clock the doors to the patio de cuadrillas swung back, the band boomed into "La Morena de Mi Copla" (more customary in Spain, I learned, than Mexico's traditional "Vírgen de la Macarena"). Led by the *alguacil* on a prancing horse, the three matadors strode into the arena as the crowd roared.

"There he is," said Sidney, "the one that looks like an undriven nail!"

As the matadors came closer, followed by their banderilleros and picadors, I saw instantly which was Manolete. It was hard to look at anyone else in the ring. He was tall and gaunt with an apologetic look on his sad ugly face, as though saying: "I know bullfighters should be handsome hero types

and I apologize deeply." But he walked regally and assuredly, as though this arena were his—his home, his business office, his domain.

The parade came right toward us and the matadors shed the dress capes and their sword boys handed them up to friends in the first row who proudly spread them out on the rail in front of them. I could see the white scar on Manolete's forehead and the other one that ran from the corner of his mouth down the side of his chin. The other two matadors simply didn't matter.

"How old is he?" I asked.

"Twenty-seven," said Franklin. "And look at that map, will you? Looks as dreary as a third-class funeral on a rainy day. Imagine looking that unhappy with all those millions of pesetas."

There was a white streak on the left side of his jet black hair, and it was hard to believe Manolete wasn't at least forty. But despite the heavy-lidded eyes and the big nose and the melancholy expression and the scars, I saw that it was a sensitive face, a good face that didn't like being ugly. And the truth was that after a while it wasn't ugly any more.

The trumpet blew and into the ring came the first Spanish bull I had ever seen. It was from the Urquijo ranch, Sidney said. I'll never forget the emotion it aroused. How big it was compared to the *novillos* I had seen in Mexico! It was enormous. Its hide was black and shiny, the tail was silky and hung to the sand, the hooves delicate, the tossing muscle, the *morillo*, swollen with the desire for battle. I exclaimed about its speed as it dashed around the empty ring looking for an enemy.

"Fast?" said Sidney. "Why this baby could beat any race horse in the world for the first hundred yards. And he can turn faster than any polo pony going, too. That's the way the bulls are here in Spain."

Manolete, hugging his cape to his chest, took the collar in his teeth while he adjusted his hands on the folds, never taking his eyes off his adversary.

Sidney predicted (so correctly), "You watch, every young torero in Spain will be copying that mannerism."

Manolete signaled with a jerk of his head and a banderillero slid out from behind the *burladero* shield. He "doubled" the bull a few times, trailing the cape in front of the animal's face.

"It hooks to the right," said Sidney. "Perfect for *naturales*."

Even he seemed nervous and expectant.

"*Ya, tápate,*" Manolete's deep voice boomed out. "Now, hide yourself!"

The banderillero ran for the fence and vaulted it. Manolete stepped quickly into the arena. The animal charged hard. Manolete, his feet together and flat on the sand calmly floated the big cape in front of its head. He did it with a grace and insouciance I never would have believed possible. I roared "*Olé*" along with the rest of the 25,000 throats. It was the most beautiful verónica one could imagine. Then he followed it with seven or eight more, hardly adjusting his feet between each pass, and ending with a languid half-verónica that was sheer poetry. The audience roared and stamped and were still cheering when Manolete went out with the muleta and sword.

Sidney was right—the animal was perfect for *naturales*, and Manolete showed us all exactly how that dangerous pass should be done. We were all too delirious to count but he must have executed twenty *naturales* out there in the center of the ring, the *palillo* stick resting delicately in the fingers of his left hand, his right hand, with the sword in it, arrogantly on his hip. Manolete made the animal circle around his body again and again and again like some wind-up toy that could do nothing else but move around a circular rail.

Holding the muleta spread with the sword in his right hand, Manolete now reached behind his back with his left hand and took hold of the red cloth. His entire body was exposed to the bull in front of the lure. He shook the cloth and the bull charged, the horns skimming under his arm as the man revolved in place. He repeated the pass several times as the crowd roared. It was his own invention, the *mano-letina*. But then he added something. He cited the bull, shook the cape and shouted "*Toro,*" and then turned his head, looking completely away from it!

"I don't believe it," said Sidney under his breath. "He's out of his mind!"

"*Toro!*" shouted Manolete, looking impassively up at the crowd. The animal charged. Manolete kept looking up at the crowd. Automatically he swung the muleta and revolved as the horns went by. The animal's horns somehow missed him. Three more times he did that without once looking at the bull, and three more times he should have been killed. It was impossible. The audience was babbling more than cheering. Then Manolete took the sword out of the folds of the muleta, sighted down the blade, and charged the bull slowly and straight on. He sank the steel up to the hilt between the animal's withers, it lunged once, wandered over to the fence, and died leaning up against the boards.

The next day the newspapers described the arena as "an authentic insane asylum."

Sidney slumped down in his seat from the tension and emotion of it all as we watched Manolete stride around the ring with both ears and tail of the animal in his hands. The matador still didn't smile. In fact, his face showed no emotion whatsoever as he walked regally around the arena solemnly acknowledging the plaudits of the wildly cheering audience.

"He's good," said Sidney finally. "God, is he ever. He's as good as I was in Sevilla."

He thought about this tremendous pronouncement for a moment; then he added with reluctance, "Hell. He's *better* than I was in Sevilla."

After Manolete had killed his second bull, he was again awarded the ears and tail. We were emotionally drained.

In the taxi on the way back from the arena Sidney said, "They say he fights so suicidally because he has TB and knows he's going to die anyway. But I don't believe it. His father was a mediocre bullfighter till he started to go blind, began seeing two bulls instead of one, and ended up dying in the poorhouse. Don't know if it's true, but they say his sister was making a living in a profession even older than bullfighting till Manolete started making it big. He didn't know anything about it until one day somebody took him to a cat house and the girls come down the stairs and one was his sister." Then he said, "Want to meet him? We'll go to his hotel."

After a drink we went to the venerable old Palace Hotel and went up to Manolete's suite. It was jammed with people and many were waiting outside. But when the sword boy saw Sidney he ushered us in. Manolete had taken a shower and was in his bathrobe with a black ascot around his neck. He gave Sidney Spain's standard masculine embrace and Sidney introduced him to me by his real name, Manuel Rodríguez. He gave me what seemed like a warm smile after watching his impassive face all afternoon.

"Call me Manolo," he said, after I had addressed him as Señor Rodríguez.

A photographer's flash bulb went off and a French news-paperman said, "Matador, how is it you never smile in the ring?"

Manolete's smile faded. "*Señor, esto de los toros es algo muy serio.*" "This business of bullfighting is a serious thing."

"The gorings," pursued the newspaperman, "Aren't you always afraid of being gored?"

"El Espartero first said it," Manolete answered, "Hunger gives worse wounds than the bulls."

He introduced us to several people around the room—they were from all walks of life: other toreros, politicians, writers, actors, his manager. He poured Sidney and me a drink from a Scotch bottle—a great luxury in Spain in those days—and a big one for himself. He cleared coats off the bed for us to sit down. He was very gentle, very courteous with enormous dignity but never with that coldness he exuded in the ring. Sidney told him about my knee and my *afición*, and Manolete asked polite questions.

"I will be fighting in Sevilla in the fair next month," Manolete said. "Please do me the honor of dining with me."

The man's personality made a great impression on me—the contradictions of melancholy and warmth, tragic yet triumphant, heroic but humble. I would see him perform some ninety times on two continents in the next years but few corridas could equal the thrill of that first time in Madrid. He seemed so sure, so invulnerable; if someone had told me that he and a bull would kill each other within three years' time I would have laughed at the idea. It was true he had the aura of tragedy about him, but of tragedy past, not future.

Sidney felt so, too. "This man thinks like a bull—they'll never get him. Never."

Manolete

My first day in Madrid had been an aficionado's dream; it seemed to me that I had met half the dramatis personae of *Death in the Afternoon*. But it wasn't over.

The next day I dropped in at Sidney's hotel room before catching my plane. Sidney's wizened little sword boy was there shining his boots and cleaning and sharpening the swords and combing Sidney's seldom-used toupee which was on a wig form on the dresser. A newspaperman was just finishing an interview, and Sidney poured us a glass of sherry. A knock came on the half-open door and in came a shabby and totally bald, pot-bellied man of forty. He was so hairless I was surprised to see that he had eyebrows. Sidney introduced him as Cayetano Ordóñez, "Niño de la Palma." The man stood there, his bleary eyes shifting uneasily, and Sidney told him to take off his coat and stay awhile. The man ran his hand over his shiny pate. "Just dropped by to say hello, Sidney," he said. He pronounced it "Seed-nay." But when Sidney offered him a glass of sherry he took it with a trembling hand.

He held it up in a toast. "Salud—"

"And love without a mother-in-law," Sidney added traditionally, as the man finished the sherry in two gulps. Sidney filled his glass again. Then in an aside to me he said, "You know who this guy is, don't you? That's all right— he doesn't speak any English. You read *The Sun Also Rises* —he was the hero."

It was a shock. Hemingway had described the then twenty-year-old curly-haired matador who had the affair with Lady Brett as "the best looking boy I had ever seen." He must have had too many Lady Bretts, or too many Robert Cohns had beat him up, for at forty he looked sixty.

The man put down his again empty glass. He put his hand on the toupee on the form on the dresser.

"Y e'to que e'?" he said in a heavy Andaluz accent that I could barely understand. "What's this?"

Sidney grinned. "That's my antimacassar. For publicity photos. Try it on, Cayetano."

The man took it up gingerly in his trembling hands. It was like a homeless merkin. He turned it over and examined the netting. Then, looking in the mirror on the bathroom door he solemnly donned the toupee.

"Hey, you got it on backwards," said Sidney. He turned it around and with a laugh said, "Now you got it right—"

But the laugh faded in his throat. It made Cayetano look funny, but it took twenty years off him. He stared fixedly at himself in the mirror. It was amazing. If one blurred one's eyes one could easily see "the best looking boy I ever saw." In spite of the defeat in the eyes and the pouches under them, the sag of the jowls, and the slumped shoulders, one could see him. Cayetano could see him very clearly. He drew back his shoulders. He was unconscious of the people in the room. He sucked in his stomach. His eyes burned and the corners of his mouth went down in that arrogant expression matadors get when they know they have the bull dominated and the crowd in ecstacy. The fingers of each hand joined together the way they do when one makes a swan when playing shadow pictures against the wall with a lamp. Then he raised his hands slowly, his chest out, shoulders way back, spine arched. I didn't realize it for a moment, but he was placing banderillas. When his hands arrived at the level of his head he twisted his shoulders to the right. His head never moved, his eyes never left his mirrored eyes. Then he turned his shoulders to the left. It was his special way of inciting a bull to charge for the banderillas. Unconsciously, his lips silently mouthed the challenge: "Toro."

And, for a few minutes, he was lost in another generation.

Then he reluctantly slid the wig off. As he laid it on the dresser, the sag came back in his body, the stoop in his shoulders, and without saying anything he shuffled out of the room.

Nobody spoke for a while. We kept staring at the door. Then Sidney sighed. He picked up the bottle of sherry and studied the label. He started to pour himself a glass, then turned to me and filled my glass with the brown liquid. He poured his own drink.

"Welcome to Spain," he said, holding up his glass. "Remember that song of the Duncan Sisters—? 'Spain, Spain, beautiful Spain—when I get my health I'll go back there again.'"

"Great song," I said.

And we drank.

CHAPTER 7

El que no ha visto Sevilla / Ha perdido una maravilla—
He who has not seen Sevilla / Has missed a marvel . . .

I HADN'T BEEN IN SEVILLA FOR TWO WEEKS before I had a telephone call from Cagancho, the gypsy matador I had met with Sidney Franklin in Madrid. He reminded me of his promise to help my taurine career and said, "Meet me at Los Corales at one—there's a certain person I want you to meet."

I didn't know it but "the certain person" would have a tremendous influence in my life. The Consulate General used to close from noon till three so, after cleaning off my desk, I left the handsome building at the edge of the park (reputedly the most beautiful of America's sixty-eight Consulate Generals around the world). Since I had plenty of time, I ambled along the sluggish historic Guadalquivir River until a carriage came by. There were far more carriages than automobiles in this city of 300,000 and it seemed very fitting to travel across town in this anachronistic vehicle.

Sevilla was the most exciting city I have ever been in. If Vigo was the antithesis of Spain, Sevilla was its synthesis. It looked the way Spain should look, and I was elated and glad to be alive as we clopped down the Paseo de las Delicias Boulevard along the park and past the Tower of Gold where Columbus had stored the treasures from America. (Columbus himself was stored nearby in a tomb in the huge cathedral.) Everywhere there was history; as we drove past the tobacco factory where Bizet and Merimee told of Carmen's having toiled, the coach driver pointed out an ancient hag leaving the building and said: "People say she is the original girl the story was based on." (Possible, I suppose, but she would have had to have been almost one hundred!)

The carriage bounced pleasantly over the cobbled streets through the interminable herds of goats, the faggot-laden donkeys, and past Peter the Cruel's magnificent fourteenth century palace, the Alcazar with its sun-filled Moorish chambers and its labyrinthine Gardens. The spectacular Giralda tower, once part of a Moorish mosque, and the inspiration for nearly every American university's campanile, reached up into the hot Andaluz sky dramatically. The driver reminded me that Murillo and Velázquez were born in the city as were the Roman Emperors Hadrian and Trajan. I found the blending of Roman, Moorish, Gothic and gypsy cultures a heady mixture.

I even liked the many medieval smells of Sevilla: the rich odor of the churros—a snake-like type of doughnut—frying in pungent olive oil on the street corners, the ever-present sweetness of carnations, the almondy smell of turrón candy sold by the urchins, the smoked hams from Granada hanging in the food shops, the acrid aroma of coffee made mostly of acorns, the good smell of manzanilla sherry being poured at sidewalk cafés, and the strong clouds of black tobacco cigarettes.

The only unpleasant thing was the way the driver would rap his skinny nag on its rib cage with the butt of his whip. I told him I was in no hurry. I usually gave the driver an extra tip to not beat the horse; I hated the way the carriage drivers always abused their horses.

There were a few regular cars and taxis on the streets but these were ancient wrecks, some of them twenty-year-old museum pieces. Nearly every car had a huge contraption on the back that looked like a water heater called a gasógeno, a wood or coal burning device developed because of the scarcity of gasoline. The ingenious apparatus, invented by some Hispanic Rube Goldberg, did in fact cause the cars to move forward much of the time.

These automobiles would set off bravely in a cloud of sparks, but their speed and dependability were subject to change without notice: their drivers were frequently required to stop in the middle of an intersection in order to run to the back of the car and stoke it up. In general it was pleasanter to take a carriage, as I was doing.

It was the most romantic of cities, a picture postcard city, a series of wonderful clichés, a set from *Carmen*. Gypsy women sold flowers on every street corner—even the babies sported carnations taped to their hairless heads! And everywhere there was music—the strumming of a guitar floating from a grilled window, gypsies in a café wailing out the "deep songs" of their tribe, an *organillo* in the park, the piano-sized hurdy-gurdies cranked to rattle out stirring paso dobles,

Gitana Sevillana

women singing *coples* as they swept off the cobbled streets in front of their houses. Peddlers, instead of shouting their wares, sang of them in strange atavistic cadences. Wherever one went, people were singing. Driving through the crooked streets of the Santa Cruz district one could hear such songs as:

"From your window to mine, the street is so narrow, the carnations can intertwine and kiss all day . . ."

And: "The bed where I sleep is bathed by the sun when it rises, and upon wakening I amuse myself by counting the beauty spots on a little gypsy girl that I keep . . ."

And: "Woman, what worse punishment could you wish for—to be sleeping with one man and dreaming of me?"

Even the names of the different kinds of music made music when one said them: *verdiales, sevillanas, granadinas, alegrías, tarantas, guajiras cubanas, seguidiyas, seguiriyas, soleares, fandangos, serranas, malagueñas, rondeñas, bulerías, peteneras, sambras, tientos, zapateados, panaderos, boleros, martinetes, saetas, caracoles, alboreas, rumbas flamencas, pasodobles, farrucas, fandanguillos* and *tanguillos de Cádiz* and *Huelva* . . .

Nearly every house had its own courtyard with an arched wrought-iron grille gate leading to the street. Every window had its ornate grillwork: come evening and flirting time the swains would court their girls who would appear at the bars. This was called *pelando la pava*—plucking the turkey. Being very heavily chaperoned, the boy and girl often would become engaged with few if any actual encounters except through the grillwork.

Gerald Brenan, who writes better than almost anyone about Spain, tells a poignant story in his book *South from Granada*. When he was a young man in Andalucía, he met

Carmen, a beautiful girl, through the bars of her small window. Every day he could hardly wait till it was time to call on her. She was lovely, bewitching, gentle, and soon they were officially *novios*—sweethearts. Week after week he would beg her to see him in some other setting, to meet him some place. She demurred, protesting that her family was very strict. Finally, at his insistence, she agreed to meet him the next day in the park. In a touching scene he tells how he sees her there on a park bench waiting for him; she is a dwarf. She does not see him, and he leaves Spain the next day on the pretext that his mother is dying, and he never sees her again.

By now I was almost late for my engagement with Cagancho. My carriage finally came to a little square where it could go no further. I paid the driver and set off on foot down crowded Sierpes Street, where no vehicles were allowed. It was a very "flamenco" street—the street of bulls, of the clubs where the bull breeders gathered, where the tickets to the corridas were sold, where the toreros themselves met at cafés. Most of the men wore boots and the flat-topped broad-brimmed hats and many of the women wore black mantillas. And what women! Far darker than their Northern sisters, they had the flashing Moorish eyes and raven hair pulled back in a chignon that archetypical Spanish women are supposed to have.

I turned off a side street as I'd been instructed and there was the café Los Corales. It was a sunny, undistinguished little restaurant with hams and sausage hanging behind the bar and a few bull posters around and many photos of the immortals of the ring. I would spend a lot of time here in the next years.

Through the cigar smoke I saw Cagancho standing at the

marble bar, his bronze face animated as he talked with the barman. His sombrero *cordobés*, complete with the mandatory toothpick in the band, was cocked over one eye. With his tie-less, white ruffled shirt, his high-heeled flamenco boots, and the black suit tight on his lithe gypsy body, he looked every inch the classic matador he was. His bright green eyes saw me come in and he greeted me in a friendly fashion, introducing me to the bartender as "*el nuevo vice-cónsul.*"

He ordered me a glass of manzanilla sherry—he called it "the treacherous blonde" because of its unexpected strength —and asked how I liked Sevilla. I answered *maravillosa*, and then asked who the certain person I was to meet was.

At that moment a little man—a very little man—with a great barracuda jaw and a hat with the brim pulled down all the way came into the café. He was the complete opposite of the handsome Cagancho. He walked over to us without changing his mocking prognathous grin.

"Ah there, Joaquín Cagancho," he said in a voice with great command in spite of a congenital stutter. "B-b-breaking training are you?"

"Hola, Don Juan," said Cagancho. "What's this I hear about their offering you a million pesetas to fight in Madrid?"

The man coughed a breathy laugh as he put his hand on Cagancho's shoulder. "That, my friend, is the price I've offered to anyone who could get me into *condiciónes f-f-físicas* to be able to fight in Madrid."

The city was always pronounced "Mah-three" here.

"Let me introduce you, Bernabé," said Cagancho. "This is Don Juan Belmonte."

The name sent a shiver through me.

I should have known, of course, after all the photos and

descriptions in *Death in the Afternoon* and elsewhere. There were at least a dozen biographies written of him, all of which I had poured over. Yet even though I had read that Belmonte was small I was not prepared for how completely puny the man was. It was not that he looked out of shape; it simply appeared that he had never had any shape to be out of. Could this man ever have fought a single bull, much less some 2,000? Was this the hero of all Spain?

About his fantastic popularity Belmonte wrote in his autobiography:

Those waging a losing struggle for existence remembered that I had been even more handicapped and had overcome my handicaps. Those aware of being ugly and misshapen consoled themselves with my ugliness and misshapenness. They looked at me and saw me so feeble, so insignificant, so opposite from what one would expect a conquering hero to be, that their own weaknesses seemed much less of an obstacle to overcome.

He was fifty-two years old but his hair was jet black and he looked no different from the photos in *Death in the Afternoon* when he was young, except his face was craggier, his jaw more jutting, and he was more humped. But there was humor and pathos in his face and the black eyes still blazed with the look of *El Número Uno*.

"*Bernabé es un aficionado práctico,*" Cagancho said, pointing to my cane. "He had bad luck in Mexico with a half-breed."

"Would you care to try out some of my h-h-humble cattle?" said Belmonte. "We are having a *tienta* Saturday—I would be pleased if you would come out to the ranch."

Gómez-Cardeña, Belmonte's 4,000-acre ranch, was about an hour from Sevilla, near Dos Hermanas, on the road to Cádiz. His chauffeur picked me up in a Mercedes at my

Don Juan Belmonte

hotel and drove me there, giving a running commentary as he did:

"Over there is where Don Juan—when he was young—used to swim the river at night and fight bulls by moonlight. It was his only chance to learn . . .

"Over there is where some fans of his carved a huge profile of him in the cliffs, like the ones of the Presidents in your country that I've seen photos of . . ."

I was so nervous that it was hard to concentrate on what he was saying. I had not had to depend upon a brace for my knee for some months now. I used a cane almost more out of habit than anything else. But to help strengthen the knee I had bought three *rodilleras*—elastic supports—the day before. All sorts of doubts began to assail me—not so much physical fear as fear of making myself ridiculous. Had I ever really been trained as a torero, had I ever really fought a bull? It had been so brief and so long ago. Was it all a schoolboy fantasy that I had come to believe?

Finally we came to two white pillars and turned off the main road. Three hundred yards more, and we pulled up in front of the ranch house, a large whitewashed dwelling crouched and shining in the sun.

Inside the arched entranceway, the front door was open. Belmonte appeared as we got out of the car. He was dressed in a *traje corto*—the black bolero jacket of the gentleman torero—and he wore ornate leather *zahaones* chaps and boots. He looked more like a bullfighter now—but not much more.

"Welcome to Gómez Cardeña," he said, shaking my hand with both of his. "We are just starting—come along."

We stepped into the big living room. It was tastefully done—the big fireplace with the stag's head over it, the provincial Andaluz furniture and bookcases everywhere.

There were none of the bulls' heads, crossed swords and corrida posters one might expect in a matador's house. The only taurine element I saw was a marvelous life-sized painting of the young Belmonte striding across the ring, his jaw thrust out defiantly against the world, a trickle of blood going down the calf of one leg. One could almost hear twenty thousand people cheering him.

"Isn't that by Zuloaga?" I asked.

Belmonte smiled appreciatively. "By the great Zuloaga himself. I myself don't feel he's caught my t-t-towering beauty, but my wife liked it."

There was nothing else in the room to do with bulls, except for a copy of *Ferdinand the Bull* on the cocktail table. On the bookcase were photos of his children and grandchildren, and one of himself with the last King of Spain. Another showed him with Douglas Fairbanks and Mary Pickford. In a special frame were the immortal brothers, Joselito and El Gallo.

Into the room came a twenty-six-year-old duplicate of Belmonte.

"My son, Juanito," said Don Juan.

Shaking hands, the son smiled the same smile as his father, but there were none of the ravages of hunger and struggle in the younger man's face; the only tough part of his life had been to be the son and namesake of such a famous father.

"Where is your *traje corto*?" asked Belmonte. "Time to get dressed."

I felt the fear clutch inside that I hadn't felt for some two years. "I don't own a *traje corto* outfit," I said.

"And you a torero?" exclaimed Belmonte. "A matador not owning a *traje corto*?"

"Don Juan, I'm not really a torero," I said, "I really—"

"But I've heard about you," Belmonte protested. His eyes were twinkling. "Your fame has preceded you—Cagancho and others have told me"—

"I've only fought two animals in my life," I said, "and I've got this knee, a very bad—"

"Of course, if you don't want to fight we have plenty of people here who will." He was enjoying it. "My son and I will fight all six of them, won't we Juanito?"

"Come," said Juanito, "We'll see what we can find for you."

I followed him through the door to a wing of the house. In one room there were many costumes hanging from a rack, covered with white slipcovers. Juanito lifted up the cover on one of them so that I could see the beautiful gold encrusted blue silk of the suit of lights underneath.

"The one I wore the day of my alternative," he said. "Six years ago."

I had forgotten that he, too, was a matador, and a good one, but burdened with his gentleness and the terrible responsibility of his name.

"How was it that day?" I asked.

"Good, good," he said. "And I had several good years, one really good one. Not so good lately. Manolete"—he shook his head in begrudging admiration—"he's too much for all of us. He's pushing us all to suicide."

He found a black *traje corto* jacket for me, plus the gray striped trousers, the flat-topped sombrero, and the boots that went with it. As I was dressing he saw the six-inch scar of the operation on my knee and whistled.

"You weren't joking, were you," he said. "Maybe you shouldn't try this."

"No, I'd like to try," I said.

"You should see my father's body," Juanito said, "covered with scars—maybe fifty gorings."

We went through the living room and out the French doors. On the porch were a dozen people, marquesas, bull breeders, the gentleman torero Alvaro Domecq, and the ex-matador Marcial Lalanda. A liveried butler was passing drinks on a silver tray to the guests. Juanito introduced me, and then the guests went back to being spectators. The balcony overlooked a perfect little bull ring, and it was apparent that the *toril* gate was about to be opened. Around the circular wall there were sitting perhaps thirty of the ranch hands and their families. A picador on a padded white horse waited, lance in hand. There was no *callejón* fence in the arena, but at three strategic points were red *burladero* shields and behind them were at least two men dressed as I was, with capes. One was Don Juan.

"Ya," he called. The man on the wall over the *toril* gate jerked on the latch rope and the door swung open. Down the chute from an adjacent corral pounded a two-year-old heifer. It seemed to *explode* into the arena in billows of dust. It was not much larger than a white-tail doe, but its ferocity made it seem larger. It had no visible udder and except for the lack of a tassel, it could have been mistaken for a young bull. It caught sight of the horse, dropped its head and charged. It made a great "thunk" as it hit the mattress padding hard. The picador pricked the withers of the animal with his lance, not too deep but deep enough to draw a little blood. Still the animal kept driving with its back legs, banging its horns against the steel stirrup, shoving the horse around the ring.

"*Muy brava!*" Belmonte exulted from down in the ring.

Juanito picked up a large notebook on the railing, opened it to a page entitled "Brujita, No. 120."

"That's her name," Juanito explained. "They all have names and numbers since birth."

Underneath some other statistics Juanito wrote "Brave entrance." Under "Number of pics" he made a mark.

Juanito answered my naïve questions while keeping his eye on the ring action.

"It's important we find out how brave the heifers are," said Juanito. "Bulls get their size from their fathers, but they get their temperament and courage from their mothers."

"What happens if they aren't brave?"

"Slaughterhouse," said Juanito succinctly.

A *novillero* was now luring the heifer away from the horse by swirling his cape at her feet. She pulled her head away from the target reluctantly, in spite of the irritating pain of the lance. She charged hard at the man. He did a few undistinguished verónicas and led the animal back to the horse. It charged again, and Juanito made another mark in the book.

In the next five minutes he had made four marks and a diagonal across them, and still the ferocious animal tried to get back at the picador. Finally, Belmonte raised his hand and said, "That does it, girlie, you've proved enough to us—we believe you!"

The picador removed his lance and rested the butt of it on the ground. Then Belmonte himself stepped out from the *burladero*. The audience watched expectantly. He took his cape in both hands, exaggeratedly bent his head and caught the collar in his teeth while adjusting his fingers. It was obviously a parody of Manolete's mannerism and the spectators laughed. Grinning at himself, Belmonte walked across the ring toward the heifer whose head was still buried in the horse's padding. The man walked as though his feet hurt him. I remembered the line from his autobiography: "My legs were in such a state that before moving one had to request permission from the other."

Yet he seemed to grow as he approached the animal.

"Ah-hah, Brujita," he called softly, "Come pretty girl, leave the horse now."

The voice caused the heifer to whirl around. She charged. Languidly, Belmonte floated the magenta cloth in front of her nose, stepping out on his left leg majestically as he did. He swung his arms so smoothly and she followed so obediently that it looked as though he and the heifer had rehearsed this maneuver for months, whereas actually today was the first time the animal, except for her branding, had ever encountered a dismounted man.

Ten more times he did that, taking the animal so close that it seemed impossible for the horn to miss his legs. They were not like Manolete's verónicas; the hands were held higher and there was an austere, classic sort of old-fashionedness about them. But they were no less good. While doing it, he seemed to have grown at least another foot, to have acquired all the grace in the world, to have borrowed another body from somewhere.

We who watched were first transfixed and then, suddenly, like people gone mad we were all yelling "Olé!" Belmonte finally strode away from the heifer. There was a big grin on his craggy face. As he walked over to the fence, he was sweating heavily; he once again looked humped and as though his feet hurt him. We had witnessed some kind of a miracle.

A novillero entered the arena after Belmonte, but no one paid much attention to him. Happily, everyone had forgotten about me, and I tried to make myself as inconspicuous as possible among the group on the balcony. With a little bit of luck, all the animals would be fought and I wouldn't have to—

"Señor Vicecónsul"—

Belmonte was calling me. There was no place to hide.

"Here," said Juanito, sweeping a cognac off the butler's tray and handing it to me. "It's an easy animal. Luck."

I swallowed it in two gulps and would have liked five more glasses like it. I got up and went down the steps. I came out behind the *burladero* where Belmonte was. He handed me his big cape. I thought of Felix's admonition the last time I had fought—that it was safer to start with the muleta, but it seemed appropriate to do whatever Belmonte told me to do.

"Now" said Belmonte.

I also got the collar of the cape in my teeth á la Manolete and adjusted my hands, which drew a titter from the audience. The heifer was across the ring, in her *querencia* next to the *toril* gate. I stepped out of the *burladero* and walked towards her. She lowered her head and stared at me suspiciously. Lordy, she had grown enormously in just the short time it had taken to get down on her level.

"*Toro*" I called, and this brought another laugh. I amended it as I shook the cape. "*Vaca!*"

The animal suddenly lunged into a full charge. Clear across the arena she came, her hooves rataplanning on the sand. I didn't move—I made myself not move. I kept my feet together as I had seen Manolete do. At the last moment I swung the cape in front of the horns. I had gauged the speed correctly and the animal went by and I heard a big surprised "*Olé*" from the audience. It worked! It was easy! I could do it!

I stood without moving, ready for the next charge, this time from my right. But what I hadn't figured on was the speed with which the heifer had whirled. It was so much faster and agile than the two larger animals I had fought in Mexico. It whirled and was on me like a cougar. I could only watch it as it crashed into my thigh. I was slammed hard to the ground. I felt my cheek scraping on the sand, the stubby horns jabbing at my body, the hooves punching on my chest. I grabbed the horns and tried to wrestle them away from me. In its rage the heifer even bit me on the arm—a final indignity.

It left me as quickly as it had attacked; Belmonte was twisting its tail, and another bullfighter was shoving a cape in its face. The calf was suddenly gone and somebody helped me up. Only one pass! I felt humiliated as I dusted myself off. I was badly bruised and bleeding a little from my lip, but I was all right.

Belmonte came over to me after the heifer was lured to the other side of the arena. "You must adjust, Bernabé," he said. "You must adjust your f-f-feet after each pass! It would be very pretty simply to stand in one spot and do twenty verónicas. It would be l-l-lovely. But you can't do that with these little animals. If she had a big bull's momentum and weight and slowness that might be different."

"I'd like to try again," I said, "and with a muleta."

The small red flannel cape with the stick handle in it was produced, plus a wooden sword. I spread it wide with the sword to make a bigger target and walked across the arena toward the heifer.

Belmonte called after me between cupped hands: "Be ready to adjust!"

The heifer needed no encouragement to charge me; it had

enjoyed the last encounter immensely. Once again I stood absolutely still, feet together, as it bore down on me in the Pass of Death. The horns went by my knees, and I didn't move until after the head had gone by. But then instead of standing there and admiring myself, deafening myself with ovations as I had done with the verónica, I quickly took two steps back toward where the heifer had charged from. This maneuver gave the animal room to whirl in without hitting me in the process and also gave me space and time to get ready for the next charge.

"*Eso es!*" I heard Belmonte call, "That's it!"

I was ready for the next attack, and this time I did a high *Pase de Pecho*, drawing the animal across my body. It merited an "*Olé*" from the audience.

I felt so much more secure with the muleta, even though theoretically it is much more dangerous because of its smallness. I did three or four more fair passes. Then suddenly I found myself in a compromised position. I had done something wrong and found myself located so that if I were to complete the pass I had cited for, the heifer would have to pass between me and the fence; the probability of her complying was small. When I tried to change positions the heifer attacked abruptly. I had to retreat back across the ring, swinging the muleta back and forth across the animal's face —"fanning it"—in a desperate defensive action. Juanito started out of the *burladero* to my rescue, but Belmonte waved him back with a slash of his hand.

"*Déjalo!*" I heard him shout. "*Está toreando*—leave him! Let him work it out!"

And I did, finally, by seesawing the muleta back and forth in front of my adversary's face from horn to horn until I finally brought its charge to a bewildered halt. I walked away in a sweat from the heifer.

"That's the best thing you've done today," said Belmonte. "We can't always make p-p-pretty passes—sometimes we have to really *torear*—get in and fight, face-fight them—*por la cara*. You learned something. You will learn m-m-more. Come again tomorrow." (I never learned exactly why Belmonte was so kind to me, why he was willing to waste so much time on me. I think he was intrigued mainly by the fact that I was an American—he'd never known an American well. I asked about Sidney—he'd never met him. I asked about Hemingway—he thought maybe he'd run into him a few times in Madrid. Belmonte was a curious man. He was curious to see how much of "his invention," modern bull-fighting, a foreigner like me could absorb. He had an interest in all people of varied backgrounds. He told me that once he'd even tried to teach a Chinese magician how to bull-fight!)

Then he waved to the man over the *toril* to open the gate. "This pretty little girl has had enough. Go out in the meadow, *guapa*, make yourself attractive, get yourself d-d-de-flowered, and raise me dozens of great bulls."

A cape was flared out in the entrance of the gate, the brave heifer charged at it, and the gate was slammed behind her as soon as she entered the chute. Her pic wounds would be disinfected and then she would retire to the calm fields never again to be molested by man.

I was pale and wobbly in the knees. Not out of fear, but the excitement of it all and the unaccustomed actions. I retreated to the porch, as another heifer was let into the arena. I had not exactly been what one might term great, but I had salvaged a little of my honor. Juanito patted me on the back and handed me a brandy. Next to the one he had given me before going down, it was the most appreciated drink I'd ever had.

CHAPTER 8

THE NEXT DAY BELMONTE HAD AN-
other program arranged. He announced that we
were going to *derribar*. Three of his magnificent
horses were saddled and waiting in the cobbled courtyard.
They were large chesty Jerezanos, with plenty of Arabian
blood in them. The saddles were totally unlike American or
English saddles, sheepskin covered and with big metal stir-
rups. There were three boys to help Belmonte, Juanito and
me mount and to hand us each a lance.

Since I was a child I had owned horses and done a lot
of riding in my life in California and on the ranch in
Montana, but this was something new. We rode through
the forest of olive trees and then galloped across the fields to
where the herds of fighting cattle were. We carefully made a
wide circle away from the big bulls which looked placid
enough but which eyed us with innate distrust. Belmonte

led us to a special field where a group of young heifers grazed. They took off when they saw us, and Belmonte singled out one to pursue. Crouched over his horse's neck, lance leveled, he sped after it, with Juanito riding herd on one side and me bringing up the rear. At exactly the right moment, when the animal's back legs were on the rise, Belmonte jabbed the blunt end of the pole a little to the left of the of the base of its tail. The heifer pitched forward, tumbling head over heels. It arose blazing with fury, and this time instead of running it charged Belmonte's horse. Belmonte zigzagged away, then turned and cut inside the heifer's charge, dragging the lance as a lure. Guiding his horse mostly with his knees, he manged to bewilder the heifer and avoid every charge. Meanwhile, Juanito had undone the muleta and wooden sword tied in back of his cantle, and he handed it to me. He held my horse while I got off. I took the muleta and walked toward the heifer. She was very brave and cooperative, and I tried every pass I could think of. Belmonte called advice to me from his horse:

"Run that hand, Bernabé, run it as far as you can! Now—follow through the pass with your upper body! Plant those feet!"

It was a different sensation, a primitive thrill, fighting this wild animal out in the middle of nowhere. I was much more relaxed and confident, and I performed better than I had the day before.

Belmonte made notes of the heifer's performance in his notebook, and then we galloped away after another one. When we came close to the second one and Juanito had tilted it over, I tried maneuvering my horse around it as Belmonte had done but my mount skittered nervously. I felt it trembling under my knees.

"Be careful," warned Belmonte, "That mare isn't used to wild cattle yet."

Juanito fought this one on foot, and I realized how much I still had to learn about capework; he was no Manolete, but he was very very good. We tilted and caped five more animals; and then Belmonte said, "Let's go home for lunch."

As we rode by a herd of bulls, I noticed one big brown *novillo* slightly separated from the others, eyeing me; a bull in a herd is usually docile—a bull away from the herd is usually dangerous. I was behind Juanito and Belmonte, and I kicked my mare to catch up. To my surprise the horse stopped dead. And to my horror it refused to move. The bull, which would have done nothing had my horse continued, now started walking toward me. I jabbed my heels into the mare's ribs. It stood frozen, quivering under me. I brought the rein ends down on its flanks as hard as I could. The bull had now gone into a trot toward me. I slapped the hypnotized horse back and forth across the neck as hard as I could with my bare hand. It didn't move. I leaned forward and pounded frantically on its head with my fist. It only stared wild-eyed and mesmerized at the bull which was now in full charge.

"Don Juan!" I yelled in panic.

He looked back just as the bull struck. I felt the horse and myself lifted up in the air. And then dropped back down again. The bull's horns, luckily, were the wide flat kind, not the upturned type. Miraculously, the horns didn't penetrate the horse and it came down on its feet. But now the bull backed off and charged again, this time its head held higher. I got my leg out of the stirrup and swung it back out of the way as the horn hit the saddle leather with a smack. The tremendous impact slammed the mare back and over. I was thrown eight feet clear of the animal. The mare, out of its trance now, sprawled on the ground and flailed its legs in the dust. The bull hesitated, not knowing whether to charge me or the horse. I remembered Felix's teaching and lay absolutely still. The bull opted for the larger, moving target and prepared to rip open the horse's unprotected belly.

"Toro!" a voice shouted.

Suddenly Belmonte was there. Swerving in between the bull and the fallen mare at a dead gallop, he leaned off his horse and slapped the bull across the face with his sombrero. The bull whirled to gore this new adversary but the target vanished as quickly as it had appeared. And then Juanito was there on foot with the muleta in his hand. When the bull charged this new adversary, Juanito ran backwards leading the bull away. When he had lured the animal a hundred feet away, I got up and grabbing the reins I tugged the uninjured horse to its feet.

As we rode home Belmonte's only wry comment was: "I suppose now we'll have to buy you a card in the p-p-picador's union."

At luncheon was the famous old gypsy El Gallo. Belmonte enjoyed recounting our adventure to him, embroidering it shamelessly to make El Gallo chortle. Though totally bald and older than Belmonte and a sort of serene elder statesman of matadors, El Gallo was a friend of Belmonte's youth and I was fascinated to hear them talk.

"Rafael, what in the world would you have been if there'd been no bullfighting?" asked Belmonte over the cognac.

And it was a good question because while one could possibly see Belmonte as something other than a matador, it was difficult to imagine El Gallo as anything but what he was.

"If there had been no bullfighting," said El Gallo puffing thoughtfully on his cigar, "I would have invented it."

The months went by and it was an exciting time. Every weekend there was a *tienta* party someplace, either at Belmonte's ranch or at the renowned haciendas of Concha y Sierra or Miura or Peñaflor or Benítez Cubero or Urquijo or Pepe Escobar. I was nearly always invited to participate in the arena action. This was not due to any prowess of mine, but simply to the fact that I was the American vice-consul— that I liked to bullfight made me even more of a rarity. At these affairs I was fortunate enough to perform along with some of the greats of all time such as Pepe Luis Vázquez, Cagancho, Lalanda, and Manolete: it was an aspirant bullfighter's dream come true, and I was properly grateful. Though I was constantly improving my technique with the young animals, I never deluded myself that I would be included in such fast company were I some unknown Spaniard.

Just being an American in Spain was an attraction during those years. Because of the country's political turmoil resulting from their Civil War and now the World War, Spain had had virtually no tourism in ten years. (As opposed to the seventeen million tourists who poured into Spain in 1968!) Counting the embassy and the consulate personnel, there were probably not more than 300 Americans in all of Spain. There were many practical reasons why the Spaniards wanted to be friendly with American consular officials: it was clear that we were winning the war and that they would be dealing more with us instead of Germany as it had appeared in the beginning; Andalucía was desperate for tractors and any kind of modern farm machinery that now could only come from

America; also, the United States was Spain's greatest outlet for sherry, olive oil and other produce.

But quite apart from that, the Andaluz people were genuinely hospitable. They were sincerely pleased that a Yanqui would bother to learn their language, customs and music, and amazed that one would acquire and practice the national passion, accustomed as they were to foreigners "rooting for bull" at a corrida and decrying the spectacle as barbaric.

Every day I was freshly impressed with the character, humor, dignity and hospitality of the Andaluces. It was incredible to me that only a few short years ago they had been engaged in one of the bloodiest civil wars of history. They preferred not to talk of it—but when they did it was chilling.

"See that street there? Franco's men took fourteen of us Loyalists, laid them down on the pavement and ran a steam roller over them.

"See that place over there in the park? That's where the Reds took seven nuns, injected plaster of Paris up them, then tied them down till it hardened in their wombs."

People on each side seemed to have a more horrendous atrocity to recount about the other side. Sidney Franklin had come down from Madrid in an attempt to secure a contract to fight again in the city of his first triumph. We had many discussions about the Civil War; I asked him what side he'd been for.

"Both sides were Spanish," said Sidney, unhappy at the memories. "I was for both."

Yet the country was ostensibly calm and working its way out of poverty. "Dictatorships always do prosper," said Sidney, when I commented on the many progressive steps Franco was taking. But it did not seem like a dictatorship, certainly not a dictatorship like Hitler's or Mussolini's. There was no great military display or build-up. The press was muzzled, but freedom of speech wasn't. People complained of Franco openly, yet they admitted he was the only person to hold the country together and keep it from communism. I met The Chief—*El Caudillo*, as he was called—at an official reception and it was hard to believe that this portly little fellow who looked like a kindly dentist had been the fierce soldier, vicious enemy and shrewd head of state who had guided his country through the tricky waters between combatants, playing on all sides of warring nations without becoming involved himself.

My consul general struck me as being about as up-to-date and as lively as a coelacanth. He had a very socially-minded European wife and they catered to the aristocratic element of Sevilla. In the large consulate building they would hold elegant soirees for wealthy celebrities such as the Duchess of Alba, the Duke of Medinaceli and the Infanta. Like so many of our Foreign Service personnel, the consul general couldn't even speak Spanish, though he had been assigned to Spanish-speaking posts for twenty years. (Once, when his car hit a cow, he tried to explain to the farmer what had happened and ended up using sign language, plus bellowings of "moo, moo," since he didn't know the word for cow.) We did not share the same enthusiasms, apparently.

As soon as I could finish my work, similar in its tedium to my routine tasks in Vigo, I would take off on the uninhibited paths of the flamenco world.

There were no women in my life. I had had two letters from Betty Layne since my arrival in Spain. They were warm, amusing and affectionate. But they shed little light on her marital problems, status and future plans. Then my letters began coming back marked "address unknown." I wrote mutual friends and none had heard of or from her.

Roberta Cameron had come over from Lisbon for a pleasant but too brief weekend.

And that was all. In Spain one didn't "date" nice girls as in America. One either indicated serious intention and plighted one's troth to the proper young ladies or one consorted with singers, actresses, night club waitresses or lower echelons of women. The brothels of Spain were of a superior order, being very flamenco, lively and untawdry. They were elegant old-world establishments, much like one's grandmother's living room with crystal chandeliers, overstuffed sofas and antimacassars on the armchairs. The Madam also looked like one's grandmother and was also overstuffed. More like a club than a bordello, they were establishments where businessmen would frequently drop in at six for a manzanilla or two and a pleasant chat with the girls before going home. Though there were large comfortable bedrooms upstairs should passion bestir a visitor, their occupancy was not a requirement. A guitar was always present and usually there was a guitarist amongst the clients; the girls would dance *sevillanas* enticingly—vying with each other in the sexy whirls and dips while castanets chattered like the machine guns at Chateau Thierry. The girls were extraordinarily attractive, mainly, I suppose, because with Spain's still shaky economy it was almost impossible for the average girl to make a living solely as a stenographer or a salesgirl and they would augment their salaries in this time-honored fashion. They were young and clean-looking; and they wore large crucifixes around their necks even while at their work. I was interested to see that the Spanish men would treat these girls in the same courtly manner they treated all women; though all they had to do was to plunk down the few pesetas and take them upstairs, the customers would flirt and woo them as though they were virgins, finally conduct them upstairs as though to the nuptial couch. Afterwards they'd slip the money to the Madam surreptitiously to avoid the crassness of it all.

There is in my mind no doubt but that Spanish men are better lovers than Anglo-Saxons: they glorify women, all women, enjoy their society, and each thinks of himself as the reincarnation of Don Juan Tenorio. Every woman is a challenge, a fortress to be assailed, an Everest to be surmounted simply because she is there. Every woman on the sidewalk, regardless of class or age, merits a stare and a careful assessment of her retreating figure from the ankles up.

I used to enjoy listening to the great variety of the Sevillan man's *piropos*—the compliments he would bestow upon a passing female: "*Tantas curvas y yo sin frenos*"—"so many curves and me without brakes!" Or, while looking with mock wonder at a girl's bosom: "*Demasiado redondo para aguacate pero demasiado largo para huevo . . .*"—"too round to be an avocado yet too long for an egg!"

If for no other reasons, the Spanish lover would probably excel his Anglo-Saxon counterpart because of his enthusiasm for sex and his lack of Victorian prudery. Also, the intelligent use of alcohol would be in his favor; in Andalucía I rarely saw anybody tipsy and never any out-and-out drunkenness.

The friends I made were gay and humorous companions, most of them connected in some way with bullfighting. I rarely saw my fellow vice-consul or the consul general outside of the office and rarely spoke English, except with Sidney, with whom I usually lunched. I learned, the hard way, that *gracioso* meant funny, not gracious, *embarrasada* meant pregnant and not (necessarily) embarrassed, and that *constipado* simply meant one had a cold. My speech became more and more Andalú' and more and more gypsy expressions became standard talk. Caló—the strange gypsy language—replaced many of the proper Castillian words: for example, kids was not *niños* but *churumbele*, nose was not *narices* but *nacles*, and mouth was not *boca* but *muí*. I was generally referred to as *"el Yanqui agitanizao"*—the gypsified American —by the townspeople.

I could have continued happily forever in the mileu of Servalavarí (as the gypsies always called Sevilla), but one day, after nine months, a cable came transferring me to the consulate in Málaga. I was crestfallen, but the cable had said "temporary assignment" so I assured my friends that I would be back.

I had acquired a trybrid motorcycle, one third American, a third English and a third Spanish. With its various and unrelated parts it resembled Tom Swift's Electric Bicycle, and it was not of a very much younger vintage. But though dilapidated it was functional. I allowed two days for the trip, taking the long scenic way around to Málaga, via Cádiz and Algeciras. The motorcycle threatened to resign several times but managed to keep sputtering along, kilometer after kilometer. The stretch from Gibraltar to Málaga along the Mediterranean was beautiful and could very well have been the California coast. Málaga itself was a beautiful port city, tree-lined and sleepy; I actually made the city limits before the Harley-Norton-Soriano collapsed. Ingloriously, I had to hitchhike the rest of the way to my new post.

I soon found that the consul and his wife were far livelier than their counterparts in Sevilla; also, there was an attractive secretary from Virginia in the office. Although there was little of the bullfighting atmosphere of Sevilla, I decided that

Málaga would not be such a bad temporary assignment. Especially when the British consul telephoned me at my hotel and asked if I'd be interested in renting a completely furnished house of which he was the custodian. Five minutes' drive up in the hills from the sea, it was a charming old Mediterranean villa overgrown with purple bougainvillaea and surrounded by four acres of terraced garden and an orchard. A sign outside said Villa Inocenta; since by custom the places were named after girl's names, a female named Inocenta must have lived there once.

"Belongs to an Englishman who was declared *persona non grata* some time ago by Franco," the consul explained. Inside it was musty and dirty but potentially attractive. (I subsequently learned that it was the home of Sir Peter Chalmers Mitchell who, along with Arthur Koestler, had been arrested in 1937 and almost executed here by Franco's men as enemies of the Revolution. Mitchell subsequently wrote a book called *My House in Málaga* about his experiences.)

"It's splendid," I said. "But I am sure I couldn't possibly afford it."

"We're anxious to have someone in it," he said. "Would you think eighty dollars a month excessive?"

I moved in that day.

There was already a cook and a gardener—at eight dollars each a month. But I would have to have a maid; someone would have to supervise the shopping for food, an all-morning process in those days before *super-mercados*. I asked around and was told to advertise. I put an advertisement in the morning newspaper.

Mauricio Fogler was the breezy, randy petroleum atttaché, a great friend, who was as enamored of things Spanish as I was; although he was usually on the road, he wanted a base and agreed to go in on the house with me.

The day after the ad appeared we interviewed a stream of assorted females and finally decided upon a dumpy peasant girl with a jolly round face, named Concepción Inmaculada. That is, I decided upon her; Mauricio wanted the blondish one with the good legs. I had to point out to him that we weren't picking Miss Málaga of 1945, that the blonde didn't have a single callus on her hands, and that Concepción looked as though she'd rather work than eat.

He agreed reluctantly, then announced that he was departing that afternoon for Tangier for a couple of weeks. There was a suspicion that while the German subs no longer actually dared to come into the Spanish ports to refuel, the Falangists were getting the oil out to them in big fishing boats. While he checked on this, I would have the pleasure of training Concepción. Before going out the door, he added, in an attempt at an English accent, "And mind there's no funny business going on between you two whilst I'm away!"

I had started to arrange some notes on a political report when Mr. Morales, the chief clerk, stepped up to my desk to say there was someone to see me. I got up and walked towards the counter, noticing two figures. One was a little white-haired woman in widow's weeds, with mean squirrel eyes. Beside her, even smaller, dressed in a rough black dress with long sleeves, was one of the most beautiful girls I had ever seen.

She stood mute and childlike, one hand at her side and the other nervously fingering the gold cross at her throat. Her hair was black—as black as a *guardia civil's* patent-leather hat— and it was pulled back and fastened in a large knot at the nape of her neck. Her eyes looked out uneasily from under ebony eyebrows, unplucked and thick.

"*Buenos días,*" said the old woman, holding up a crumpled newspaper and jabbing at it. "I have seen this of the *periódico* today. I have brought my Chelo to apply for the position of housekeeper in your and your Señora's house."

"I'm very sorry," I said, "but the position has been filled already."

"Work, decent work, is so hard to find now."

"I'm sorry," I said.

The mother sighed and said, "Well then, Señor, forgive the molesting and good day."

I went back to my desk and the consular invoices that had piled up to be signed. I found that it took me fifteen minutes to check and sign one sherry invoice; that oval face kept interrupting. What did her mother call her? Chelo, Chelo. Short for Consuelo.

Concepción didn't appear the next morning as scheduled: I ate my meals in the big gloomy hotel. The house was still the way it had been when I'd moved in—filthy. I had been too tired after work to even think of tackling the gigantic task of cleaning it up. I had straightened the upstairs bedroom —shaken the piles of dust off the big double bed's canopy and tried to get most of the debris out the balcony doors. But it didn't matter for the moment—I preferred to sleep out on the terrace on a mattress anyway.

When Concepción didn't appear on the third day, I decided to insert the ad again. Then as I drove back after lunch, I caught a glimpse of a small figure with a black mantilla coming out of the shadows of the cathedral.

I swerved the motorcycle and drew up alongside the sidewalk on the wrong side of the street.

"Señorita!"

"Hola, Señor Vicecónsul." Her voice was low.

"Look, Señorita—are you still interested in that position?"

"*Cómo?*"

"Do you still want the job as—as *ama de llaves* in our house?" It wasn't really "housekeeper"; but *criada* was not a pleasant word, somehow—not for her—and it didn't hurt to dignify the business a bit.

"Sí, Señor," Chelo said.

"When can you come?"

"When the Señor wishes."

"This afternoon then. I'll tell the gardener to let you in."

"*Muy bien,*" she said.

She was there in the courtyard when I turned down the driveway. Dressed in the same black dress and canvas *alpargata* sandals, she was beating the rugs on the line and enveloping herself in clouds of dust. She had undone the knot and her hair spilled down her back and swirled around her head in ebony waves as she assaulted the rugs with a wicker beater.

"*Qué tal?* How do you find the place?"

She paused in her work and looked up at me. "I like it. Has the Señora come with you?"

"I have no señora."

"But the newspaper said the place was to be kept for a *matrimonio.*"

"No—it just said for two. We are two señores."

"Oh," she murmured. "I think it best that my mother does not learn that I'm working for—that I'm not working for a señora."

"I'm sorry if it was misunderstood. He's away, but he should be here in a few weeks."

We'd said all we had to say.

I went into the house and was amazed to see how it had changed. She had done a prodigious task in that single afternoon. The mustiness and drabness were gone, the furniture was in a more attractive arrangement and the walls, floors and windows had been scrubbed. The ugly clay color of the walls was three shades closer to being attractive. Flowers from the garden filled every vase; even the stuffed bull's head had been dusted, its horns shined. And a rose was tucked behind one of its ears.

The first week before the storm we barely spoke. I'd give her money, and when it was gone she would show me the bills and I would give her more.

G. K. Chesterton once remarked that less French was needed to carry on a philosophical discussion than to buy a safety pin. My new domestic situation required the acquisition of a whole new vocabulary, for while I was quite capable of discussing something like Spanish literature—ancient and modern—I now had to learn how to say such mundane things as "We need a new collander" or "Buy some fire tongs."

In the morning, breakfast would be on the table, and she would be an unseen clatter of pans or dishes or a humming from the kitchen. At noon I didn't come home, preferring the hotel or a restaurant.

But when the end of the day came, I found myself looking at my watch and getting restless.

The first Sunday in the house I came down from the terrace about eleven, in my pajamas and bathrobe. The curtains in the living room had been taken down, and all the furniture had been moved into the dining room.

"Forgive the liberty, Señor," she said, "but this dark color is so *triste*. I thought perhaps the Señor might want to paint the room a lighter color."

"But we have no paint," I said, "and today is Sunday."

"Señor, I bought some yesterday." She showed me the buckets and brushes. The paint was a yellowish-orange. "I meant to ask the Señor yesterday, but I forgot until I was downtown. So I just bought it."

I looked at her dress and realized it must be the only one she owned. I went to my room, found a pair of old blue jeans, a tie for a belt and a blue denim shirt, and brought them down to her. She took the big trousers delightedly, held them shoulder-high and started to march solemnly around the room stiff-legged and kicking the pants legs out in front of her. Then she remembered that she was a servant and went upstairs. I ate breakfast, shaved, put on an old shirt and pants and went into the living room.

She was already perched on top of a ladder like a sprite on a mushroom. She was slapping paint against the wall and dragging the big brush down in long sweeps with fierce intensity. She was having a marvelous time.

Her yard of hair was piled in a black knot on top of her head, there was paint at the corners of her mouth where she had sucked the end of the brush handle, and her bare calves were speckled with yellowish-orange. The pants were rolled up to her knees, but there was nothing to be done about the waist but try to gather it up with the tie as best she could. Her young breasts stretched the shirt so tight and the buttons were so far apart that I couldn't help seeing gaps of bare flesh.

I started painting the opposite wall. We painted in silence for an hour or so. Then I went into the kitchen and got two apples. I threw one up to her.

"Gracias, Señor."

We went back to painting our respective walls.

One night I arrived home later than usual. Since it wasn't

cold, I decided to sleep out on the terrace. All the stars were present and accounted for, but half an hour later I saw them beginning to disappear as gray flats of clouds slid across the sky.

I heard Chelo walking slowly up the stairs humming and going down the hall to her room with tired steps. And then I could hear her heating the water and running a bath in the big bathroom.

About two in the morning a storm lashed the house—one of those wild warm storms that sweep across the straits from Morocco, from Tangier and Ceuta and Melilla, crisscrossing and twisting over Málaga. I was awakened by sudden shafts of rain slanting down into my face. I sprang up and started to drag the mattress inside. Then a door banged and through the pelting downpour I saw her step out onto the terrace in her nightgrown. She caught one end of the already soggy mattress and helped me drag it inside. I heard shutters slamming furiously and we raced to the patio to close them.

I shut three and then quickly went to the other side of the house to help Chelo who was wrestling the wind for the last one. I put my arms over her shoulders and pushed the shutters together, flipping the curlicue iron latch to bolt them. As she turned around, I suddenly felt the touch of her. I pulled her against me and kissed her on the mouth. The warm rain had made our clothing like another layer of skin, and as I clung to her, I could feel every contour of her body on my own.

She wrenched away with a gasp and ran into the living room. I followed her, closed the big door, and switched on the lights. Her breasts showed tawny through the wet transparency of the nightgown.

"Here." I took my overcoat from the closet.

"Very kind," she murmured, enveloping and buttoning herself in it. Then she squirmed out of the wet gown and let it plop down around her feet. She was so little that she could get her arms into the sleeves without unbuttoning the coat.

"I will make some coffee," she said.

We drank our coffee standing up, about a yard from each other. Once our eyes met over the rims of the cups.

She took the cups when we had finished and put them in the sink.

"*Buenas noches, Señor.*"

As she started to go past me toward the stairs, I took her by her shoulders and pulled her to me. She fought for a moment, twisting her head to avoid my lips, and moaning, "No, no, Señor, *por Dios* . . ."

Suddenly she turned her face to mine and our mouths met. Then we went upstairs together.

CHAPTER 9

WE WERE YOUNG AND IN LOVE, AND I thought it would never end.

In the morning I would drive off on my motorcycle and work at the Consulate until 1:30. Then home for lunch in the sun beside the fish pond on the terrace overlooking the Mediterranean and a siesta until 3:30. Then back to the Consulate until 7:30. (Andalucía stays light until ten o'clock several months of the year.)

In the evening Chelo and I would walk arm in arm through the grounds of the villa. From the hills we could see the lights of the town and the torches of the fishermen out in their boats catching the delicious boquerones and chanquetes—tiny fish typical of Málaga. Sometimes when there was a *nocturna*, a second-rate night corrida, we would climb the Gibralfaro, a steep promontory overlooking the yacht harbor and the bull ring, and watch it from there.

Chelo

Then we would wander back for dinner, which in usual Spanish fashion would not be served until around eleven, unless I had some official function to attend or unless the Consul and his wife were entertaining. I was not able to take Chelo out publicly; it was made quite clear to me that we American Consular officials were living in goldfish bowls and any untoward behavior would instantly get me removed from the post, the country and possibly the Service. Living with one's maid would definitely come under the heading of scandalous behavior. Therefore, she had to be excluded from everything. Whenever I entertained, which I was required to do often, not only could she not join the party but she had to don a maid's uniform and wait upon me and my guests. The consular corps, and in fact everyone in town, knew I had a beautiful maid—they would see her shopping downtown or their servants had informed them of the fact. When they came to my house, Chelo had to be on display and very much as a maid. It must have been degrading for her. But she tried to make light of it. Nevertheless, I arranged to give the minimum of fancy parties.

When Mauricio or Sidney Franklin or any of my other friends from Sevilla were in town the pretense was dropped. We would have gay little flamenco parties and Chelo would dance in her ruffle-trained, polka-dotted dress as I tried to accompany her on the guitar. I was taking lessons at one dollar per session from a young man named Celdonio Romero (who has since, with his brilliant sons, formed one of the most successful and sought-after guitar groups in the world).

Chelo attracted strays, and little by little the villa was transformed into a zoo. We started with a kitten named Cantinflas, then came two dogs named Manolete and Cagan-

Zorro

cho, then four pigeons all named Moriarty, two love birds
named Pelleas and Melisande, one turkey, aptly named
Condemnado, seventeen goldfish named Goldfish and a delightful young goat named Zobeida, who would leap around
the furniture in the living room, rarely touching the floor.

I had to go to Tangier on business one weekend and I
came back with a woeful monkey which was christened E.
Poor One. A total alcoholic; E. Poor One could not be left
in a room with wine or whiskey without our having a drunk
monk on our hands. Also, he used to see ghosts; he would
suddenly look up and "see" someone or something come
through the door. One could almost see the handle turn as
he riveted his attention on it. Intently he would watch the
ectoplasm walk across the room and go out another door.
Then he'd go back to picking fleas from the dog or whatever
other simian hobby he'd been indulging in.

When Mauricio went to Morocco on a petroleum matter,
he brought back a desert fox for Chelo. This creature was
shy but affectionate and was called Saharaguy, which I was
told meant "desert man" in Arabic. (I have always had a
weakness for wild animals, but especially foxes; as I write
this in 1969, my three-year-old Zorro, a gray tree-climber,
lies curled at my feet asleep.)

At Christmas I gave Chelo a parrot named Cotorrita. The
Spanish Christmas was quite different from the ones I'd
known in the United States. The emphasis was on religion,
introspection and contemplation, and not on the exchange of
expensive gifts, multiple Santa Clauses and egg nog parties.
Chelo had never heard of present-filled stockings or Santa
Claus, so I drew a large picture of him for her and put it in
the dinning room. Luis Morales, the wonderful long-time
clerk of the Consulate, told me that on the eve of the day

of the Kings, Epiphany, the sixth of January, the children of Spain put their shoes out on the window sill, hoping that the Wise Men would call and leave a gift, as they had for the infant Jesus. When the children would wake up they'd run to the mirror to see if they had a soot mark on their forehead, "left there by the touch of the Negro Wise Man, Balthazar." When Chelo woke up on the morning of the sixth and went to the bathroom to wash her face, she gave a little squeal of delight; there was a soot mark. She ran to the window and saw her shoe where I had put it. In it a note said to go to the dining room. In the dining room was the little green parrot on a stand. And several other packages, including a new dress, the finest I could buy in Málaga. She was thrilled. She gave me several drawings she had been working on plus a photo of herself which I had wanted her to have taken. It was a very nice Christmas. Or rather, *Reyes*, as it is called.

I tried to teach her English with notable lack of success. I taught her a few answers to questions such as "How are you?" and "What are we having for dinner?" I would call her from the Consulate and try her out. "Where's the dog?" I would ask, and she would reply brightly, "Meat!" We went back to Spanish.

On weekends we would drive down to the sea by back roads, fearful of being seen together. I now had another motorcycle, one with a sidecar for Chelo; all vehicles were so old and undependable in Spain that one needed two— one for use and one for the mechanic's shop. Chelo loved to ride in "el siday-car," as the appendage was called.

On some remote beach we would have our picnic and a bottle of Marqués de Riscal. I made a crude wooden mask with a glass face plate and bought an Italian fishing spear. In the crystalline Mediterranean waters I first discovered the fascinating world of fishes, a world I would visit again and again over the coming years in Peru, Jamaica, the Virgin Islands, the Bahamas, the west coast of Mexico, Hawaii, Tahiti, Moorea and Bora Bora. It is a startling and enchanting world.

I introduced Chelo to it. Though she could not swim and was timid, I led her out into the water up to her waist and convinced her to look through the goggles at the galaxy around her. She was astounded and delighted.

"It's like looking through a cathedral window!" she exclaimed.

There were round fish and flat fish, fish as rectangular as a box, fish as thin as a pencil and fish as obese as a soccer ball. There were fish of a solid bright yellow and yellow fish striped with black. Many didn't look real at all but like designs for fish to be submitted to God for approval. There were black fish spotted with blue and blue fish striped with red and red fish edged in white and white fish spangled with silver and silver fish flecked with gold. And there were octopi whose color you could never be sure of since they changed it to conform with whatever rock cluster they undulated against. There were shy soles who buried themselves in the sand so that only their eyes were visible. There were the brazen fish who swam up and bumped against the mask to stare at this invader of their realm. And everywhere there were clouds of tiny silvery fry which caught the light of the shafts of sunlight and looked like handfuls of new dimes being thrown into the water.

Usually I could manage to spear a robalo or some other delicious fish and we would either put it on a stick and roast it on the spot or take it home.

The next month, Mauricio had business in Sevilla and invited us to go with him in his chauffer-driven official car.

I thought we could get away with it that far from Málaga. Chelo was excited. She had never been out of Málaga in her life. She dressed in the dress I had given her for Christmas, an attractive blue and white floral print; she looked stunning. With a white carnation in her lovely hair and the few pieces of jewelry I had given her she looked like the essence of the aristocratic Spanish woman. Mauricio whistled when he saw her; he bowed and kissed her hand as he opened the car door for her.

"Enter, Baronesa," he said. "I christen thee la Baronesa de Málaga."

We took the shorter more dangerous way to Sevilla, through the mountain passes. Since the Civil War, many soldiers had taken refuge in the mountains and had become bandits, preying on the occasional automobile that came along. We had been warned against this route as there had recently been several murders. Mauricio kept a rifle across his lap for part of the five-hour trip. But we saw no one emerge from behind the giant boulders.

In Sevilla, we went to a *tienta* party at Juan Belmonte's. Mauricio introduced Chelo to everyone as "la Baronesa de Málaga." She got away with it, accepted even by the titled people who were at the party. She enjoyed it, putting on a regal expression as she held her hand out to the men to be kissed. She charmed everyone by doing little else but smiling; she was smart enough not to talk too much, so that the "rine in Spine" elements in her speech wouldn't be detected.

Manolete was there and when he was introduced to her he said gallantly: "Señorita, *es Usted un monumento de mujer*"—a monument to womanhood.

There was one sticky moment when an elderly Marquesa came over to her and said, "You're absolutely lovely, my dear!

But regarding the Baronetcy of Málaga, I have always been under the impression that since the war there has not been . . ."

"Excuse me!" Mauricio broke in as he led Chelo away hurriedly, "but Don Juan wants to see the Baronesa outside on the porch."

The *tienta* began and Chelo was momentarily forgotten as Belmonte and several other top toreros caped the animals. The big season was only a few weeks away and the matadors were eager to get in some practice after the winter layoff. One couldn't ask for a better show: Pepe Luis Vázquez executed the best verónicas to be seen anywhere, Manolete practiced his *manoletina*, and Lalanda did the classic butterfly pass which he invented. Mauricio and I relaxed with several extra glasses of cognac, since it was clear that today there would be no place for amateurs in the ring. I was having a magnificent time—my girl was a great success, we were watching the best bullfighting one could see, and the butler kept the glasses filled.

The *duquesa* sitting on the porch next to me offered me a cigarette from a handsome Toledo-worked case made of gold. I declined, and she asked if I would be so good as to hold the case for her, her purse was inside the house. I complied by slipping it into my breast pocket and went back to explaining to Chelo what was going on in the arena: like so many Spaniards, she had never seen a bullfight.

After a while they must have run out of pros, because all of a sudden Belmonte was looking up from the arena at me and saying: "My protege, El Señor Vice Consul, will now honor us with a few passes."

I was flabbergasted. I wished I hadn't had that last Fundador. But I couldn't un-drink it, and I couldn't weasel out.

Certainly not in front of Chelo. I wasn't even dressed in *traje corto*. I loosened my tie and got up.

"You'll show 'em," said Mauricio, who was also well taken in wine.

I went down into the ring and took the big cape that Belmonte handed me. Suddenly I decided I'd *really* show them. In an aside to Belmonte down behind the *burladero*, I asked: "Don Juan, how does one do a *larga cambiada?*"

He grinned as he replied: "Frankly, it's never occurred to me to do a *larga c-c-cambiada.*" Then he added, "Watch yourself on this animal—it's larger than you're used to and the horns aren't docked."

Before the *toril* opened, I ran across the ring and knelt down, swirling the cape out on the sand in front of me holding the corner in my right hand. I tried to remember exactly how I'd seen Felix do it. I knew the basic principle, of course, of the pass known as "the long changeover": the bull would charge to my right, and at the last moment I would swing the cape over my head and to my left, thus changing the animal's charge in mid-flight from right to left. It is one of the most spectacular and breathtaking maneuvers one can see in the ring. I was well aware of the inherent problem: if the cape is swung too soon there is suddenly no other target but the man's exposed body; if it is swung too late and too slowly, the animal changes his charge over only part way, sending a horn straight into the man's body. I had heard that the commonest reason for failure was that nervous *novilleros* became rattled when they saw the animal bearing down on them, couldn't wait out the proper time and swung too soon. I was grandly and drunkenly determined not to commit this error.

The *toril* gate opened and nothing happened. Then a

shape filled the doorway. It was a big three-year-old heifer, the biggest of the day, with long sharp forward pointing horns. But I did not quail. It spotted me, dropped its head and hurtled straight at me. I was magnificent. I stayed there calmly on my knees, my right hand holding the cape at the ready for the big changeover, waiting for the precise moment. I would not be tricked too soon; I would not be hurried into an untimely and pusillanimous maneuver simply because I was on my knees and a horned animal was hurtling at me with murder in its black eyes. I waited. And I waited. Seven feet, six feet. Still I waited. Four feet, three feet . . .

NOW!

Languidly I made my move, smoothly flipping the cape over my head. The animal responded as I knew it would. It swerved off its course after the cape, just as it should have. And then, just as it should have—since there simply wasn't time or space, traveling at that terrific speed, for the heifer to change over all the way—the left horn slammed into my chest.

The impact was tremendous. It felt like being struck by a sports car, since the animal weighed only slightly less than a small automobile. It was as though there had been a wire attached to my belt and several strong men had suddenly yanked it. As the crowd screamed from very far away. I flew fifteen feet—five long yards—through the air and fell in a crumpled heap on the sand.

Manolete attracted the animal away with his cape and Belmonte was the first to reach me. He looked worried; that horn was sharp and I had been hit near the heart. I was dazed and content to lie there—was I dead already or merely dying? They pulled back my jacket and looked for the wound which would surely be pumping out my life's blood.

"*Cómo es posible?*" Belmonte exclaimed. "There's no wound!" He ripped open my shirt. "No blood! But I saw the horn strike!"

I sat up and felt my chest. Then I removed the cigarette case from my breast pocket. There was a deep dent in it, almost all the way through the metal. Belmonte took it and turned it over in his hands. Then he began to laugh his great wheezy coughing laugh and I thought he would never stop. He was still laughing as he helped me back up to the stands and showed people the case. He finally gave it back to me, saying: "I'll order half a dozen—one for each p-p-pocket. Should have had them years ago."

I sat down sheepishly and wearily next to Chelo.

"Sometimes I do better," I said.

She patted my arm. I turned to the *duquesa* and handed her the case with thanks, but she said, "No—I wish you to keep it as a memento of an Andalusian afternoon." (And I still have it, not so much as a souvenir of Andalucía but as a reminder never to do *larga cambiadas*—ever!—and never to mix bulls and Fundador.)

America was not through distinguishing herself this afternoon. Now Mauricio was in the arena. He was holding a *garrocha*, the long pole used for tilting animals from horseback. It was quite clear that he was going to attempt the *salto de garrocha*, that ancient, spectacular maneuver glorified by Goya in his Tauromaquia series of etchings. Where Mauricio got the idea I don't know, for while he had tried his hand, sober, at caping calves at various *tientas*, he had never attempted this. Nor had anyone else I'd ever known. The crowd clapped in anticipation of seeing such a rare feat.

With both hands Mauricio held the pole under his right

arm like a star pole-vaulter, which indeed he had been in high school back in Manhattan. The heifer was across the arena where Manolete had it hypnotized by his cape; when the matador saw Mauricio was ready, he ducked behind a *burladero*, calling, "All yours!"

Mauricio wagged the pole and shouted, "*Ah hah, vaca!*"

The heifer broke into a run across the arena, building up speed as it ran toward him. Mauricio started running hard straight at it. When the end of his pole was three feet from the charging animal's snout, Mauricio jabbed the pole into the ground. His impetus swung him up into the air in a high graceful arc. The man vaulted completely over the animal which passed under him, wondering where its victim had disappeared to. Mauricio landed on his feet behind the animal's stern and ran to the shelter of a *burladero* before the heifer could recover from its surprise.

We all clapped delightedly, and Mauricio took a bow with mock solemnity. But the applause went to his head. Instead of gracefully retiring in triumph to the stands, he grabbed the *garrocha* and prepared to repeat the maneuver. Everything went as before except with one exception that Mauricio hadn't figured on: fighting bulls, and especially heifers, have good memories. For example, a bull which had, as a calf, been pic'd severely at its testing by a man on a white horse might, when in the arena, charge horses of every color except white.

This heifer remembered; she had learned from the first *garrocha* experience. Now when Mauricio confidently grabbed his pole and again sailed blithely into the air, the heifer did not charge on through like the first time. Instead, it slammed on the brakes and skidded to a stop, looking up at Mauricio and waiting for him to come down. Mauricio tried to delay this eventuality as long as possible. When he saw the horns waiting underneath for him, he clutched his pole frantically trying to shinny up it, defying gravity as long as humanly possible. But down he had to come. And back up in the air he went, this time impelled by a butt of the heifer's head. Again he came down and again he went up. The dangerous farce could have gone on all day had not Manolete lured the animal away, and allowed Mauricio to sprawl on the sand unmolested. His clothing was ripped, his body was bruised, but luckily he hadn't been punctured.

We left the rest of the afternoon's activity to the Spaniards, where it belonged.

I did not get back to Sevilla and bullfighting myself for more than two months. But I did have a lucky meeting three weeks later.

Mauricio and Chelo and I drove three hours along the coast to Algeciras to see the first big corrida of the season. It would star Carlos Arruza—no one cared who else was on the program. This twenty-five-year-old Mexican had taken Spain by storm for a few months the previous year. More and more people were saying he was greater than Manolete. Others scoffed and said that while brave, he was only fit to be Manolete's banderillero. The publicity build-up was unprecedented in the history of bullfighting. He seemed to have come from nowhere in answer to the obvious need for someone to compete with Manolete on his own level. It was almost too good to be true—different styles, different countries, but two great toreros. The impresarios loved the idea and so did the public.

When we got to Algeciras it was raining and we went to the Hotel María Cristina. The fight had been called off,

Carlos Arruza

and many of the fans were milling disconsolately around the lobby hoping for some miracle in the weather. I saw my friend, Eduardo Miura, the famous bull breeder, standing near the bar with another man. Eduardo waved to me.

"Eduardo, *que mala suerte*," I said, as I came up to him. "Damn this rain—I was hoping we'd find out today once and for all if this Mexican clown's really any good or if it's all been publicity."

Eduardo's friend spoke up gloomily. "I was hoping to find that out also, Señor."

"Permit me," Eduardo said, clearing his throat, "to introduce you to Carlos Arruza."

I recovered sufficiently to shake hands. Arruza smiled to make me feel better. He didn't look Mexican. He didn't look Spanish. With a lock of brown hair over his forehead, a boyish grin on his handsome face and a red sports shirt, he looked like the prototype of the Midwestern American college boy. He was tall for a bullfighter, as tall as Manolete, and slender. But he didn't have that tubercular fragile look that Manolete had. Arruza looked like an athlete.

"May I buy you a sherry to help excuse my gaucheness?" I asked.

Eduardo had to leave but Arruza joined us for sherry, and afterwards lunch. We found we had friends in common in Mexico and we talked long and pleasantly.

I asked him where his next fight was.

"Castellón de la Plana, day after tomorrow. Come with us —I'll pick you up in Málaga on the way."

He was as good as his word. Chelo and Mauricio couldn't go; big and grand as the Buick station wagon was, it was still a squeeze with several of Arruza's cuadrilla in there. Arruza's manager, Gago, and the rest of the team had gone ahead. On the long drive Arruza was very tense. He kept talking about a new pass he'd thought up. He thought it might work. It sounded strange and impossible.

"I've got to come up with something different," he kept saying. "You don't know how it is—all this publicity. It weighs on you like a load of coal. I've just *got* to be good. You can go down in this business a lot quicker than you came up."

As it turned out he was good. He was sensational. That day he held the muleta *behind* his legs and created the fantastic *arrucina* pass, the most dangerous that had ever been seen.

News of Arruza's triumph in Castellón spread over Spain. The papers were saying that Arruza was far greater than he had been the previous season—his style had jelled, there were no raw edges now. But Castellón, people argued, was only a town of 50,000. What did they know of real bullfighting? Wait until he tried that fancy business in a big city—any big city.

He fought next in Barcelona on April 2. Unfortunately, it was too far for me to go and I had work to do. How I regretted not having gone! It was probably the most resounding success ever recorded there.

We were very flattered that he stopped in Málaga on his way back. Over dinner he told Chelo and me about it elatedly. He had been awarded both ears, the tail and a hoof. It made the front page of every newspaper in Spain. Manolete had only been awarded one hoof in the entire previous season. It is difficult to imagine the excitement that swept over all Spain. World Series emotion or heavyweight championship interest in our country cannot approach the epidemic fever created by these two men in Spain in 1945.

The great epochs in bullfighting history have always been based on the rivalry of two men: Lagartijo and Frascuelo in the old days, Joselito and Belmonte in more modern times. Now, for the first time in more than a quarter of a century, two men of equal talents would be striving for the coveted title of *El Número Uno*. Adding to the interest was that Arruza came from a democratic country that was harboring Spanish refugees and, in theory, bore little love for the fatherland. That it was no secret that Manolete and Arruza had hated each other from the moment they first met did not hurt the box office either.

"You'd like him if you knew him," I argued with Arruza. "He just appears to be a little aloof; he's shy."

"Shy?" snorted Arruza. "He's shy like Attila the Hun. He's glacial!"

So, besides the natural rivalry of two highly skilled technicians we had the added factor of personal antagonism. It made for great copy and violent conversation in the cafés.

Manolete had also started his season, but in five corridas he had been awarded only four ears. That would be fine for an ordinary matador, but not for the god Manolete had become. Already the crowds were demanding more from him because of Arruza. Yet while they had fought together eight times the year before, they still hadn't met on the same program this year. Just how great was the "New" Arruza? How would the two men compare when seen together with the same bulls on the same program on the same day?

Finally, it was announced that they would fight on the same program on both April 18 and April 19 in the most demanding *plaza* of them all—the Real Maestranza ring of Sevilla—with the finest and largest bulls available.

Arruza seemed confident now. "I am looking forward to

it," he said quietly. He told us that all 30,000 tickets for the two days were gone, in spite of the astronomical prices, six hours after they went on sale, but that he would have tickets set aside for us. It seemed the eighteenth would never come.

On April 6 I came home from the consulate for lunch as usual. Pepe, the gardener, opened the grilled gate to the garden for me. He had his beret in his hand and tears were running down his wrinkled cheeks.

"It's so tragic, Señor," he said. "Our sympathy . . . "

All I could think of was Chelo. I grabbed him by the shoulders. "What's happened to her?"

"Not her," he mumbled. His watery eyes blinked at me. "That great man, your President—we just heard on the radio . . . "

"Rosey-belt," as the Spaniards called him, had died. The reaction in this country so far from America, so far from democracy, was extraordinary. Long lines formed in front of the consulate building that afternoon and for a week, people from all walks of life streamed through the consulate to express their sorrow. It was touching and impressive.

We were all worried about what would happen now to our country and to the prosecution of the war. It seemed that there simply had never been a time when Roosevelt had not guided the country for better or for worse. How could this haberdasher possibly fill the breach? Our most recent impression of the Vice-President was the tasteless photo in the previous week's *Life* magazine. At the keyboard of an upright piano, he was smirking at Rita Hayworth who was draped sexily on the top of it.

A directive from Ambassador Armour "suggested" that all consular personnel observe a two-week mourning period (reelections). Women should dress in black, men in dark suits. No one was to appear in any public places, such as restaurants, night clubs, theaters, or bullfights . . .

BULLFIGHTS!

I went into the consul's office. Harold Quarton was a decent, bald, stout man who looked like Henry J. Kaiser and who said everything, no matter how nice, with clenched teeth, as though he were terribly angry at something.

"Mr. Quarton," I began, "I mean no disrespect for our late great President, but couldn't I just mourn like the devil for twelve days instead of half-heartedly for all fourteen? I mean, I'll fast and go to bed at eight and mass on Sunday and . . ."

"I'm sorry," he said. He was always a good friend. "I know how much the two corridas mean to you. But a suggestion from the ambassador is an order. We'd all be in hot water."

"How about a disguise? Maybe a beret and glasses . . ."

"No chance."

"and a great big nose . . ."

"No."

"and a beard down to . . ."

"No!" He slammed his hand down on the desk. I gave up.

For the next eleven days I listened to the radio and read the papers—the interviews, the predictions—and I died a little inwardly.

I had a commiserating letter from Roberta in Lisbon:

Are you in mourning, too? I suppose you are and maybe—horror of horrors—you can't go to the fair in Sevilla! I know we have been told "not to be seen enjoying ourselves in public"; I don't know whether that means we can go out to night clubs if we act as though we're not enjoying it. Maybe they'll let you go see the fights if you promise to keep the corners of your mouth down and not to shout "*Olé.*" We have been told to wear all black for two weeks. It's been only eight days now, and I'm so damned sick of my three black dresses that I don't think I can hold out. It affects my mental outlook. Last night I went to dinner at the embassy all black and mournful, but what they didn't know was that I'd gone home first and put on red shoes, a pink shirt and a yellow sweater, and did a Charleston all by myself—which relieved me somewhat. (Remember Iris March in *The Green Hat,* who used to wear red shoes because she said she could walk faster in red shoes?)

The day of the first fight I dragged myself gloomily into the consulate. The newspaper on my desk had large photos on the front page of Arruza with his big grin and Manolete with his tragic face. Underneath it said, "Which will triumph?"

"Who gives a damn anyway," I muttered and tried to busy myself with a report on the tobacco industry of Granada.

Mr. Quarton appeared in my office suddenly. He appeared especially and ferociously angry, as he always did before doing something nice. He hemmed and hawed and then he burst out with it.

"Goddammit Conrad, if you think I am going to continue to look at that woebegone, wretched, self-pitying, imbecilic face of yours for one more day you are wrong! Now get out of this office and get your tail over to Sevilla for those stupid corridas!"

If he had looked just a little less like Henry J. Kaiser I would have kissed him. As I wrung his hand and dashed out of the office I heard him say: "But take the long way around!"

It was ten o'clock. The fight would begin at five o'clock. Sevilla was far away. I would just be able to make it. As usual, the Harley-Norton-Soriano was in the shop, its *queren-cia*. But the toothless young mechanic had finished fixing whatever had been wrong with it and assured me it was "*absolutamente perfecta*," as he always did. To prove it he started the engine on only the sixth hard kick of the starting pedal. As he was gassing it up, I telephoned Arruza, told him I'd be there after all, and to leave a ticket at the hotel for me.

After phoning Chelo, I roared out of town heading for the mountains. I disliked disobeying the Consul after he had been so decent in letting me go, but it was going to be hard enough to cover the distance going the short way. The long way was out of the question except perhaps in a very fast car.

I had gone quite a distance, almost an hour of travel, before anything vibrated off the motorcycle. The first thing to go was the hand lever that worked the clutch. That was all right. I stopped, put it in my pocket and by pulling the cable with my fingers was able to shift gears adequately. An hour later, as we climbed steeply, the exhaust pipe fell off and clattered behind me on the road. I didn't want to lose my momentum, and the motorcycle seemed to operate as well, though considerably noisier without it, so I didn't even stop. Half an hour later the cable to the accelerator broke, but I found this little problem could be surmounted by simply pulling on the wire inside the cable, by-passing that fancy turnable grip on the handlebar. After awhile, my fingers felt as though they were ready to drop off also. But I consoled myself that I was almost over the mountains and the rest would be much easier. The crest was just ahead.

Suddenly, as I was going through a rocky gorge, a remarkable thing happened; with a great crack my headlight exploded. I stared down in wonderment at the tangled mess of metal where there had been a nice shiny headlight a second before. The motorcycle never paused in its headlong flight, so I didn't worry. But I was perplexed. I was never of a mechanical bent, to say the least, though I was aware and accustomed to the strange vagaries and frailties of my Harley-Norton-Soriano. But what on earth could be inside of a headlight to cause it to explode like that for absolutely no reason? Internal combusion, I decided sagely, just before I heard the whine of the second bullet.

I crouched low over the handlebars and looked back. There in the shadow of a giant boulder were several men. They had rifles and, quite incredibly, they were shooting at me. I had never been shot at before. I didn't like it.

The trouble was that I still had a long straight section of road up to the crest of the hill. I was like a metal duck in a shooting gallery, I was traveling at a given rate of speed on a steady course. They could not fail to hit me again before I got over the other side of the mountain.

Ahead on my right, I saw a dirt side road. I swerved off the paved road on to it. At full speed I skidded down its winding turns. But after a few hundred yards I saw that the road narrowed down into a hunter's path where the motorcycle could never go. I spun the machine around and went back two hundred feet to a growth of dense foliage and trees off to the left. Careening off the road I crashed ten feet into the middle of the brush. I killed the engine and tried to rearrange the branches in front to shield me.

In what seemed like a very few moments, I saw the men coming. There were seven or eight of them. They were not dressed as I had expected brigands to be dressed, with gold rings in their ears and silk bandanas on their heads. Unshaven and dirty, they wore berets, cartridge belts slung across their chests and the white clothes of the Andaluz peasant. Some wore tattered remnants of military uniforms, one a general's cap which I assume was captured since he didn't look like a general in *anybody's* army. One had a leather wine bottle from which he was drinking with the hand that wasn't holding a pistol. They were strolling along chatting and laughing; they knew that the road ran out and that a motorcycle couldn't get very far. Rather than appearing in hot pursuit of anything, it was more like a pleasant holiday rabbit shoot—if they got something, fine. If they didn't, that was all right too. (In retrospect they seemed like the semicomical bandits in the film *The Treasure of the Sierra Madre*, when the besieged Bogart called out, "If you are law officers as you say, show me your badges!" and the bandits shouted back: "We don' have to show no steenkin' badges!")

But there was nothing comical about these brigands at the time. Closer and closer they came. At one point they were not three yards from my hiding place. The dirt road was baked hard, but perhaps I'd left some tracks. I thought if they couldn't hear my heart pounding, they would surely hear the little "pings" my cooling motorcycle's engine was making.

There is a bit of nauseating but true nature lore which says the giant sloth is so afraid of his enemy, the tiger, that when it is up in a tree and a tiger is prowling in the vicinity below, the terrified sloth catches and eats his own droppings rather than risk detection. I quite suddenly had acquired a deep understanding and compassion for the sloth.

But the men went on by me. The moment they turned the corner in the road, I raised myself up in the saddle. Coming down with my full weight on the starter pedal I gave it the most vicious yet prayerful kick an inanimate object ever received. For the first time in its life, the Harley-Norton-Soriano started on the first attempt, as though it, too, was scared and wanted no more of its parts shot off. I jerked the bare clutch wire, shifted, and the engine roared into life as I pulled the accelerator wire out to its fullest. We crashed out through the brush onto the dirt road, and by the time the brigands came running back, I was out on the main road. It would have been far safer to go downhill back to Málaga, but I was headed for Sevilla. I made the crest just as the bandits came running out on the road. They fired, perhaps into the air, and shouted. The shouts almost sounded happy, as though they could show they were sportsmen too, and it was only fair that the rabbit had got away—this time.

I patted my mechanical friend as we coasted down the long grade and resolved never to curse it again. I pondered on what I should do about my narrow escape; an attack on a consular official was not a minor matter. A report should be made to the embassy. On the other hand, the Ambassador would immediately want to know why I was allowed to go to Sevilla and that would get Mr. Quarton in trouble. And Mr. Quarton would want to know why the hell I had disobeyed him, and that would get me in trouble. Better just to forget the whole thing.

I continued on my way in the blazing sun, parched, stiff, saddlesore, sweaty and grimy. Only one more part fell off before we got to Sevilla. But it was a relatively important one. It was the bar that one rests one's feet on. I suppose I could have stopped, picked it up and gone back to look for the nut and bolt that had been vibrated free. But it was already almost four o'clock and I had many kilometers to go. I kept going at my breakneck pace.

I was relieved and grateful that the last part to go did not influence the running capacity of the engine or something else that would force me to quit altogether. Nevertheless, I sorely missed some place to rest my feet. It is not easy to hold your legs off the ground for almost an hour. The muscles screamed for relief after a short time. It was agony, but I kept going, through towns and villages and herds of cattles and goats. Finally, unbelievably, Sevilla loomed into sight. I could see the Giralda tower jutting up arrogantly out of the flat land and the giant silhouette of the cathedral. I sputtered into its cobbled streets at twenty-five minutes of five.

The fair was on, everyone was dressed in gay costumes, and I could barely get through the streets thronged with revelers and fancy carriages and horses in their fine trappings.

One hundred yards from Arruza's hotel the front tire exploded. I spilled off the saddle and had trouble standing up for a moment. The motorcycle sprawled in the gutter like a stricken pterodactyl. I picked it up and wheeled it into a little open bar, shoved some bills into the startled owner's hands and gasped, "Take care of it till tomorrow!"

Then I lurched on down the street toward the hotel. I must have presented an interesting sight. I'm sure I looked not unlike a modern day Quasimodo. My knees were bent and feeling as though they would never again straighten; the muscles were frozen at half their standard length. My back and shoulders were humped in the same position that they had been in since ten that morning. My fingers were locked in a predatory attitude like the talons of a peregrine falcon on the attack. My face and neck were black with dust and grease except where my dark glasses were.

There was a crowd around the entrance to the hotel and a shout went up as I got there. Arruza's men, dressed in costume, were shoving open a path for their matador to the waiting station wagon. Carlos, resplendent in a cinammon and gold suit of lights, strode by me as people clapped him on the back and wished him luck.

"Carlos," I croaked.

He didn't recognize me.

"It's me," I said. "Bernabé."

He stopped. "But Chico, what's happened to you?"

"I came by motorcycle," I said, "All the way."

He couldn't help grinning at my appearance. "The concierge's got your ticket. Use my room to clean up. There's a bottle of brandy there, too."

"Good luck," I said, and he nodded and got in the car. Vargas, the sword boy, gave me the hotel key as he got in the front seat.

I was in better shape by the time the fight started. A face wash and a couple of pulls on the brandy bottle made me relax and straighten up and almost forget that a short while ago I had been target practice for a band of thugs. The hotel was near the bull ring, and I managed to get into my seat just as the band struck up "Morena de Mi Copla." No other ring in the world can compete with the Maestranza for setting and architectural beauty. The sand, actually crushed rocks from the mining district of Huelva, is a true golden color the way the fight posters like to depict it. There is no advertising permitted as in most *plazas*. One of the oldest in the world, its classic form was built in 1761 and its history of great fights is unequaled. New chapters in that history were soon to be added.

It was unquestionably the finest day of bullfighting I had ever seen, both men being awarded ears and tail off both bulls. Could it ever be better?

The first time I had seen Arruza perform the year before, I asked Belmonte what he'd thought of Arruza.

"*No me ha c-c-convencido,*" he said. "He hasn't c-c-convinced me."

Today, as we all left the stands jubilantly, I again asked him what he thought of Arruza.

"Well," said Belmonte, jutting out his jaw, "the lad is beginning to c-c-convince me."

The following day both men outdid their previous performances. And there were added thrills.

Manolete, in trying to outdo Arruza's spectacular performance, worked in so close to the horns of his second bull that it seemed impossible that he would not be gored. And it happened. While doing one of his supremely languid natural passes out in the middle of the ring, the bull hooked slightly to the left. It was only a few inches but it was enough. Suddenly there he was on top of the horns and flung into the air. It was doubly shocking because he had always appeared so invulnerable. The bull's act seemed like sacrilege. Manolete lay sprawled on the sand and as helpless as any other man as the bull whirled to spike him. None of his men were near him to help, and it looked like an inevitable goring.

Suddenly a gold streak shot across the arena. It was Arruza. He had nothing but a banderilla in his hand. He reached the bull before it got to Manolete and whacked it across the nose with the stick. The bull swerved away after Carlos, who zigzagged to the fence and vaulted it just in time.

Manolete lurched to his feet and was helped to safety by his men. He was dazed but not hurt.

Carlos told me after the fight that "Even though we're enemies, I was glad he didn't get gored. I wouldn't wish that on anybody. As I passed by him I started to tell him that. But then I said, what the hell. I thought for a minute he was actually going to thank me for saving his stupid life, but then his sword boy handed him his muleta and sword and he went back out in the ring and we still haven't spoken to each other. Maybe it's better this way."

Even though shaken up by the tossing, Manolete killed perfectly and was awarded both ears. Both men were carried on the shoulders of the crowd all the way to their hotels. But Arruza had been awarded the ears and tail, so it was his day. I saw Belmonte on the way out.

"Now what do you think of Arruza?" I asked.

Belmonte grinned. "The lad has c-c-convinced me."

"Which one is the better?" I had the temerity to ask.

He hesitated a moment.

"*El que mas c-c-cobre*," he replied quietly. "The one who gets paid the m-m-most."

Belmonte and Arruza and I had a drink afterwards at the elegant Alfonso XIII Hotel. But it was difficult because hordes of people, even in that sophisticated bar, kept coming up to shake Arruza's hand. We had to leave finally. Arruza was fighting in Almería the next day, so he agreed to drop me off in Málaga on the way. We loaded the corpse of the Harley-Norton-Soriano on top of the car and set off.

"The bastard could have thanked me, at least," Arruza muttered before falling into an exhausted sleep. He had fought eighteen straight days in a row. Just the constant traveling from one side of the country to another would hospitalize the ordinary man, without even the nerve-wracking and physically exhausting fighting of the bulls. But it was only the beginning.

CHAPTER 10

O
N THE NINTH OF MAY, ONE OF THE
greatest corridas ever recorded happened in Valencia. During that fantastic afternoon, Manolete, Arruza and Manolete's great protege, Parrita, were awarded twelve ears, six tails and three hoofs. Only six sword thrusts were needed for the six animals. The matadors shared the trophies equally, and the next day the newspapers referred to the *plaza* as "*un manicomio*"—an insane asylum.

To try to describe it would be impossible. But the next day there was another event of note. I was invited to a little luncheon the impresario gave in a patio back of the corrals. It was in honor of the matadors and their men; of course, a luncheon for matadors who are to perform later that day is more a tribute to the honor of the occasion than a banquet, since toreros don't eat much if anything the day of a fight.

As I started to sit down I was horrified to see them seat

Arruza next to Manolete. They still had never spoken to each other. It looked as though it were done diabolically to watch the fireworks, perhaps for publicity purposes. I was across the table and tried to keep them distracted from each other as they sat down. But Arruza nodded at Manolete coldly and Manolete nodded back. This, compared to their previous salutations, was practically an embrace. Arruza made some remark about the food, which seemed to break the ice.

"You missed a fine opportunity to let me get killed off there in Sevilla," said Manolete laconically. "I've wanted to thank you for not doing it."

"What would I do for a rival then?" said Arruza offhandedly. "I need the stimulus of the little competition you manage to give me."

There was a brief silence. Then the impossible happened. Manolete's mouth widened and he gave a low rumbling noise. Everyone looked up from the table. Manolete was laughing! Few people had ever seen or heard Manolete laugh. And then Arruza laughed, and they started to talk. They talked all through the meal and stayed on afterwards for another hour. They would have stayed longer but they both had to leave for Barcelona where they were fighting that afternoon. They shook hands warmly. When they met again later that day they were once more bitter rivals.

And so the friendship was born. As Arruza wrote about it in his autobiography,

That was how I began to know Manolete, the other Manolete, the charming, friendly, humorous one who existed only away from the *plaza de toros*. I had never met anyone whom I liked and admired so much as this man to whom bullfighting was a religion.

. . . Away from the ring we became like brothers, but inside the ring it was each man for himself.

Forty-four more times they appeared on the same program together in that fabulous season of 1945, and eight of those times *mano-a-mano*—hand-to-hand with no other matador. It was one of the most brilliant—if brief—rivalries of all time. Once started, it could only be ended by one of their deaths.

Manolete was a magnificent fighter and a good friend. He probably was the greater fighter from a standpoint of sheer perfection and majestic execution, just as Joselito was probably better than Belmonte. But there has never been a more versatile or more exciting bullfighter than Arruza. If they were both fighting the same day in different *plazas*, I might admit that Manolete was the better fighter—but I would go to see Arruza! No one ever quite knew what would happen when Carlos was in the ring.

About this time I was summoned to Madrid by the new ambassador, Norman Armour. Unlike so many ambassadors appointed only for political reasons, Armour was a cultured, intelligent and charming man who handled people as well as his assignments. Five minutes after I stepped in his office, I felt I'd known him for years. The consul in Sevilla was being recalled to the State Department, he said. Did I think I could accept the assignment of acting consul, in charge of the vice-consul and the other fifteen employees?

"I realize you're only twenty-three," he said, "but we feel you can handle it. If you don't let too much bullfighting get in the way, that is. And speaking of bullfighting, I'm flying up to Pamplona today on a little matter—how about joining us so you can explan what's going on?"

I knew this much about Pamplona: it is the only city in the world whose entire male populace is made up of psychopaths. In case there is any doubt about this fact, they annually demonstrate their madness in the streets from July 7 to July 15 during the traditional fiesta of San Fermín.

Pamplona, which is about two hundred miles from Madrid, has always been a bull-conscious town. In fact, one of the very first documents we have regarding professional bullfighting pertains to Pamplona. It is a royal order, dated August, 1385, by Carlos II, in which he says that fifty libra are to be paid "to two men, one Moorish and one Christian, that We have had come from Zaragoza to kill two bulls in Our presence in Our city of Pamplona." But although Pamplona, with its *plaza* holding 13,000 and its top programs every year, is a major bullfighting town, its fame is clearly based on what happens in its streets.

Along for the jaunt also were the naval attaché, and a friend of mine, Sam Dodge, a mild, plump little lieutenant (j.g.) from the naval attaché's office who had been a history of art instructor at Yale before the war. He hated any form of bullfighting with a passion, so I couldn't imagine why he had come along.

When we landed on the small Pamplona field, officials immediately whisked us off to a large cocktail gathering. The people were charming and it was hard to believe that they could be an enthusiastic party to the traditional savagery that was to take place in the morning. I was just beginning to assign Hemingway's accounts to tourist lore, when the young mayor of the town came over to us.

"I am going to bed," he said, shaking hands, "so as to be fresh for the bulls tomorrow."

"Bulls?" Sam asked.

"Yes," said the *alcalde*, with a twinkle in his eye. "Surely you are going to run also, *Teniente* Dodge?"

"Surely I am not!" said Sam coldly and aggressively, his

bull phobia blinding him to the fact that the *alcalde* was jesting, for no one would ever seriously dream of an *Americano* running in front of the bulls. "Furthermore," Sam announced vehemently to the assemblage, "I think it's barbaric and degrading and I refuse to get up at an ungodly hour to even watch those . . . those "—mustering up the proper loathing in his voice "—those *bulls!*"

Ah me, the best laid plans *do* gang aglae in Spain as well as Scotland.

At seven the next morning, the ambassador, the naval attaché, two Pamplona officials and I gathered in front of our lodgings in the cold light of morning ready to set off for the main part of town where the bulls were enclosed. The night before we had gone to a boisterous dance after the cocktail party and had retired at about two o'clock. But not Sam; Sam had disappeared. We had been discussing bulls at the table and when we looked around, he was gone. Exactly where he went nobody knew.

He didn't come in at all that night, and we wondered about him as we got into the car in the morning. Then, suddenly, there loomed in the road three weird figures. They each carried a blown up bladder on a stick and they would hit each other on the head with it from time to time saying, "*Riau, riau,*" which for some unaccountable reason Pamplonicas like to do at fair time. (What "*Riau, riau*" means is not known, unless it means "Look what a capital fellow I am— I am hitting you on the head with a bladder!") They were like any other group of Pamplonicas, except that in the middle, dressed in the traditional Pamplona bull-fleeing costume of *alpargata* sandals, white trousers, red sash, white shirt, red neckerchief and red beret, was Sam. From the brightness of his costume, his ashen face stared out at us, while two similarly dressed Pamplonicas flanked him, weaving unsteadily. (Unlike Andalucía, the people are inclined to drink in the North of Spain.) We piled out of the car and stared unbelievingly at Sam.

"He is our *hermanito*," said one of the Pamplonicas. "He is our little brother and he is going to run. *Riau, riau.*"

"Run where?" I asked, dreading the answer.

"In front of the bulls, of course!" the Pamplonicas chorused delightedly. "Come, we must hurry, they will start soon."

"Sam, what's this all about?" asked the ambassador.

Sam started to answer, but one of the Pamplonicas broke in: "He's told everyone in town that he's going to run, everyone is waiting to see the *Americano* run in front of the bulls. *Riau, riau.*"

"Is that right?" the captain asked. "Have you told everyone that you're going to run?"

Sam swallowed. "Well, maybe not *everyone*, sir."

The captain paced up and down.

"Are you really going to run, Sam?" I asked, incredulously.

"Of course he is!" broke in the Pamplonicas who knew some English. "He is mos' brave *Americano* who live. *Riau, riau.*"

"Are you running, Sam?" I repeated.

He paled. "Well, I guess I am, unless the ambassador wants me to grease up the plane or something." Louder. "I say I guess I will unless maybe the ambassador thinks its undignified and forbids me to."

The ambassador turned around and said quietly, "No, Sam, I'm not going to forbid you to." Sam's face fell visibly. "And I'm not going to order you to do it either, but it seems to me that you've got yourself and America into a hell of a mess if you've told it all over town that you're going to run. At least 10,000 people will be on hand to watch this thing and you know yourself how much stock Spaniards put in personal bravery and what they'll think of Americans if you back out at the last minute."

"Well, I am not as charitable as the ambassador," said the captain. "Lieutenant Dodge, I order you to honor your word as an officer and a gentleman. Now get in the car!"

None of us said a word the whole way. Upon arriving at the starting point, we got out and shook hands with Sam silently. Then he climbed over the thick board fence that blocked off the side streets, keeping the crowd safe from the bulls, and joined the leaders of a mass of about two hundred sleepless Pamplonicas, most of them in various stages of intoxication. No one was really plastered, however, for a *guardia civil* was stationed at each entrance to prevent any falling-down drunks from getting in.

"That one's the *Americano*," I heard them buzz as we pushed through the jammed crowd safely up to a place selected for us where we could see the whole half-mile course. "There, that small one in front of the other runners is the *Yanqui*, the poor little one!"

We didn't speak among ourselves but the ambassador kneaded his hands and the captain kept looking at his watch. It was seven twenty-eight. The other runners were wandering nervously around, occasionally glancing back at the end of the street where the bulls were to be released. But Sam was down in a sprinter's crouch, looking up the long gray street with grim determination on his face and not daring to look at the giant bulls that were bellowing and pawing restlessly in the enclosure back of him.

"In the blind wound of the dawn" runs a song about the running of the bulls, "they are waiting, waiting . . . "

Bang! At exactly seven-thirty the pistol was fired, the bulls were released, the crowd let out a great roar and the runners sprang forth with a speed that was in direct proportion to the amount of wine they had consumed the night before. The veteran Pamplonicas around Sam were calm and unruffled because they knew the bulls were a hundred yards behind them still, and that there were hundreds of enticing Pamplonicas between, so they jogged along as though their biggest immediate worry was not to step on the squares. But not Samuel; it was enough for him that there were bulls at large in the town site, and he shot off from his crouching start like puffed rice from a cannon, quickly taking the lead and pulling away from the mob, trying to run easily as the old track coach had taught him at Yale, chin up, elbows close to the body and on the balls of the feet.

The string of one of his sandals came untied as he rounded the first corner. He stepped on it and sprawled on the cobblestone street. As he got up a wave of Pamplonicas caught up with him, knocking him down to his knees. Again as he tried to rise Spanish feet battered him flat to the street. He lay stretched out trying to protect his head while wave after wave ran over and around him. As he lay there, unable to rise and panicky, he heard a great roar go up from the crowd. Twisting his head around, he saw, through the maze of legs, the flashing black of the gigantic lead bull as it swung around the corner, followed by seven others, not five yards away.

Up to that point Sam had been scared, but I don't think the rules of the game had been made quite clear to him: it hadn't really been impressed upon him that he was playing for keeps. But now, after one look at that horny tribe, he clawed, fought and slugged his way to his feet and you could see the horrible import of the situation etched on

his face. If he had been white before, he was pale chartreuse now.

Sam shuddered afterwards: "I could feel the beast's hot alfalfa breath on my neck."

The lead bull was two yards behind—and gaining, gaining terribly fast. At first when Sam began to run, it was like the nightmare when the tiger's after one and the legs won't work. But then he began to stride out and soon was almost holding his own with the bull whose great horns were now just a few feet astern. The bull was still gaining, when the boy next to Sam tripped and fell. The bull lost time by slowing down to take a jab at the prostrate figure. But in a moment the lead animal plus two others were up to Sam again, and he ran as never before in his life, throwing form to the wind, his legs going like rubber pistons and his arms flailing the air. Some other runners gave up running and took refuge in doorways or cringed in niches or crouched in the gutter, trying to grow gray and inconspicuous like the street itself. Then a youth just a bit ahead of Sam tripped and fell, and the bulls again slowed down, like wolves halting in their pursuit of a drotsky to eat a tossed-out occupant.

The new delay gave Sam a real chance to open up and gain a lead of about five yards. The end was in sight. Ten yards ahead of him was the bull ring and safety, but before him lay the toughest stretch of all. The first part of the half-mile course is tough enough, running through the forty-foot-wide street, but where the real casualties come is at the entrance of the *plaza*, where the street funnels down to the *plaza* gate which is about twenty feet wide. When a couple of hundred frantic Pamplonicas converge on the *plaza* entrance and try to fight their way through to safety, it's like trying to get ten pounds of guano into a five-pound bag.

When Sam got to the entrance, the struggling forms were piled five feet high, blood was spattered on the plaster walls, and it looked like suicide to try to get through. But then he glanced over his shoulder up the street and saw bearing down on him that spearhead of bulls, some of their horns glistening red with blood. Sam hurled himself, without hesitating, on top of the seething mass, crawling over heads and backs and arms and legs, until finally he spilled out into the sunlight of the arena.

The bulls were right behind him, ploughing and trampling and goring their way through the Pamplonicas. As they surged into the ring Sam scrambled off the arena sand, beat it to the low wooden barrera and vaulted to safety. There, with considerable dignity, he threw up. His head was swimming, his mouth felt like emory paper, he was covered with bruises, but as he settled happily to the ground he offered up a prayer of thanks, white of face and wet of pants. He'd preserved the honor of the United States and the American Navy—and he smiled.

I transferred back to Sevilla the next week, but I kept my house in Málaga. Chelo was very upset. I tried to explain that it would just be for a few weeks.

"No," she said. "It will be for a long time. Then you will be sent someplace else. And then some other place. And then you will go back to America. And then I will never see you again."

I assured her that she was wrong, that I would come back and see her every weekend, and in a few weeks the new permanent consul would arrive in Sevilla and then I would come back to Málaga forever. But we were both despondent when she saw me off on the train.

I missed Chelo in Sevilla. I telephoned her every day. But being the consul had its compensations. I had a grand car, a day and night chauffeur and a palatial dwelling with several servants. I gave some extravagant parties in the ballroom, which were quite different from the stuffy affairs of my predecessor. Best of all, I was my own boss.

I tried to initiate some reforms in the consulate. It had long struck me that most of our missions in the world were overladen with unnecessary personnel. (In 1949, when the Communists in Czechoslovakia ordered our government to cut our embassy staff there from eighty to thirteen, the ambassador stated that his skeletal operation was "probably the most efficient embassy [he] ever headed." More recently, Ambassador Tuthill suggested that our embassy of 924 people in Brazil be cut by fifty percent, proposing his own corollary to Parkinson's Law—"Any organization that grows to a thousand people no longer has need of contact with the outside world.")

It was hard for me to understand why we in Sevilla needed five people in the press and public-relations department, plus four Spanish clerks, plus one American secretary, plus two vice-consuls, plus one consul. I winnowed the personnel, and we seemed to get the necessary tasks done as well, if not better, than before.

I, myself, would get up early, get my work done by noon and have the afternoons to attend a bullfight or to go out to the bull ranches and fight. I appeared on the program of several *festivales* and gained more and more confidence. I was seriously considering quitting the Foreign Service to become a professional torero. But Sidney Franklin discouraged me. He had managed to get only one corrida in the previous year (at San Roque, where he had performed excellently).

Whether it was the pressure of Manolete and Arruza or politics or because he was "old hat" or whatever, he simply could not get booked. Finally, however, on July 18, in Madrid, he "confirmed" the alternative he had originally taken thirteen years earlier in Mexico. Although I was unable to get up for it, I was told he performed adequately, if not brilliantly, and thus realized his great ambition: he was now a full legitimate *Matador de Toros*, the first American ever to earn the title. But still he could not get contracts.

And if Sidney could not, with his long career and his contacts, how would I ever be able to?

CHAPTER 11

ONE SATURDAY AT BELMONTE'S, AFTER I'd caped half a dozen heifers as well as I'd ever done in my life, I came panting up to the porch and Belmonte introduced me to a well-dressed, mustached gentleman.

"I am organizing a corrida for September 23 in Castillo de las Guardas," he said. "It will be for charity and it will star Belmonte."

I was excited because although I had seen Don Juan fight many calves in this private ring, I had never seem him perform in a real corrida.

"Who will be fighting on the program with you?" I asked.

Belmonte said it deadpanned: "You."

"No, really," I said, "who else?"

"You," confirmed the impresario.

I felt that terrible clutch—half thrill, half fear. But I

gulped and managed to say, "If you're serious, I would be honored."

"We will christen you 'El Niño de California,' " said Belmonte, raising a glass of sherry. "The California Kid— that is the way it will appear on the posters."

I had never killed a bull. Belmonte worked on that phase of the fight with me for hours.

"It's very easy," he said, "as long as you remember that it is the left hand that kills, not the r-r-right."

As a boy wheeled the mechanical bull at him, Belmonte showed how the left hand holding the muleta must move slowly and steadily in order to guide the bull's head under the man's chest. At the same time he must concentrate on reaching over the left horn to slide the sword in the small place between the withers.

"The trouble is," said Belmonte, "one gets so busy putting the sword in, one forgets to swing the muleta. Then, d-d-disaster."

It was like rubbing one's head and patting one's stomach. I practiced hitting the opening in the cork hundreds of times a day while swinging the cloth in a *pase de pecho* movement. I could see why it was called "the moment of truth."

"It is no great feat to kill a bull," said Belmonte, "if that is all you w-w-want to do."

Yes, it would be no trick to run off to the side, stick the animal in the lungs and produce a cruel and lethal hemorrhage. But thousands of people would be watching you do it the cowardly fashion. The correct way was to go in from a short distance away and to go in straight over the left horn, maximizing the risk to the man, at the same time plunging the blade down toward the heart so that it would cut the big aorta artery and produce a quick death.

"*Corte y derecho*," Belmonte would order as I would line "the bull" up. "Enter to kill from a short distance and go in straight!"

He pointed out that although the bull is bloody and tired at this point of the fight, he is desperate and fighting with defensive choppy lethal charges. It is the most dangerous time of all. Most of the fatal gorings in history have occurred at the kill. As Belmonte put it: "Be careful—this is the best chance that the bull has had all day to c-c-collect you."

The day before the fight, I arrived at Castillo at about seven o'clock with the two banderilleros and sword handler I'd hired. The town is about sixty kilometers from Sevilla. We looked over the *plaza de toros* first, to find out where the *presidente's* box and the entrances were and what they had in the way of *burladeros*. The arena itself is made of stone and holds about six thousand spectators. There were big posters all around advertising the fight. Below Belmonte's name there it was, irrevocably, "Bernabé Conrad—Niño de California."

Jesus!

We drove through the towered fairy-tale town up to the bull breeder's finca, a three-hundred-year-old ranch that probably didn't look much different, complete with its courtyard, carriages and quaintly costumed farm hands, than it had when it was built. We arrived in time for dinner in the patio with the large family of the *ganadero*, and afterward a guitar was produced and we sang. Chico, the sword boy, wailed out a gypsy song but stopped midway, saying he wasn't in voice. He was as nervous as though he were fighting the next day instead of just being my sword boy. Cascabel, my banderillero, did a stamping dance with Sona, the rancher's pretty sister, but we couldn't seem to clap in rhythm for him. I asked Manolo, my number one banderillero picked by Belmonte, to dance a *bulería*, but he said he wasn't in the mood. We were all jumpy and quarrelsome. We went to bed early.

I soon fell asleep but tossed restlessly and fought a hundred bulls before waking at dawn, sweaty and tired and with a sinking feeling. I made myself go back to sleep. When I awoke again, the sun was pouring in the window; there was the good hot scent of the fields in my room, and the swallows were wheeling and crying about the barn. What a fine day for everyone else, I thought; what a hell of a fine day! For the first time I asked myself if the glamour and excitement were really worth it.

For the month before the fight I'd thought of little else. When going over some consular invoices or passport applications, my hands would suddenly begin to tremble as I thought of the onrushing date. Or when I'd go to the movies and relax enough to laugh, right in the middle my brain would remind me, "You're fighting on the twenty-third!"—and the laugh would stick in my throat.

And now here I was in Castillo, and today was the day, and there was no getting out of it. On the telephone Chelo had cried and begged me to get out of it. I think if there'd been an honorable way to do so, I would have.

I got up and went down to the patio and practiced with the cape in the sun. Manolo came down and watched me. "You're crazy to practice on the day of the fight," he said. Manolo was a nice young Sevillan who had tried to be a matador but who gave up after one disastrously cowardly exhibition in Madrid. Now, he was content to resign himself to the unspectacular and comparatively safe routine of a banderillero.

I did some verónicas with an imaginary bull. "Don't do verónicas today, Bernabé," said Manolo.

"Why not?" I asked irritably.

"Because it's your weakest pass. They're no good and you get caught when you do them."

"Who the hell is the matador around here?" I snapped.

I practiced until my arms got a little tired. Then I went back up to bed to rest. I could hear the others down below eating lunch in the patio while I had a coffee with milk. I heard some laughter. It seemed incredible to me that anyone could laugh today. I fell into a fitful sleep about two. I dreamed I was back in America, in San Francisco, riding on the cable car with Betty.

"Come on! To the fight!" Manolo had a rough hand on my shoulder and was shaking me. I had the idea that maybe if I kept my eyes closed and picked up my dream again, Manolo would vanish and there wouldn't be any fight. He shook me again and I got up quickly. It was five o'clock, and the fight was at six-thirty, since it stays light in Andalucía so late. My costume was laid out neatly on the chair, and after I'd shaved, Manolo helped me into it. I wore the big broad-brimmed hat and sash and white jacket used in festival fights. Manolo was serious and white and suddenly efficient.

"You look like a third-class funeral," I said, as we went down the stairs. I wanted to see if I was too scared to talk. "You'd think you were going to take the chances."

"I'm not going to take any chances," he answered.

"I know," I said. "Then why are you scared?"

"I'm always scared," he said, "You know that."

"Why do you keep fighting then?"

"I can't help it," he said. "That's why."

We came down to the courtyard, and the rancher's family clapped and said, "Olé, matador!"

They took some photos of us when Chico and Cascabel came down. I looked at my watch. "It's almost six."

They all came up and shook hands seriously, wished me luck and hoped I'd "get at least one ear." Except the foreman who shook his head and said pleasantly but positively, "He won't kill that animal. I raised that creature and I tell you he won't kill it with anything less than a hand grenade." My heart sank lower.

"Of course he'll kill it," said Sona. She was little and dark, with black Spanish eyes. "You'll see him come back with the bull's ear." She took a religious medal from around her neck and pinned it on the inside of my jacket. Then she kissed me on the cheek.

"Sure he'll kill it," said Manolo uncertainly.

We stood around awkwardly for a few moments.

"Let's get going," I said. It was six-ten. We swung on the truck and rattled down the road. I could see Sona waving in the courtyard. She wasn't going to the fight because she said she couldn't stand it. We drove very fast, and on one of the curves, Manolo said, "This uncle's driving is scaring me to death!" It struck me funny he should be worried about anything but the bull that was waiting for us, and I remember trying to laugh. All the way in, as we passed the big posters for the fight, I was constructing a wall of false courage, detaching myself from this person who was trying to be a Hemingway character, who was going to kill a bull with Juan Belmonte. But the sight of the gray and forbidding coliseum rising at the top of the hill brought me back into myself with a rush, and there was a sickening knot in my stomach.

It was six twenty-five when we arrived at the foot of the plaza hill, and the cathedral bells were starting to ring. We started up the cobbled street, and the big crowd that was milling toward the plaza gave us a great ovation, shouting, "Suerte, suerte"—Luck, luck—and patting me on the back as we pushed ahead of them. I forgot the knot for a moment and smiled and waved. Then a great shout went up as Belmonte's Fiat pulled up and the Earthquake of Triana stepped out of his car in fighting costume and hurried after us.

"*Buenas tardes,*" he said, panting, smiling his great smile.

"*Muy buenas,*" we said.

"Who has seen the bulls?" he asked.

"I haven't," I said, "but I understand they're big."

"What do you mean, big, Bernabé?"

"I've heard they're about three hundred.

"*Jesús, que miedo!*" he said, with his barracuda jaw jutting out. "Jesus, what fear. What a tragedy."

One never could tell what Don Juan was thinking. Had he expected them to be bigger or smaller?

"They say there will be no picadors."

"No picadors!" I exclaimed.

"That's what I understand," said Belmonte. "Originally the bulls weren't going to be big enough to warrant them."

This meant the bulls would arrive at the muleta part intact!

"Use your punishing passes," Belmonte said, "don't forget your *pases de castigo.*"

We got to the ring, and it was already filled to overflowing. Belmonte's banderillero was holding his horse for him, a good-looking skittish chestnut. I saw a bronze plaque on the wall that read: "The *novillero* José Hernández 'Parraito' was killed in this *plaza* on February 28, 1885, may he rest in peace." It wasn't the sort of data I most wanted to be informed about at that moment.

As we lined up in the entrance to the ring, adjusting the capes over our shoulders, the third matador came up. He was a young *novillero* and he looked nervous.

"*Holá,*" he said, as he puffed rapidly on a cigarette.

"*Holá.*"

"I'm Chávez," he said, "you must be El Niño de California."

"Yes," I said.

He smiled wanly. "You have a rare name."

"I thought El Andaluz was fighting third today?" That's what the posters had said.

"No," he swallowed dryly, "he's not. I am."

"What happened to the Andaluz?"

Chávez was working his feet in the sand like a boxer in a rosin box. I figured it looked pretty professional, so I did it too.

"El Estudiante got it bad in Logroño yesterday—right through the lungs. Andaluz had to substitute for him in Linares." He ground out the cigarette on the sand under his boot.

"So you're fighting third."

"Yes, I'm fighting third." He yawned, a sure sign—often observed in soldiers at the front—that one is scared. I started to yawn myself, but swallowed it before it was out.

"No picadors?" he said.

"No picadors," I said.

"What a rare name," Chávez said, frowning at its rareness.

"At least there's no wind," I said.

"No," he said, "at least there's no wind to blow the capes."

I remember thinking throughout the whole day that it seemed as though everyone had read Hemingway and was trying to talk and act like it.

"Better take your watch off," said Belmonte. "You don't want to get it b-b-broken!"

There was something ominous sounding about that. I took off the watch and handed it to someone to keep.

Belmonte got on his chesty horse. We lined up in back of him on foot, Chávez and I in front and our cuadrillas—sword handler and banderilleros—in back of us. The crowd was getting impatient; they were stamping their feet. It was six-thirty.

Belmonte swung around in his saddle. I'll never forget the chillingly calm way he said, "I don't know any reason why we shouldn't start this thing."

I knew a hundred reasons and would have been delighted to suggest a few. But his horse moved forward, and we all automatically started forward on the left foot. The band struck up with a clash of cymbals as we strode to the center of the ring, then wheeled and walked to the fence, bowing to the *presidente* as we did. We got behind the fence, and I looked over the crowd. It seemed that everyone was looking at me because I was American, and not at Belmonte, who was waiting for his bull in the center of the sunny ring. The look in their faces was a combination of amusement and commiseration and relief that it was I and not they down there. I saw Eduardo Miura and the newspaper critics and all my friends from Sevilla, and they waved and smiled. I nodded back to them and tried to look casual. They seemed so damnably safe up there.

There was an ominous roll of drums, and a trumpet split the warm air. The *toril* gate banged open. Belmonte's bull ran in, black-and-white and bigger than we had been told. He fought it Portuguese style, on horseback first, making the trained horse dodge the bull's charges skillfully while he placed banderillas, and then he got off to kill it on foot. But first he did a dozen of those special Belmonte passes which no one has ever been able to duplicate. They transcended his physical limitations and age, individual little works of art that contributed to the larger work of beauty, the perfectly designed *faena*. He was magnificent. The *presidente* granted him the ears and tail of the animal, and the crowd gave him a tremendous ovation. The next day the newspaper would headline in the taurine section: "We have seen what it means to fight with the muleta!"

I saw all this through a haze, for drumming in my head was, "You're next, you're next, you're next!" But the crowd seemed in a receptive mood, and they weren't expecting much from an American.

Belmonte sent his horse outside the ring and climbed up into the stands. The trumpet blew for my bull, and the gate clanged open. Manolo and I stood behind a *burladero*, El Chico and Cascabel behind another, as we waited silently for the bull to come out of the long, dark *toril*. I felt a little dizzy. It didn't come and it didn't come. People began to laugh. Finally, Cascabel went over and cautiously flopped a cape in front of the passageway. Then he raced for the fence as a black shape skidded out of the *toril* in a wave of dust. The bull hurtled around the ring jabbing and feinting with his horns and snorting; the dust from the corral blowing off its back.

"Line him up for me," I said to Manolo. He took his cape and went out to run the bull up and down so that I could see which way he hooked. After doubling him two or three times at a safe distance, Manolo got in trouble; the bull was almost on top of him and he had to throw down the cape and duck inside the *burladero*.

"I can't see which horn he favors," I said.

"He hooks badly on both sides!" Manolo panted. "Don't go out there!"

I don't know how he expected me to arrange *not* to go out

there. When he saw me getting the magenta and yellow cape firm and right in my hands, he said, "All right, all right, but don't take him close and don't try verónicas! Face-fight him! For God's sake, no verónicas!"

Manolo didn't know that Belmonte had never really taught me much about face-fighting, the only way to fight a bad bull that won't pass. I'd always had good animals and never had to learn how to trick the bad ones.

Holding the cape for a verónica, I stepped out from behind the fence. "*Huh-hah-ah-ah-ah, torito!*" I called. My voice sounded like someone's else's. "*Huh-hah!*" It wheeled and charged for me, blowing out air as it did. It swooshed by, its horns much closer to my legs than I had intended, as I swung the *capote* just ahead of its nose. It came by again, this time even closer. It had obviously been fought before, and I couldn't control it because it went at my body instead of the big cape. It kept crowding me, making me back up. The third time it charged, it hooked to the right and slammed me up against the *barrera* with its shoulder. I heard Manolo call, "Get the hell out of there!"

I was shaken up, but I changed the grip on the cape and called the bull again, stepping away from the fence. This time it came with its head high. The side of the left horn struck my chest a glancing blow and the right horn caught in the *capote* and yanked it out of my hands. I was disarmed. I fled for a *burladero* and ducked behind.

The crowd was laughing. This is what they expected of an Americano who was trying to invade a Spanish art. They weren't laughing cruelly; they liked the fact that I had tried and they were glad that I hadn't been killed—but then again they were glad that I had been knocked around. It was very funny to see me get knocked around, as long as I didn't get killed.

"*Sabe latín*," said Manolo, coming over, shaking his head. They say a bull that's been fought before is so smart that he knows Latin. Bulls, of course, are supposed to be simon-pure when they come from the range, but sometimes ambitious kids have sneaked out on moonlit nights to practice on them with capes.

Since there were no picadors and the trumpet had blown for the banderillas, Cascabel had to go out to try to put in the barbed sticks. He ran at an angle toward the bull, holding the banderillas high. The bull knew enough to lead Cascabel by several feet. The banderillero ran sideways frantically like a crab and managed to miss the horns, but he also missed putting in the banderillas and looked ridiculous.

"For God's sake," I yelled to Manolo, "go out there and show that *tío* how to put in a pair!"

Manolo went out. By sneaking up on the bull from behind, he managed to put in the banderillas with great difficulty, getting his pants ripped as he spun away. The crowd was still laughing as the trumpet sounded for the third and last part of the fight. Chico handed me the muleta and the wooden sword.

"Let the burros laugh," Manolo growled. "The animal was impossible with the cape and sticks, but with the muleta, I swear you can dominate him."

"I don't know," I said.

I found Belmonte in the crowd; I went through the ceremony of extending my hand with the hat and dedicating the bull. "Thank you, Don Juan, for not having hidden," I started, and the crowd laughed—with me this time. "For you, master of the great masters, who has taught me what little I know, I am going to kill this bull, this difficult, cross-eyed bull." I turned in the classic way and flung my hat back up over my head. He leaned forward to catch it. He had looked worried, and that made me even more worried.

The bull was against the wall in his *querencia*. Under no circumstances did I want to take him on in there, as I'd learned well that a bull fights a defensive and more dangerous battle in his *querencia*. I told Manolo to lure him out and into another part of the ring. He went in as close as he dared and cautiously flopped the cape at him several times. "Get in closer!" I shouted.

"You get in closer, he's yours!" he answered without turning his head. But he got in closer and swirled the cape out on the dust in front of the bull again. The animal pawed the ground and shook his horns, but he wouldn't move out of the five-foot circle.

About this time I got mad, mad at the bull for being so rotten, mad at the crowd for not seeing that it was rotten, mad at the *ganadero* for raising such a rotten bull, mad at myself for being so rotten with the cape and mad at Manolo for not being able to get the bull out.

"Hide yourself!" I shouted. When Manolo left the ring, I stepped out quickly from behind the fence in back of the bull. I took the sword and smacked him hard across the rump with the flat of it. The bull whirled around, his tail went up and he shot toward me. I waited with my back pressed up against the fence, offering him the cloth, spreading it wide with the sword, shaking it, and praying to God that he take it and not my legs, for there was no way out for me if he didn't. Swoooosh, he went by, his head in the muleta. The crowd froze. The bull wheeled, came at me again, and setting my teeth, I made myself hold my ground as he hurtled by, the horns about five inches away from my legs.

"*Olé!*" screamed the crowd as I made two more closer passes without moving, and now that I think of it, it was a very sweet sound, but then I was too busy with the bull. I wanted to get away from the fence, so I worried the animal out across the ring, away from his *querencia*, with choppy, punishing passes. Once in the middle, I gave him every pass I could think of. I even made up one. On the most difficult, the whirling *afarolado*, he tore my sleeve off and raked down my arm. It didn't hurt, but it made me mad, and on the next pass I took the wooden sword out of the muleta and broke it across his stern as he went by. This left me with just the limp rag and nothing to spread it with, so four times I had to pass him with the dangerous natural and *pase de pecho* passes. The crowd was going wild and I savored their cheers. Finally, I walked away from the bull and Manolo ran out into the ring with the real sword.

"Kill him!" said Manolo.

I lined up the bull with its front legs together, so that the shoulder blades would open, as Belmonte had taught me to do. I sighted down the blade, shook the muleta to make him charge and ran at him as he ran at me. But the bull had moved its leg position at the last moment and closed the small opening. The sword hit bone and flew out. There was a sigh of disappointment from the crowd, but it had been an honest entry; I hadn't lost the ears yet. I lined him up again.

"*Corto y derecho*," I heard Belmonte shout, "short and straight!"

I had to do it this time. As the bull charged, I flung myself over the right horn on top of the animal. The sword sank into him up to the hilt, sliding in easily, as though into a barrel of honey. The bull sagged, reeled, headed for the fence drunkenly and then flopped over dead.

A roar went up from the crowd, and Manolo ran out and threw his arms around my shoulders jubilantly. I staggered over to the fence, and Belmonte tossed my hat down from the stands.

"*Bastante bien*," he said quietly. "Not bad, Bernabé."

The *presidente* signaled with his handkerchief that I was to be granted both ears. They dragged the bull out of the ring with the mules, and the crowd kept applauding and yelling for me to take a lap around the ring while they threw hats and cigars down to me. Already in my mind I was composing the triumphal cablegram to my brother. I started around shakily, the notched ears in my hands and Manolo in back of me throwing the hats back to the owners and keeping the cigars. But suddenly a trumpet blew, the *toril* gate opened, and we had to beat it for the fence as Chávez' bull skidded out into the pale sun, blinking its eyes and looking for something to kill.

CHAPTER 12

IN DUE TIME, THE NEW CONSUL ARRIVED in Sevilla and my brief reign of glory was over. I returned to Chelo in Málaga, and we tried to resume the halcyon days we had enjoyed before. But things were somehow different. Theoretically all was serene and wonderful, but there was an aura of insecurity underlying our daily lives. The war was over, jubilantly, incredibly finished; there was a sense of restlessness and change in the air. Chelo seemed to feel it—or express it—more than I. Whereas before she had occasionally said with a wince, "If you should leave," she would now say matter-of-factly, "When you leave."

I had thought of marrying her. But that was a crazy idea, I kept telling myself. I was very convincing in my arguments; our backgrounds, education, language, interests, everything was too different. It was all very romantic here in sunny postcard Spain, but how would she like America? How would she fit into San Francisco life—she who had never been further away from Málaga than Sevilla, geographically or mentally? As a consular official I was not permitted to marry a foreigner, according to a new rule. I would have to resign from the Foreign Service, and then how would I support a wife? It was madness to think of marrying her. Also, always present in the back of my mind was the thought that Betty Layne and I were destined for each other and would someday get together, even though she seemed to have disappeared from the face of the earth.

After my success at Castillo de las Guardas I thought more about becoming a professional matador. Several promotors offered me fights for the following season and two managers of successful toreros wanted to take me on. One day I would think yes, I should, and the next I would say no, quit while you're ahead. I was not sure I wanted to fight bulls for the rest of my life. But, then, I was not sure what I wanted to do for the rest of my life. I only hoped it would be something creative.

With an eye toward making some money against the time when I would quit the Foreign Service, I sculpted a little statue of Arruza doing his now famous *teléfono*, resting his elbow on the bull's forehead. It was the first sculpture I had done since art school but it didn't turn out badly. I decided to have it cast. I was told that the best man to cast statues was a midget named Antonio in a village outside of Sevilla. I drove there and made arrangements for him to make some and to keep making them until we had a good batch. I planned to return that week and try to sell them to some store. If they sold I would complete and have cast the little statuette of Manolete I was working on.

But before I could get back to the midget, I had a cable

from the embassy: I was to go to Barcelona immediately as a temporary commercial attaché.

Commercial attaché! At best, my acquaintance with any sort of commerce could be described as furtive. And attachés —weren't they the ones who carried those narrow leather briefcases?

I was upset; I'd been back in Málaga less than a week. Chelo gave a resigned sigh, but there were tears in her eyes.

"You see," she said, "It will always be like this. Until you go away for good."

"It won't be long," I said, "I promise."

"That's what you said about Sevilla," she said.

I thought about how many other Consular men must have gone through this same sadness with women in all parts of the world and how cruel it was.

The day I left, I received a letter with the depressing news of the death of Dick Westdahl, one of the most important friends of my teens. I thought about him on the plane to Barcelona.

Several of my friends had been wounded badly in the war, including Dick Young, who had lost a leg in heroic action in Germany and was now back at Walter Reed where the doctors were trying to save his remaining leg. But I would see them again. However, my two best friends at prep school, Nion Tucker and Jerry Baker, were gone irrevocably, killed on Iwo Jima and in Germany. School and college friendships loom so large, and as Dos Passos has written, "The people involved are quite out of scale with the rest of the world. When one of those early friends dies your universe is irreparably diminished."

My longtime friend, Herb Caen, the widely known newspaperman, was still unscathed even after landing the day after D-Day on Normandy. He had written me a jubilant postcard: "When we landed at Carentan it was so great—I was elated and excited and scared and I had to go to the bathroom desperately. I saw an old guy there who was too old-world-French to be true, with the smock and the white mustache and the beret, and I rushed up to him and said 'Monsieur, pardon, où est le lavabo?' And he answered, tears of happiness streaming down his cheeks and gesturing around him expansively: 'Mais, toute la belle France, mon ami, toute le belle France!' "

But it was Dick Westdahl's death that I couldn't get out of my mind; he'd had a great influence on me, encouraging my interest in such diverse subjects as boxing and piano playing and the pursuit of pretty women and respect for the written word, whether prose or poetry.

"Like Scaramouche," he said once with his buccaneer's laugh to his bewildered father, "I was born with a smile and a sense that the world was mad!"

Now he was dead and I felt sad and a little guilty; I hadn't asked for this soft, safe life in Spain—but I had to keep reminding myself of that fact.

I was met at the Barcelona airport by a grizzled veteran vice-consul named O'Flaherty, one of the pathetic group who attain that level by diligence but lack the personality to ever rise to a higher class of consular officer. As we rode to town in the chauffeur-driven limousine, he drew out a flask, had a nip, wiped it off with his sleeve and proffered it to me. I shook my head.

"What's the consul general like?" I asked. "The Ambassador said he was a great guy."

"Probably is," said O'Flaherty ominously, "to ambassadors." He took another swig. "Yesterday. Consul general and I are waiting for the elevator. Rings. Rings again. Elevator doesn't come." He belched. "Rings again. Then kicks the door down."

I was installed, with the questionable help of O'Flaherty, in a small apartment. ("Neat but not Guadí, he punned.) I called on the consul general, Mr. Nash, in the large and bustling office. Very Bostonian, tall and with a waxed gray mustache, he seemed agreeable enough as he outlined the functions of the office. But on the other hand, it wasn't too hard to envision his kicking a door down.

The first few days were not very eventful as I was shown the usual routine ropes. But the fourth night I was there I had an interesting bit of serendipity. I had taken an American secretary to dinner and then had dropped her at the Ritz where she lived. I went back to my apartment around ten, took a hot shower, and when I got out I noticed that the bathroom had one of those nice large European towels. This one had the size and heft of a *capote* and after drying myself I couldn't resist taking it into the bedroom where there was space to swing it. I did a series of verónicas ending with a swirling *serpentina* that blossomed the towel out around me. Then I heard a soft *"Olé"* and three hand claps. Startled, I covered my nakedness and peered out the picture window. I hadn't realized the curtains weren't drawn all the way. I saw a rather tall woman of perhaps thirty-five, very well-dressed, who looked up at me with a half-bemused, half-embarrassed smile. She was about to get into a cab but she hesitated and then with the pleasant accent of the upper-class Spanish woman, spoke the traditional compliment to a torero: *"Vaya estilo y arte!"*

I recovered from my embarrassment long enough to say *"Gracias."* And then I gathered some courage and said,

"Won't you come up for a drink?" She gave a little laugh. "I don't drink—even with men who are dressed." But she did not get in the cab, so I said, "I will be dressed and I have coffee." I turned on my best smile and said, not completely untruthfully, "I am lonely."

She said she would not stay long but she dismissed the cab. I put on a bathrobe and pressed the button that opened the door to the apartment and she came up. I took her hand and introduced myself. She said, "*Enchantée*," in a perfect French accent, but didn't say her name. She was terribly handsome in an old-fashioned, almost Gibson Girl sort of way, and formidable in her elegance. I was very nervous and had a quick drink when I went to the kitchenette for her coffee. We sat on the sofa and talked, now in English. She asked me where I was from and what I was doing in Barcelona. She said she had been in New York and that she longed to go to California. She seemed not at all ill at ease and at one point rested her white gloved hand on my knee. Then she put down her coffee cup and in the next moment I was in her arms, or she was in mine, I'm not sure which; it really didn't matter. What mattered was that the elegant clothes shortly came off to reveal a figure that deserved to be recorded in marble, as well as a libido that warranted mention in the *Decameron*.

Two hours later she left, refusing to let me accompany her to a cab. I didn't know her name still, not even her first name, and it was a long time before I learned exactly who my charming visitor had been.

The next day I was sitting at my desk reliving the pleasure of the night before and going through the routine tasks of a vice-consul, when I remembered the midget.

He was six hundred miles away in Sevilla, frantically reproducing those statues! I had forgotten to tell him to stop making them when I'd been transferred from Sevilla the week before, and every statue he finished would cost me one-eighth of my monthly salary.

I put aside the passport case I was working on and hurried through the big outer room where the clerks worked, past the senior consuls' offices and into the consul general's lair.

"Go right in, Mr. Conrad," his secretary said. "Mr. Nash has just come in."

He always arrived at four minutes to ten. Not three minutes or five minutes, but always four minutes to ten. I gave my tie a nervous tug before opening the door.

I was still only twenty-three. Consuls general to me were like brigadier generals to a second lieutenant.

"Good morning," said Mr. Nash cheerily, leaning back in his swivel chair, his hands clasped behind his head. "How are you finding Barcelona after a week? Isn't much like the gay gypsy life in Sevilla, is it?"

"No, sir, but it's very pleasant." I hesitated because I knew how fantastic this was going to sound. "Mr. Nash"—

"What can I do for you?"

"I was wondering if I could go back to Sevilla this weekend."

The consul general frowned. "You've only been here a week." He paused and scratched his head. Then he looked up at me with narrowed eyes. "If this has anything to do with bullfighting"—

"No, sir," I said, and launched in. "You see, last month I made a statue of Arruza. I only wanted a few cast until I found out whether they would sell. Then this transfer came through and in the excitement of getting here I stupidly forgot to call off the man who's casting them. He'll be up into the hundreds unless I can stop him."

"Send him a wire!"

"I don't know his name, except Antonio. He's a very small man—a midget, in fact. He lives in Gelves, a village near Sevilla. There's no telephone. I only know how to get there. I don't know the address."

It sounded so phony I didn't blame him for not swallowing it. He smiled knowingly.

"You know, we've heard about your bullfighting for the two years you've been in Spain." He chuckled and lit a cigarette. "I'm a great aficionado and I must say it all sounds very colorful. But"—he brought his fist down on the desk—"not while you are a member of my consulate."

"But, sir"—

"I have no intention of having the State Department land on top of me just because you've been injured in some fool bull ring."

"Mr. Nash, can't you see"—

"There are some things, young man, which an officer in the Foreign Service cannot permit himself to see."

"But, sir, honestly—I am not going to Sevilla to fight bulls."

He looked at me skeptically. "It's just a coincidence that there are some big fights there this weekend?"

"Mr. Nash, I give you my word of honor that I will not fight any bulls."

He swung away in his chair and tapped his teeth with a pencil for a few seconds. Then he turned back and said, "All right. A vice-consul's word of honor is good enough for me. But if you're not back here in this office early Monday morning you will no longer be a vice-consul."

"I'll be back," I said.

The next morning, Saturday, I caught the plane to Madrid. There I transferred to one of the corrugated and archaic tri-motored Junkers of the Iberia Line and arrived in Sevilla in the afternoon.

I wanted to call Mari Harcourt, a girl I knew, but after leaving my suitcase at the hotel, I grabbed a taxi and headed for Gelves; my midget could probably turn out a statue or two in the time it would take to phone Mari.

I arrived in the adobe village of Gelves about five, after frequent stops for stoking the taxi, which was propelled by a coal-burning *gasógeno*. I knocked on the door where the midget lived. A little girl answered the door.

"*Papacito no 'tá, Señó Vice*," she lisped in her Andaluz accent. "He's gone to the stove to cook a big load of statues."

My heart sank, for I could see beyond her into the house. Everywhere there were replicas of my bullfighter busy resting his elbow on a bull. They were perched on the mantel, the chairs, under the bed, on the stove, on the window, above the sink. There must have been seventy-five of them—and now the girl was telling me another load had gone to the kiln to be fired!

"Where is the stove?" I asked her. "I have to stop him." I didn't know how I was going to pay for these, much less another batch.

She shrugged. "Another town." But she didn't know which. Anyway, the statues were already made. It was too late.

"Papa will return tomorrow at five," she said.

"Not until tomorrow?" I exclaimed.

I took one of the statues and got back into the taxi. I was supposed to take the ten o'clock plane the next morning. Now I would have to catch the evening train at six-thirty. It would be a tight squeeze, but I could probably get back out to Gelves, stop Antonio, discuss arrangements to pay him by the month for the statues and make the train. I had to make it. It was the only one that could get me to Barcelona before ten Monday.

Back in Sevilla I called Mari and made a date to meet her at the Bodega Bar in the Hotel Cristina. She showed up looking very American and pretty with her saddle shoes and white sweater and brown hair. Half English and half Madrileña, she was an art student in Sevilla, and though she was a bad artist, she was a nice person.

We had danced once and toasted each other with a sherry when Carlos Arruza came in with his manager.

"*Hola!*" he shouted when he saw me. "Just the uncle we're looking for!"

Arruza was on top of the world. He had just finished the season with one of the most astounding records of all time: he had fought 108 fights, one less than Belmonte's record 109 set in 1919. (He could have equaled or broken the record but didn't out of respect for Belmonte.) Of those 232 bulls, he placed banderillas in 190 of them and was awarded 219 ears, 74 tails and 20 hoofs!

"Look, Chico," he said as they sat down at our table. "Tomorrow we're having a big festival fight. It's for charity and it's supposed to be international. I'm fighting for Mexico, Montani is representing Peru, Alfredo Pickman for Spain and now you'll represent America."

I would have given anything I owned to fight on the same program with Arruza. "Look, Carlos," I said. "I can't. I'd really like to—but my leg. It's acted up again."

I felt Mari looking at me, and I knew she was thinking that it hadn't hurt my dancing a few minutes ago.

"But these are going to be really small animals," Carlos protested. "And the civil governor is going to give a gold bull's ear to the uncle who puts up the best *faena.*"

I shook my head. "I can't do it."

"What an uncle you turned out to be," said Carlos. "I thought you were the big 'Niño de California.'"

"Listen," I said. "I'd like to, believe me, but I can't. I . . . I promised someone I wouldn't."

"Your mamacita?" Carlos' manager grinned.

"Or some little girl up there in Barcelona?" said Mari.

There was an awkward pause. Then Carlos said, "Speaking of mamacitas, would you mind bringing my mother out to the fight tomorrow?"

"Sure, I'll be glad to take her," I murmured.

We had dinner and I went to bed fairly late. I couldn't get to sleep. I kept fighting a mythical bull—a wonderful, brave, cooperative bull that I could make do everything but sit up and moo. And up in the stands, applauding deliriously, was Chelo and the consul general. I finally fell asleep at dawn and slept almost till noon.

After lunch Mari and I picked up Arruza's mother at her hotel. I warned her that I would probably have to leave early as I had to take care of my statue problem and catch the six-thirty train. She said that was all right, she'd come home with Carlos.

She was hardly the pathetic, barefoot, telling-her-beads type of bullfighter's mother that one visualizes from literature. She was modern, attractive, and youthful and had made a success of her children's clothing business in Mexico City long before Carlos became famous. But she looked worried today.

"Carlitos has been fighting since he was thirteen years old," she said as we left the outskirts of Sevilla. "And I've never seen him in the ring. All the others, yes, as I am a great aficionada. But never Carlos. So finally I have said to myself,

'Look here, you are ridiculous, you just go watch today like any other spectator.' "

"You picked a good day," I said. "This is just a private ring and Carlos says the animals are very small."

"Small!" Señora Arruza snorted. "Remember, these are fighting bulls! The animal that killed Joselito was no more than a calf." She bit her lip as though in anger for having voiced these thoughts. "I just hope he doesn't try to show off and do those *cositas* I read about—those little things."

"Please ask him not to do *cositas*," his mother said unhappily, as we drove through the pillars of the entrance to the ranch. "No little things."

We saw herds of fighting bulls in the enclosed fields, and they raised their heads and snorted at the car, as if to say, "How dare you trespass!"

We drove past the white ranch house that hadn't been changed in two hundred years and down to the small bull ring. We were late, and as we hurried up to the stands we heard a shout of "*Olé*" from the crowd.

Since it was a private festival fight, the audience was composed mainly of bull-wise people. There were professional bullfighters, bull breeders, promoters and several *duques* and *marquesas* who dedicated themselves to amateur fighting. People squeezed over to make room for us on the stone seats when they saw it was Arruza's mother, and someone passed us a bottle of sherry and some crayfish.

Down in the ring the Peruvian, Montani, was putting up a good performance with a two-year-old bull. It would charge the muleta time after time, and Montani gracefully managed to make the horns graze inches away from his legs.

The man next to Mari turned while applauding and said to us, "Too bad you came late—you missed a good performance by Alfredo Pickman. But this Peruvian is even better. He's certain to win the golden ear, unless Arruza decides to cut loose."

Señora Arruza looked very unhappy.

"I hope Arruza decides *not* to cut loose!" she said.

Montani's animal was wearing down, and he lined it up for the kill. This was just a festival, and the animals weren't to be injured, so he threw away the sword. Then, pretending he had the weapon in his hand, he lured the bull into a charge and flung himself over the right horn. He did it well and managed to slap the animal exactly between the withers— where the sword would have gone—as the bull hurtled by him. The audience cheered and clapped and stamped their feet, for the man had risked his life to execute the moment of truth perfectly.

A gate was opened and the uninjured animal trotted out to the corrals. Montani ran around the ring sailing back the hats and cigars and purses that the jubilant people threw into the arena.

We saw Arruza come into the ring and stand behind the fence, hugging his cape. He spotted us in the audience and waved and smiled.

Suddenly a bugle blew. Montani ducked out of the arena through a *burladero* and the gate to the tunnel swung open. Out into the empty ring a greenish black shape appeared. It was a three-year-old heifer with long thin horns.

"Ai, ai, ai," Señora Arruza was moaning, twisting her handkerchief. Then as she saw her son getting his big magenta cape ready in his hands and preparing to fight, she couldn't keep from crying out, "No *hagas cositas*—no little things, Carlitos!"

Arruza went out into the ring chanting, "Ah-ha-ha-ha,

vaca," to attract the animal's attention. On the first pass he knelt down gracefully. As the heifer charged he swung the cape over his head, and the horns missed his head by five inches.

"Olé!" burst from the crowd, as though from a single throat.

I glanced over at Señora Arruza. She had her hands over her eyes. They remained there for the rest of the fight—and with good reason. Arruza did everything in his repertoire, including the teléfono. A shake of the animal's head would have spiked a horn through his chest, if the man hadn't had the heifer so completely under control.

After Arruza had simulated the kill perfectly, and the heifer was removed from the ring, I persuaded Señora Arruza to remove her hands. She sat back limply.

"You still haven't seen your son fight," I chided. Then I looked at my watch. "I'll have to leave pretty soon, because I have to . . ."

I heard a voice saying my name from down in the arena. I looked down and saw Arruza in the center of the ring and heard him announcing: ". . . and so the next contestant for the golden ear will be El Vicecónsul de los Estados Unidos de América!"

He pointed up to me, grinning. Everyone in the audience turned to look at me, and they applauded encouragingly.

I shook my head. "No," I shouted, "no, I'm not going to fight!"

"Yes, yes!" cried the crowd.

"I have to catch a train," I said. "I can't!"

The tunnel door swung open and another heifer skidded out into the ring fast, shaking its head and looking for something to kill.

Suddenly it hooked into a *burladero* and with a jerk of its head it sent a heavy slat flying into the air. It did it so viciously that it broke off part of its right horn.

The crowd cheered the animal's strength and spirit and kept looking at me.

"Vámonos!" they shouted. "It's a brave animal—a good animal!"

"Come on, Chico!" Arruza yelled. "Show them!"

"He has a bad leg," Mari protested to the people around me. "He can't fight!"

When the people saw that I wasn't going to accept the challenge, a sort of embarrassed silence came over the crowd. Spaniards put personal bravery above any other quality in a man. I heard murmurs of, "Well, let's not force him," and dry laughs following the words. "It *is* a rough animal for an amateur."

One of the men, who was a known Germanophile, having been an officer in Spain's Blue Division which fought with the Nazis, said in a stage whisper: "You see, I told you . . ."

Montani went out in the ring with the heifer, and though he did some excellent passes with the cape, no one applauded. The people just watched sullenly. My failure to fight had put a damper on the whole festival.

Suddenly I knew that I had to do it. Hell, I said, if the consul general were here he'd insist that I fight! I rationalized thusly: this one action of mine, which so many Spaniards were witnessing, was ruining an inestimable amount of good will that the State Department so desperately wanted.

I stood up and pushed down through the rows. Word of honor or no word of honor, I was going to fight. The crowd cheered when they saw what I was going to do, and I'm sure the Nazi rubbed his hands with gleeful anticipation.

As I dropped down into the passageway the comforting thought struck me: I'd promised the consul general I wouldn't fight a bull, but nobody said anything about heifers.

"It's all yours, matador!" Montani called as he left the animal and vaulted the fence.

A sword boy handed me a muleta and sword, and without even taking off my hat or tie, I slid through the *burladero* opening into the ring.

"Ah-ha-ha-haaaa, vaca!" I called.

The animal focused its attention on me, shook its one sharp horn and prepared to charge. Down on its level it looked bigger and more vicious. But now that I'd picked up the gauntlet, I had to do something sensational to justify all the fuss. I'd try the "blind" pass that I'd seen Manolete do.

I planted my feet, putting them down as though they'd be unable to move even if the animal headed straight for my body. Then I turned my head away from where the heifer was standing and looked up at the crowd.

"Ahaaaa, vaquilla!" I shouted, still looking in the opposite direction from the heifer.

"No, no!" yelled someone in the crowd.

"Vaca!" I yelled once more, shaking the muleta and praying the animal would go for it and not at my legs.

I heard the heifer snort. I heard it start for me, heard its hoofs crunching into the sand. I wanted to turn to see whether it was heading for me or the cloth, but I forced myself to keep looking the other way. Then I heard swoosh as the animal expelled air, and I felt the curly short hair of its shoulders brush against my trousers.

"Olé!" yelled the crowd. And again "Olé!" as I repeated the pass.

From then on I could do no wrong. The performance

wasn't half so graceful or polished as Arruza's, of course, but it was every bit as suicidal. In fact, it was more difficult because the animal's broken horn made it hook drastically to the right.

After a dozen passes, the closest and smoothest I'd ever done in my life, I lined the animal up for the mock kill. This was the most dangerous and important moment of all and I wanted to do it right to round off the *faena*. Making the heifer focus its attention on the muleta in my left hand and pretending to hold a sword in my right, I headed straight at the animal as it charged toward me.

But I tried to do it too well. I went in too straight. The heifer swerved to the right and the horn, instead of slicing by my knee, glanced off it. It was my weak knee and the blow knocked it out of joint. I fell on top of the animal's head and then I was tossed high up into the air as the crowd screamed. After I smashed to the ground I saw the heifer wheel and drive at me, but I blacked out before it reached me.

When I came to I was stretched out on the grass outside the ring. Señora Arruza and Mari were bending over me placing wet handkerchiefs on my head. I blinked my eyes and propped myself on my elbows. I was covered with blood. I discovered later it came from the broken horn when the animal was trying to gore me on the ground.

My pants legs were torn and the pockets of my jacket ripped off. After a few minutes I attempted to get up. My knee was completely knocked out and I couldn't stand. I looked at my watch, which somehow wasn't smashed. It was quarter of four.

They carried me up to the ranch house and cleaned me up a bit and gave me a glass of brandy. I rested until I felt a little better. When I finally checked my watch again, it still said quarter of four!

"What time is it?" I gasped. "I have to make that train at six-thirty!"

"Almost six," said Mari. "But there's a chance."

They carried me to Arruza's big station wagon and stretched me out in the back. Then with Carlos at the wheel, driving the way one would expect a bullfighter to drive, we streaked through the Andalusian countryside, plowing through herds of turkeys, careening around oxcarts and honking our way through whitewashed villages.

We roared into Sevilla at six-fifteen.

"My suitcase," I cried, "at the hotel!"

"Never mind," said Mari. "I'm coming through Barcelona next week and I'll bring it to you!"

We sped straight for the station, already hearing the departing whistle and the clang of the bell. Mari ran to buy a ticket while Carlos and a porter carried me into a made-up berth just as the toy engine started to chuff and steam. They scrambled off the train, and I waved to them on the platform weakly. I was close to fainting and every bone and muscle in my body was bruised and aching. But I'd made the train.

And then as I lay back and we pulled out, I thought of the midget. I hadn't turned him off. I hadn't even done what I'd come to Sevilla for in the first place!

The train arrived in Madrid at six the next morning. With porters carrying me to a taxi, I made it to the airport. Another set of porters carried me onto the plane and at nine o'clock I was in Barcelona. I went straight to the consulate, and two of the clerks managed to hustle me into my office without any of the consuls seeing me.

There was a gabardine topcoat of mine on the coat tree. I hurriedly put it on to cover my blood-stained, shredded suit and sat shakily on the edge of my desk.

At four minutes to ten, the consul general opened my door. "Just made it back," I managed to say cheerily. I shuffled through some letters and strove for the perfect picture of the eager young vice-consul unable to wait to take off his hat and coat before seeing what the day's tasks would be.

"Everything go all right?" said the consul general with an enigmatic smile. "Midgets and statues and all?"

"Fine," I said. I put my hand to my stomach. "I don't feel very well, though."

"You do look a little pale," he said, studying me. "Probably rancid olive oil. They all cook with it in Sevilla."

I waited for a few minutes after he'd gone, and then I had myself carried to a taxi and taken to the hospital. From there I phoned in word to the consulate that I was down with stomach trouble. It was true—my stomach was as black and blue as any other part of my anatomy.

After four days of massage and hydrotherapy, the doctors fixed me so that I could walk around with a slight limp. I went back into the consulate Friday morning, thanking my lucky stars that my ruse had worked long enough to get me back on my feet.

Now my only problems were how to pay for a couple of hundred statues and how to stop Antonio from making more.

The consul general came in at his usual time and sent for me immediately. His hands were behind his head and he was staring out the window when I came into his office.

"Good morning," he said, and something about his tone made me uneasy. "Stomach all right?"

"Fine," I said.

Then I spotted the two objects on his desk. One was my figurine of Arruza. The other was a gold bull's ear mounted on a plaque. Underneath the ear was a little silver plate which said that it had been won by Carlos Arrruza, giving the date and place. And under that plate was another which read: "Redonated by C. Arruza to el Vicecónsul Americano for his brave performance of the same date."

My heart disappeared in the pit of my stomach.

"Your friend Mari Harcourt stopped here on her way to Mallorca yesterday. She left your suitcase, a note and the statue. We . . . we had an interesting chat."

The way he said "interesting" left nothing to be said. He handed me the note.

It was crudely written in pencil, but the letterhead was very fancy. It proclaimed:

ANTONIO MORALES
Caster of Statues, Religious and Secular
By Appt. to his Excellency the American Vicecónsul

I skimmed through the note and learned that Antonio had bumped into Arruza's manager while looking for me, that the manager had ordered fifty of the statues and had introduced him to the head of the largest store in Sevilla, who wanted two hundred.

It was consoling to know that I would at least have a little money coming in now that I was out of a job. But it was a poor exchange for the coveted position of vice-consul in the Foreign Service of the United States of America.

I put the note in my pocket. "Mr. Nash, I must explain how it happened. You see, the crowd at the fight"—

"What fight?" growled the consul general, swiveling his chair around.

"Why—the bullfight," I said. "The gold ear"—

"What gold ear?" he said.

I made vague motions at the gold ear glittering on the plaque on his desk. "That gold ear, sir."

"I don't see any ear."

"Right there, sir," I said weakly.

He sighed with exaggerated patience. "As I remarked a few days ago, Mr. Conrad, there are some things which an officer in the Foreign Service cannot permit himself to see."

"Thank you, sir," I said.

"Young man," he said gruffly, "stop wasting time and get back to work."

I picked up my statue, my suitcase and my invisible ear, and walked out of his office with almost no limp at all.

CHAPTER 13

IF I HAD ENTERTAINED ANY REAL HOPES OF
becoming a professional matador, this recent injury
removed them. I went out to a bull ranch near Barcelona with the ex-great matador, Gil Tovar, and tried caping
some heifers. Everything was fine when I could just stand
there and perform pretty passes. But whenever the animal did
anything unpredictable I simply could not move around
quickly enough with the assurance that my knee would not
fold under me. I would fight many more times in my life
(and be gored almost fatally) but for now my dreams of
glory in the professional arena were shelved. In all honesty,
I believe I was relieved that the decision had been made for
me.

I would have to think about making money, since I knew
I would not be content with the dull routine of a consulate
much longer. I made the statue of Manolete and sold a few

dozen, but that was hardly a dependable income. I wrote an article on bullfighting, and though I had no real hope of selling it, I sent it off to *Esquire* with some illustrations and forgot about it.

I was in Barcelona for only five weeks before the real commercial attaché arrived. Once again I returned to Málaga, and once again Chelo and I tried to pick up where we had left off. On the surface we appeared overjoyed to be back with each other. But I was apprehensive and nervous and so was she. Something was amiss, something indefinable; the rhythm of our life was out of step. I couldn't put my finger on it exactly: she'd be a few minutes early here, a half an hour late there, or not at a place she was supposed to be. It was that special variance that suburban wives are so quick to feel—more than detect—when their husband's metronome existence alters slightly, no matter how valid the reason for the delay, the sudden business trip, the "important" stay over. Truth has an unmistakable rhythm to it when it is spoken, or not spoken: I was convinced Chelo was not telling the truth about certain things. The idea suddenly came— could she be cheating on me? I tried to dismiss the thought, but I couldn't. She had every right to be looking to her future; I certainly wasn't offering her anything. Not only that, but when I would leave Spain, which I obviously would do someday, I would be leaving her "a besmirched and ruined woman" in the eyes of most Spaniards.

Then the thought would come—why didn't we just up and get married once and for all?

I continually dragged up all sorts of reinforcing reasons for why I shouldn't link my future with hers: formalized religion, for one thing—it meant so much to her and so little to me. Also, though I tried to encourage and teach her, she knew nothing of writing and had no regard for books. She had not even read her national pride, *Don Quixote*, much less *A Handful of Dust* or *The Great Gatsby*. She knew nothing of art. But she knew Art Was Good; she liked the *idea* of painting. The moment she saw a picture she would exclaim "How marvelous!" even before she'd really looked at it. Velázquez, Bougereau, Maxfield Parrish—it didn't matter. If it was in a frame she liked it. (Except her fellow Malagueño, Picasso—"I could do better than *that!*")

In general, as Browning's duke said so scornfully of his last duchess, "She had a heart too soon made glad."

However, reason plays little part in affairs of the heart. When I try to think back on how it—the end of it all—happened, my immature conduct, and what was said and done, the events, very conveniently, became a little blurry.

I had sent her to stenography school, and she seemed to love it. I gave her a typewriter and she practiced diligently. For a while. Then one day Concha, the old cook, said that a man had brought Chelo home from school. Chelo didn't mention it. I asked her if she was still going to school and she said she hadn't missed a day. I called the school from my office and they said she hadn't been there all week. I had to spend the next weekend out in Torremolinos where I was painting some murals in the bar of the hotel that belonged to my friends, the Fred Saunders, so Chelo said she would go visit a girlfriend. When I returned she was at home, but Concha could hardly wait to tell me that she had left and returned with the same man. I confronted Chelo with the facts and she owned up to it. Yes, she had gone off with the man, a used-car dealer, and she had stayed at a hotel, "but nothing had happened—not even a kiss."

Señor López had money, she said, was a married friend of

Concha, the cook

her brother's, and had offered to put her and her mother up in a fancy apartment after I had left Spain. But only after I had left. He was very nice to her and took her to nice restaurants and stage shows and dancing and other things that I had not been able to do with her. After all, she had to think about what she was going to do when I left, her future.

Intellectually I could see her position, but emotionally I was knocked for a loop. And a used-car dealer. A middle-aged used-car dealer!

We had a great row. I told her to pack up, she cried and begged to stay and said she loved only me. I went off on a bender. I ended up looking for Señor López—incredible as it seems to me now—with a snub-nosed pistol that I extracted from the consulate safe. The chief clerk, Luis Morales, caught up with me in some bar and did a successful job of talking me out of whatever vague plan of violence I had formulated.

I sobered up and went back home. Chelo was still there. She swore she was innocent, that he'd never even held her hand. She begged to be allowed to stay, repeated that she loved only me, that she would die if I sent her away, that on her father's grave she hadn't done anything bad with that man. Then she threw a fit. She moaned and screamed, grew white and red and finally hysterical. Then, when she saw me heading for the door with a suitcase, she hissed after me: "And he's twice the lover you'll ever be!"

To recover my equilibrium I went off to Lisbon to spend a week with Roberta Cameron. When I returned to Málaga, Chelo's things were out of the house and so was she, gone from my life as abruptly as she had entered it.

I left Málaga, I left the villa and I never saw her again.

That is not to say that I never thought of her again. (Three years later when I returned to Spain I tried every way to find out about her. She had gone away from Málaga and no one seemed to know anything more. Except one man who had seen her in Madrid. "She was walking gracefully down the Gran Vía," he said. "Well dressed, very beautiful and with a prosperous looking gentleman. She looked sad.")

I had been in Spain two years almost to the day. Michener has written: "Spain is a very special country and one must approach it with respect and with his eyes open. He must be fully aware that once he has penetrated the borders he runs the risk of being made a prisoner."

I was a prisoner, but it was time to break out. I had "home leave" coming to me and the government would pay my way back to Washington. I was offered the position of acting consul at San Sebastian, considered a plum of an assignment, but I had already made up my mind to resign. My brother was in Peru, and it seemed like a good idea to head for there, though toward what end I didn't know.

The freighter left from Sevilla. Mauricio and Manolete and several other friends were there. Belmonte also came down to see me off, and in a very uncharacteristic gesture—since he was usually above anything that smacked of self-aggrandizement—he brought me a photo of himself fighting, inscribed: "In remembrance of our first performance together, at Castillo de las Guardas." It meant a great deal to me, especially since the word "first" implied that there would be subsequent performances. Before I got on the boat, he embraced me as he would have a son.

There's a Spanish song: "Anyone who says partings aren't sad—tell him to go part!"

As the freighter pulled out into the muddy Guadalquivir

River, I saw the maroon consulate Chevrolet pull up on the dock. The vice-consul jumped out and waved a letter—the ship was only about twenty feet away from the dock. He wrapped the letter around a stone, secured it with a rubber band, wound up and threw it on to the deck. It was from *Esquire* and simply said: "We like your article about bullfighting in Spain. We enclose a check for $350 for the piece and the three watercolor illustrations."

No writer ever forgets that first sale—that first miraculous sale. I was stunned. I kept turning the check over and over in my hands. I read and reread the letter. It was signed by some marvelous man with the splendid magical name of George Wiswell. What a wonderful name. What a wonderful, thoughtful, discerning, farsighted old editor he must be. I could see him now: looking not so much like Mark Twain but as Hal Holbrook made up to look like Mark Twain. Puffing on his pipe, he would crustily recall how he and *Esquire* had first published Pietro Donato's *Christ in Concrete*, Ring Lardner, Dreiser, Dos Passos, Steinbeck, the best of Fitzgerald, the gems of Hemingway, the vintage Sinclair Lewis and Mencken and George Jean Nathan. And now Conrad!

If *Esquire* thought this piddling little article was good, wait till they saw what I could REALLY turn out! I went to sleep that night on the freighter full of a hundred articles and stories. Just wait till we got to New York—the things that I would outline for that crusty old curmudgeon, Mr. Wiswell! Just because he had dealt with all those landmarks of America's literature didn't intimidate me at all. Not at all.

We arrived in New York and I seemed to have a problem getting off the boat. I thought it was the monkey, E. Poor One, that I was trying to smuggle in; he was under my sweater clinging to my shirt. Maybe a steward had ratted to customs.

It turned out to be the barrel of manzanilla wine that Mauricio had brought to me on the boat in Sevilla. It was worth only nine dollars and I would have cheerfully jettisoned it to save the monkey. But no. The customs man who boarded the boat was one of those super-friendly sleazy types. He called me into the ship's lounge. "We know you have a barrel of wine. Let's see how good it is, shall we?" He ordered a steward to bring it in. Then he poured a couple of glasses and we drank.

"Hmm—delicious," he droned on. "How is Spain, as a country to visit, I mean? The Missus and I are planning a little trip and . . . "

Then we drank again. It seemed interminable, especially since the monkey was getting restless. He probably smelled the fumes and, being an alcoholic himself, wanted to join us in a quick shot of manzanilla. As long as he stayed still he couldn't be seen under my overcoat, jacket and sweater. But he wouldn't stay still. I kept rubbing my stomach to soothe him.

"Bad stomach?" asked the inspector.

"Rancid olive oil," I explained. "Does it every time."

Finally, he let me go, with both my monkey and the wine. And as far as E. Poor One was concerned, it was just in time.

After installing the monkey in my hotel room (The Algonquin has had stranger guests), I headed for the offices of *Esquire* magazine. Mr. Wiswell was not a Mark Twainish type at all. He was a heavy set, jowly, pleasant faced man of twenty-five. A boy genius of the magazine publishing world, he had already been an editor for several years. We had a long lunch (at "21"! I was a success!) during which we discussed possible articles and rewrites that I might do for the magazine. But first I had to go to Washington and go through the procedure of extracting myself from the Foreign Service, almost as complicated a procedure as getting in in the first place.

My Aunt Girlie lived in Washington and E. Poor One and I stayed with her. I thought the monkey looked very chic in his little turtleneck sweater and his hair parted in the middle and slicked down with a little Vitalis. But Girlie sighed when she saw him and said, "He looks so dreadfully common. We'll have to make some proper clothes for him and change his hairdo. And he drinks entirely too much."

There was a letter waiting for me from my brother:

Peru's great—come on down! Arruza just arrived—everybody's excited as hell. Manolete's due also, but when I don't know.

By the way, I had the damnedest thing happen at a cocktail party the other night! I saw an American tourist girl who looked like Betty. Not really, but same style. *Great* looking. I went up to talk to her and during the conversation I remarked: "You look like a girl I know in the States named Betty Layne." She looked startled and said, "That's funny—I know Betty!" I said, "She was my brother's girl and he's lost track of her completely. Where is she?" She answered, "Vassar." And I said, "Are you sure we've got the same girl?" and she says, "Long brown hair with sunstreaks, perennial tan, big brown eyes and went to St. Margaret's?" "Yes!" I said. "She's a senior at Vassar," this gal says, and moves on.

Betty *had* said in one of her last letters that she was thinking of going back to college in the East after her divorce came through.

I showed the letter to Dick Young who was at Walter Reed getting fitted for an artificial leg. (He was also acquiring a wife, having fallen in love with his beautiful, intellectual nurse.)

"Wire her," Dick said, in his wonderfully unsolemn solemn way.

"Supposing it's a different girl?" I said.

"What have you got to lose?" he answered.

"What indeed."

I sent a telegram to Betty Layne, Vassar College, Poughkeepsie, New York: JUST BACK FROM SPAIN. HUNT IN PERU SAYS YOU ARE AT VASSAR. WHAT THE HELL ARE YOU DOING THERE? OR ARE YOU A DIFFERENT ONE?

There was a two-day silence from Poughkeepsie. Then a telegram arrived saying: BACK SO SOON? HEARD RUMORS OF THAT GRANADA AFFAIR. CANNOT BELIEVE IT TRUE. DID PEDRO GIVE YOU MANUEL'S MESSAGE? THE OLD BETTY ADORED SPANISH OMELETTES. SO—SIGH—PERHAPS I AM A DIFFERENT ONE.

BETTY LANE

"She obviously thinks it's a friend pulling a gag," said Dick.

"But it's a different girl," I said. "She spells her name differently. She's not my Betty."

"Maybe Western Union just misspelled it," said Dick. "Besides, she sounds pretty good, whosever Betty she is."

I wired back for her to meet me at the Biltmore Hotel under the clock, to determine whether she was or was not the original Betty.

She countered with: WILL HAVE NOTHING TO DO WITH SCHIZOPHRENIC HEMINGWAY HEROES RECENTLY RETURNED FROM IBERIAN PENINSULA.

Dick and I perservered, bombarding the poor girl with what we thought were highly witty telegrams. Dick was cleverer than I at that sort of thing; he wrote them. She finally consented to meet me under the clock for a drink, adding, I'LL BE THE ONE WITH THE OCELOT ON A LEASH

On the train going up, I was like a nervous bridegroom. Supposing it really was my Betty enjoying a joke? Supposing it wasn't, but just a very ugly girl with a clever roommate for telegram writing? After all, Dick had written my telegrams for me.

I stood restlessly under the clock with a group of very young looking undergraduates, for what seemed like a long time. Quite obviously neither my Betty nor anybody's Betty was going to show up; it was all an elaborate hoax.

I was about to leave when she appeared. She didn't have an ocelot on a leash but she did have a leopard coat. And it was quite obviously she. Long dark brown hair with blond streaks from Long Island tennis afternoons, tall and leggy with dancing brown eyes . . . she did not look unlike the other Betty Layne. We both had excuses at the ready for other plans for dinner, had things not worked out, but we didn't need them.

"I'm glad you're tall," she said, "I had visions of a clever little midget. I'm so excited—it's my first blind date!"

We went to Greenwich Village for dinner with George Wiswell and Sidney Franklin, who had just arrived from Spain. Afterwards, just Betty and I pub-crawled. She was so sophisticated, she didn't have to pretend to be sophisticated. She was enthusiastic about everything. We found we had a lot to talk about that weekend. And subsequent ones, for she came down to Washington the following weekend and I came back to New York the one after that.

She was utterly charming, we became good friends and remain so to this day. In fact, when she was married in Paris, my wife and I were her attendants.

But she was not my Betty.

I still could find no trace of the original Betty. I spent one morning in a Washington hotel lobby going through every major city's telephone directory. There were a few Elizabeth Laynes scattered around the country, but they all ended in false leads.

Esquire had given me a couple of hack articles to rewrite, one on rodeos and one on fox hunting. With the money I bought a one-way ticket to Lima. I wasn't sure what I was going to do there, but it sounded like a good idea.

Two days later after a stopover in Panama, I was in Peru— my first time in South America. It was great to see my brother after more than two years. As always, since childhood, we had a great deal to talk and laugh about. As an employee of a successful fishing and exporting firm, he had an attractive apartment overlooking the country club with plenty of room for both of us. Lima was a bustling modern city but with enough colonial atmosphere still remaining to remind one of old Spain. Though I had just missed Arruza, there was a lot of good bullfighting in the offing.

"So now what are you going to do?" Hunt asked me.

"I don't know," I said. "Write a book maybe."

"How you going to live?"

"Sponge off you," I said. "Write some magazine articles."

I did write some articles and stories. But they came back with form rejection slips, not even nice letters from tactful editors. Apparently there was a little more to this writing game than I had figured. I started a novel called *Christmas in July*, based more or less on my time with Chelo. But that didn't solve the problem of any immediate money.

One day I went by the fancy Bolívar Hotel and on an impulse I went in to see the Swiss manager, Mr. Elminger.

I bravely asked straight out if they needed a piano player in their downstairs nightclub, El Grill. Quite reasonably, he wanted to hear me play, so we went down to the then-empty room. He asked if I knew "Sombre Dimanche," which after a moment I realized was "Gloomy Sunday," the Hungarian song the playing of which reputedly drove dozens of people to suicide.

My piano playing could most charitably be described as decadent, my rhythm is faulty and I cannot read a note. But I can play anything that I can hum, so I swung into "Sombre Dimanche" with a flourish. Mr. Elminger's eyes misted over, he stared off into space and he smiled nostalgically.

"Play it again," he murmured.

I played it twice more with schmaltzy gypsy sentimentality.

"You're hired," he said.

One hundred and fifty dollars a month was quite enough for me to live on. I went to work that night. My job was to play in the intermissions between the dance band and the rhumba combo. What they wanted were old-time ballads such as "Body and Soul" and "Smoke Gets in Your Eyes," and I had dozens of those. And of course, "Sombre Dimanche" whenever Mr. Elminger appeared. (I bumped into him last year in San Francisco—he is now a top executive of the Hilton Hotel chain—and I asked him about his fascination for that particular murky madrigal, but he merely smiled enigmatically and looked off into space as mistily as he had twenty years before in Lima.)

"El Greel" was unquestionably the most elegant night club in town and both the well-to-do Peruvians and the tourists patronized it. Here I discovered that piano players, like taxi drivers, meet the strangest characters. It would seem that every nympho, dipso and homo is compelled to accost, proposition or merely bore the piano player. Generally they ask for a song to hear themselves asking for it more than the music itself.

"Boy, play 'Star Dust.'"

"I just did, sir."

"Play it again," they slur. "Reminds me of her."

One night a strange coincidence happened. I was playing a song I had written years before at the University of North Carolina for the annual musical revue. A man sitting at the bar strolled over to the piano stand, offered to buy me a drink and asked what the name of the song was.

"Little thing of mine," I said. "College."

"I know a girl in the States who plays it," he said, "never heard it any other place."

My heart skipped a beat. "What's her name?"

"Layne," he said. "Betty Layne."

"L-a-y-n-e?" I spelled.

"L-a-y-n-e," he echoed. "Know her?"

I couldn't believe it.

"Where did you know her?—where's she living?"

"Last time I saw her was at a party in Los Angeles. Think she lives in Redondo Beach with her father."

"Where's that?"

"Near Los Angeles," he said. "Say, can you play 'Little Girl Blue?' I'll hum it for you . . ."

It wasn't hard to locate Betty now. We had a long and expensive phone conversation. A week later she arrived in Lima.

From the moment she had stepped off the plane, we were as before. I'd brought a huge corny heart made of flowers— like the ones they give winning race horses—to the airport and I had hired the little band from the Bolivar's Grill for the occasion.

I had steeled myself to be disappointed. I had always had

a febrile imagination and it had been so many years since
I had seen her. Had I built her up too much in my mind?
That thought was dispelled the moment she stepped out
of the airplane and walked down the steps. She was more
beautiful than I remembered, less the gorgeous girl but
more the radiant, self-possessed woman.

"What am I doing here?" were her first laughing words
after we kissed.

And I couldn't answer her question, but it didn't matter.
On the way back from the airport I drove her around Lima's
beautiful parks and boulevards but it wasn't a time for sightseeing. I had tried to get off work but couldn't. When I
finished my piano playing stint that night we went to a
funny little Chinese restaurant—*una chifa*—in the Oriental
quarter. She carefully avoided all mention of her ex-husband
and her life in the past years, but I told her about the second
Betty and Spain and we laughed and talked until the place
closed. Then we went back to the flat—my brother had
diplomatically gone away for the weekend—and made love.
For the first time in our lives we made love. Thus we cul-
minated the longest courtship since GBS and Ellen Terry.
We opened a bottle of champagne and drank to the historic
event. We drank champagne and made love and talked until
daylight. We stayed in bed all the next day. We had years
to catch up on and it seemed that we begrudged every month
that we had not spent together.

I never did quite understand why she had not written,
where she had been and what she had been doing. But then
I never did understand the enigma of Betty. There was always an ephemeral and mysterious aura about her—which
possibly accounted for the attraction she had held for me
for those past ten years. When I would question her too

closely, she would simply smile that great smile and say, "Yesterday's newspaper . . ."

Now that Betty was actually in Lima we weren't certain of what the next course of action was to be. We were both a little scared. First we found an apartment near Hunt's. Then, since she had spent the last of the money her father had given her for plane fare, she got a job as a secretary in the American embassy. She hadn't done that sort of work before, but she liked it and did a good job. At noontime when she was too busy to leave for lunch she would lower a basket on a string out of the third-story window and I would put in it *un perro caliente*, Peru's valiant try at a hot dog. She would haul it up and blow a kiss to me. At night she would sit in a corner of the bar until my piano playing chores were over or sing in front of the orchestra in her good throaty voice.

During the day I would paint—mostly pictures of Betty —and work on my book. I had no idea how to write a novel: I made no outline, planned no story line, mapped out no chapters ahead of time. Wasn't that the way Thomas Wolfe and Hemingway and Fitzgerald did it?

Quite honestly, I thought *Christmas in July* was going along pretty well. Betty volunteered to type up the sixty or so pages I had written. But it seemed to take forever. I finally asked her what was taking so long.

"It's hard to type fast," she said with a little laugh, "when you're holding your nose with one hand."

"Is it that bad?" I asked.

"Oh, no," she said hastily after a look at my stricken face, "it's fine. Just maybe not my type of book. After all, what do I know about literature?"

She finished typing those pages but never asked to see any more. I was very disappointed and used to watch her sullenly and jealously as she would stay glued to what I believed were inferior works—escape literature.

On weekends we would go to the country or go sightseeing or go to the bullfights. I had very soon got in with the bull-fighting group and was invited to perform three times and did with varying success. Once in the big ring of Acho, an exact duplicate of the arena in Sevilla, I fought an animal which, very sensibly, had been rejected by Manolete. At the kill I was tossed and ended up with a bad pounding and a broken rib. (But at least I could now say that I was the only American ever to fight in Mexico, Spain and Peru.)

Financially we were able to manage, what with Betty's salary and my stipend combined. But then one night Mr. Elminger came to me with tears in his eyes. It seems that he had hired a new manager of the night club, who didn't like "Sombre Dimanche," or as a matter of fact, anything I played.

"The only explanation could be that he is tone deaf," he said sadly. But . . . I would have to go, though he would give me a splendid recommendation to any other place.

Unfortunately the Peruvians had their own type of music, and there was no other place where a cocktail pianist was needed or appreciated. I was dejected. I was down to my last cent and Betty had none to spare.

Two days later I had a piece of luck. I had done a pastel of Betty, her head tilted down, her tan face glowing, her hair swirling around her head, her eyes downcast. It wasn't bad, and Betty liked it, so I had taken it to Roca, the framer. Now, when I came to pick it up, the little fat man greeted me with open arms, his shiny pate a-glisten with perspiration, as always; with his toga-like smock and his black fringe of hair combed forward like a Caesar's laurel crown, he looked like a dishonest Diogenes.

"Just the person I was coming to see!" Roca exclaimed. It seems that he too liked the picture, and after framing it he put it in the window of his shop. Yesterday, he told me gleefully, a rich Limeña, Señora Herrera, had her chauffeur stop the limousine in front of the shop. She carefully studied the picture through her lorgnette. "I like the portrait. In the window," she said to Roca. She spoke in jerky nonsentences. "I wish an oil. Done of me. The painter?"

Roca had to refresh his memory by taking a sly look at my signature.

"Barnaby Conrad," said Roca.

"The signature tells me that," she snapped, "but may I ask who is he?"

"You mean to tell me, Señora Herrera," said Roca, "that you have not heard of Conrad? You with your advanced cultural interests?"

"The name. It does sound . . ."

"Why, he's the top portrait artist in New York! His one-man show in London last year was a fabulous success! He's here in Lima just temporarily—on his way for a big showing of his in Argentina."

"How much does he charge?" she asked.

Roca barely hesitated. "Five hundred *soles*, Señora."

"Really not too bad," she said.

Roca said hurriedly, "That, of course, is not life size."

"And life size?"

"Seven hundred and fifty *soles*, Señora," said Roca. Seeing that she accepted that, he added, "But that, of course, is without the frame."

"And. With the frame?"

"One thousand."

"All right," said Señora Herrera. "Tell him to . . ."

"That price, of course, does not include the hands."

"How much with the hands?"

Roca gulped, perspiring more than usual.

"Twelve hundred *soles*, Señora."

"Tell him to be at my house tomorrow at eleven."

Knowing Roca, he would have liked to have added, if he thought he could have got away with it, "Of course, Señora, with a face the portrait will be extra!"

Mirabile dictu! In one fell swoop I suddenly had a profession, an agent and a client!

"What does she look like?" I asked Roca.

"She looks like a million!" exulted Roca.

I was very excited. I telephoned Betty and told her the good news. Then I rushed off to buy canvas and paints. I could see the stately portrait I was going to do of the handsome matron: a little Gainsborough here, a touch of Van Dyke there and a lot of Sargent everywhere. Would I be able to capture her stunning looks? I pored over those great masters' portraits in the library that evening, seeing how they had posed the celebrated beauties.

The next day I went to her mansion in the chic Miraflores district, arriving fifteen minutes late for our appointment. I did this by design, since being the famous portraitist I was, I didn't want to seem too eager.

And she kept me waiting an hour and ten minutes.

When she finally appeared in the grand salon, it was a shock. Her hair was the color of a saxophone, her dress the obscene green of a plastic garden hose and she was without a doubt the homeliest representative of the female sex I have ever encountered. I have seen many women that no one could possibly call beautiful yet whose faces could lend themselves to handsome portraits, redeemed as they were by underlying traits of kindness, intelligence, humor or whatever. This face was not even tempered by humility.

"I wish," she said imperiously, "to have a beautiful portrait made of me, and I wish it to be an exact likeness."

"Only two years' experience in diplomatic work restrained me from replying, "Madam, I'm afraid a choice must be made between those two requests."

But I was hungry. So I set to work with a sharp pencil and a dull ache. No portrait I have ever done before or since required such skill: I had to try to flatter extravagantly yet still maintain some faint relationship to the sitter's features. Bulging hyperthyroid eyes were alchemized to a look of sparkling alertness; sagging jowls became the merest hint of baby fat; a porcine nose emerged as merely retroussé; her malocclusion became a pleasingly determined chin, and her adenoidal leer with the sagging nether lip of a Silenus was transformed into a beatific smile.

After four nerve-wracking sittings I finally finished this meretricious masterpiece of deception. It was time for the subject to approve of it. With fear and trembling I placed the painting in the ornate frame that Roca had supplied. Carefully I moved the easel to the place in the living room which had the most advantageous light, and then invited her to look at it.

"Well," she hurrumphed, as she studied it through her lorgnette, "You didn't exactly flatter me while you were about it!"

My heart sank. I had invested a lot of time in this and by now I really was totally broke. Then she said, "But I suppose it looks like me," and—as my heart rose—"I'll take it!"

I cashed the check, gave Señor Roca his share and Betty

and I flew off to the glorious ancient Inca ruins of Machu Pichu for the weekend. (Now one can ascend by funicular to the ruins; we went by mule back. Now there is a grand little hotel; then we snuggled in sleeping bags.)

As so often happens with portraits after the first reaction, Señora Herrera grew to like the picture very much. She showed it to her friends, word of mouth spread and suddenly I was in business. I did another portrait the following week and two the week after that.

These new subjects were far more interesting than Señora Herrera had been, and I enjoyed doing honest likenesses of them. I have always enjoyed doing portraits. Unlike Rosa Bonheur who preferred painting horses' posteriors or Gainsborough who was bored to death with people and yearned to devote himself to landscapes, I had no desire to paint anything else; certainly not abstract art, which I felt was painted by the untalented, sold by the unprincipled and bought by the bewildered.

To me it was, and is, constantly astonishing that God has been able to work so many millions of combinations out of the simple basics of the human face; after all, everyone looks more or less alike—it isn't as though The Master Draftsman had three or four eyes, a couple of noses and rectangular or triangular shaped heads to play around with on His facial designing board. The facts are that nearly everyone's eyes come exactly in the middle of the head (not three-quarters of the way up, the way beginners draw a face), the eyes are an eye-width apart, the lobes of the ears are on a level with the mouth while the tops of the ears are on a level with the eyebrows, and the mouth comes approximately halfway between the nose and the chin. But it is the slight departures from these rules and the infinity of subtle variations of features that cause a person to look unique and different from his neighbor and which provide the portraitist with a brand new challenge every time he sits before his easel.

Not all the portraits I did in Peru were smashing successes, of course; some would always have "a little something wrong with the mouth" (the statement John Sargent suggested be written on his tombstone). When a subject would bring the painting back for some alteration I often wished I could have afforded to be as rude as Mr. Sargent who, when a woman objected to the mouth, snapped, "Well, Madame, perhaps we'd best leave it out altogether!" And when another complained of the nose, he handed her the canvas that she was paying $5,000 for, saying airily: "Oh, you can easily alter a little thing like that when you get it home."

I found out how hard it was to please everyone who is supposed to be pleased by a portrait. We all see others through a special prism. It's all very well for us to rave over a self-portrait of Rembrandt or the "King of Spain" by Goya or the "Mona Lisa" now, but one can't help wondering what Saskia Rembrandt, the Queen of Spain and Signor Giacondo had to say about those works at the time. Quite probably: "It's rather nice, dear, but don't you think there's something a little funny about the mouth?"

Goethe once said, "One is never satisfied by the portrait of a person one knows." He should have added the word *well*. I am quite happy with the likenesses of acquaintances I don't know well, whereas their wives and children are not.

In Lima I came more and more to the conclusion that only two people should have to be pleased by a portrait: the painter and the sitter. And toward the end of my stay in Peru I began to have my doubts about even including the latter. As the varied advice and complaints came in, I could hear in my mind's ear Whistler's mother droning pettishly: "But Sonny, you've made me look so drab," or the Blueboy whining, "I wanted my faded jeans instead," or Madame Recaumier complaining, "If you'd waited a week, I'd have had the couch recovered!"

I came to learn that everyone has an opinion about a portrait, though affirming the while, "I don't know anything about art, but I know what I like." (I preferred the New Yorker cartoon showing the professorial type scratching his head before a museum painting, saying, "I know everything about art but I don't know what I like.") Even J. P. Morgan is supposed to have considered himself an art expert, though Roger Fry dismissed the tycoon's feeling for art thusly: "A crude historical imagination was the only flaw in his otherwise perfect insensibility."

Not only did I have to contend with the recording of people's likenesses, but also frequently I had to struggle with their egos. One nine-year-old Fauntleroy took exception to the pastel I had worked on for two weeks and with an oath like a longshoreman, he dashed his milk into his own likeness. Needing the money, I could only sigh, pin a new piece of paper on the board and start in all over again.

Another hazard was the adoring wife who wanted to surprise her husband with a portrait. Day after day she'd sneak up to my brother's apartment (where I'd set up my studio). Then she would have to invent things to explain where she'd been to her jealous husband. It had all of the dangers and inconveniences of an affair with none of the rewards; I kept feeling that I would find a Peruvian shiv in my ribs before the portrait was finished.

All in all, I did about thirty portraits that year. I had a one-man show at a gallery and though I set no artistic bonfires, I had respectable reviews in the newspapers. The money was not exactly rolling in, but at least I had enough to live on and Betty and I could take trips and come to know the astonishingly different facets of Peru. Once, when Betty had a vacation, we went up to Pucallpa and the headwaters of the Amazon. We flew over the Andes in a single-engine plane overloaded with supplies for the Indians, and quite literally our wheels were not twenty feet above the snowy crags. The Indian pilot didn't seem worried, though.

"What happens if the engine quits about now?" I asked.

He grinned and drew a brown forefinger across his throat.

A few hours later we were on the steaming Ucayali River, paddling along in a dugout canoe with Indians so untouched by civilization that they could barely speak pidgin Spanish. The banks of the river were lined with alligators, swarms of monkeys chattered in the trees and flights of parrots flew overhead. It all seemed very colorful and adventuresome, though no real adventure occurred. Friends warned of the dread Jivaro Indians, the ones who delight in shrinking heads down to the size of a frail girl's fist. And indeed, there were quite a lot of these grisly relics in evidence. When a group of Indians tried to sell me one of the long-haired, lip-sewn souvenirs, our Indian guide showed that it was a fake, made from an animal skin. He exposed the fraud by pointing out the simplest fact: "Señor, the tufts of hair representing the eyebrows were merely left there when the rest of the 'face' hair had been shaved away." Could we not see that the hair of both eyebrows grew in the same direction? On a real human head the hair of the eyebrows would grow in opposite directions on opposite sides of the face.

When we returned to Lima we found the town buzzing

with the exciting news that Manolete was arriving for a series of corridas after a fantastically successful season in Mexico. With him was the Spanish actress, Lupe Sino. They were traveling as man and wife, but gossip had it they weren't married. We gave a small party for them at my brother's apartment. Manolete charmed the other guests with his dignity and quiet humor.

I had a painting of him that I had started in Spain and he said he liked it and would come pose while in Lima. I showed him the article I had published in *Esquire* that was largely about him, and he was pleased, but he frowned when he saw this paragraph:

Augmenting his millions, he has made a film entitled, *The Man Closest to Death*. Actually, with his fantastic control over every bull he fights, Manolete is probably farther from death than any other torero in the world.

"I hope you're right," he said. "I really hope you're right."

But in a moment he was smiling and telling us some charming anecdote about his encounter with Peruvian food.

"Whew!" said Betty afterwards. "That is the most attractive man who ever lived!"

But to me he seemed nervous and even more gaunt than before. A new scar had been added to his sad face since I had last seen him. There was a haunted look about his eyes. He had three Scotches in the time everyone else was having one.

"I want to get out of all this," he told me in private. "When I wind up these fights here, I have two in Colombia with Carlos and then I'm going back to Spain and cut off my pigtail for good. Here I am, almost thirty, and every time I go out in that ring they expect me to fight as though I were

"*I hope you're right,*" he said.
"*I really hope you're right.*"

twenty. They keep demanding more and more of me, and I have no more to give. Carlos feels the same way, he wants to quit too."

"But what will you do then?"

"Retire to the ranch in Córdoba," he said. "Raise bulls for other idiots to fight."

"Get married and have kids?"

Manolete smiled. "But have you not heard the gossip? I am married. At least that is what I hear."

Lupe Sino (or Antoñita Bronchalo, her real name) was a brown-haired, baby-faced, vivacious young woman. But, though very pretty, one felt she was cold and ambitious. Manolete's friends did not like her and thought she was the main reason he was drinking so heavily. That, plus the fact that although he knew he should retire, he hated the final stepping down from his exalted position as *El Número Uno*.

The next night the American ambassador gave a reception for Manolete and Lupe. The ambassador wasn't the most popular or tactful envoy that Peru had known, but this act endeared him to Lima. However, his hostess, his mother, almost undid the good. Manolete and Lupe went to the party with a Colonel Suárez and his attractive wife. It happened that Manolete and Señora Suárez entered the reception room together. The ambassador's mother, an old world Southerner, greeted them warmly.

"Howdy-do, Mr. and Mrs. Manaletty!" she said.

"But I am not really Mrs. Manolete," said Señora Suárez smiling, "I am"—

"Now, don't you worry, honey," said the older woman, patting her hand. "Never mind the gossip—we are all broad-minded here and you are just as welcome as though you were married."

Then she introduced them to the ambassador as Mr. and Mrs. Manolete. Señora Suárez, realizing this would be the only time she'd have the opportunity to be the wife of a top torero, relaxed and enjoyed it as they went down the receiving line. But Colonel Suárez was not amused and tagged after her saying, "But Luisa . . ."

"Pay no attention to him," Señora Suárez announced with an airy wave of her hand, "he is just my husband's sword boy!"

The story was spread all over town the next day to the delight of the Limeños.

At the party I had heard the ambassador mention that he had an ocelot which had been given to him and that he didn't know what to do with it. I said that I liked animals and he said for me to come get it the next day.

"Tigrillo" was a handsome and husky specimen. He resembled a small leopard and was very tame. We kept him on the roof terrace of my brother's apartment, where he was quite happy. He was very neat and would actually go to the toilet in the toilet. I thought this was the result of extraordinary training until one day he urinated in a bathtub I was about to get into; apparently ocelots in the jungle have a tendency to eliminate in any water or stream so as to avoid leaving traces of their presence.

A week after acquiring Tigrillo, the doorbell rang. A rather angry looking man stood there with a dead rooster in his hands.

"Do you own an ocelot?" he asked.

It seemed Tigrillo had made an incredible twelve-foot leap from our roof to a neighbor's roof. The man's fourteen-year-old daughter, who was hanging up lingerie on a laundry line, fainted at the sight of the cat and had to be taken to the hospital. The ocelot had played with the lingerie, leaving it in shreds. Then as a final indignity, the cat had killed the rooster that was tethered there.

"And that is the worst, for which I demand one thousand *soles!*" shouted the man. "This was the finest fighting cock in all Peru!"

"Why didn't it put up a better fight, then?" I countered lamely.

We settled for an amount considerably less than what he demanded, retrieved the ocelot and Betty cooked a delicious, if expensive, coq au vin that night.

CHAPTER 14

I SHOULD HAVE BEEN HAPPY IN PERU, I should have realized what a pleasant life I had. But I wasn't, and I didn't. There was a gnawing inside, telling me to move on. I felt something big was waiting for me around the corner; I didn't know what the something was, but I felt sure that the corner was not in Lima. I didn't feel that fate intended me to spend the rest of my life in Lima doing mediocre society portraits. I had that malaise of youth, that feeling of *Je ne sais pas ce que je veux, mais ce que je veux, je veux bien.* I wasn't sure what it was I wanted, but I knew I wanted it very much.

The egos of the people I had to paint was a contributing factor to my discontent, especially the vanity of the male sitters. To please a woman all one had to do was take a few years off her; the men were rarely satisfied. "You've caught the Napoleon in me," they might admit, "but have you captured the Lord Byron?"

I also knew that the longer Betty and I stayed together, the harder it was going to be for me not to marry her. In my unsettled frame of mind and with my self still far from found, I had no business getting married. Betty would have been content just to have gone on living in Lima the way we were. She had learned Spanish almost immediately, loved the country and made several good friends, including a distant cousin of mine who was married to a Venezuelan diplomat. She also expected her father to come down and join her soon, a pending visit which did not decrease my restlessness.

I felt a little trapped and I wanted out.

Even the bullfights left me cold, though Manolete had never been better. He was the idol of the country when he left. When we said good-by I was not only saying good-by to him but to bullfighting in general, a chunk of my life that was now put behind me. It was the last time I ever saw him.

"It's good to leave on a happy note," he said. "I shall never fight in Lima again. I only have a couple of fights more—then to Spain and rest, blessed rest."

But I wondered, would the crowds ever let him rest? They felt he belonged to them, body and soul, and in a way they were right.

It occurred to me that here was a great protagonist for a novel. I briefly considered abandoning *Christmas in July,* my pale account of an American vice-consul's love affair with a Málagueña girl, and writing the story of a great matador. But what would the plot be? Like all beginning writers I was more concerned with plot than character. I shelved the idea.

One day I saw in the newspaper an announcement that a freighter was leaving for New York and that it was taking a limited number of passengers. The fare was inexpensive enough for me to afford it. Impulsively, I went to the steamship office and booked passage.

"For how many?" said the clerk.

I swallowed. "For one."

Several times I started to tell Betty, but I couldn't find the words.

Finally, after a week, she said over breakfast, "Gertrude wants us for a picnic on Saturday. We'll all go to Chosica—it'll be great fun!"

"I can't go," I blurted out. And before she could ask why, I added, "I'm leaving that day for New York."

She clapped her hand to her mouth. Then she cleared her throat and managed to say "Oh?"

"Come with me," I offered lamely.

"I think I'll stay," she said; there were tears in her eyes. "I think I'll stay for awhile."

"Look—when I get settled, when I find out what the hell I'm going to do, when I get my book finished, I'll send for you."

"That'll be nice," she said in a tremulous voice.

"I've got enough for the freighter." I tried to be calm but I couldn't. "Look, I've got to talk to some publishers about my book!"

"That's nice." She brushed the tears from her eyes. As she started to take the dishes to the sink, she turned and said, "Oh, and darling?"

"Yes?"

She made an attempt at an exaggerated Noel Coward accent: "I do believe I'm preggers."

"What?"

"I'm late."

"Oh, God! How late?"

"Pretty late."

"You've been late before."

"Not this late."

This was a ruse to get me to stay and marry her!

"Why didn't you tell me sooner?"

"What could you do?"

"You spring it on me five goddamn days before I'm supposed to leave!"

She didn't say anything.

"That's pretty lousy," I said, my voice rising. "All of a sudden when you hear I'm leaving you make up this cock-and-bull story about being knocked up!"

I got up and slammed out of the apartment. I came back in two hours.

"Look," I said contritely, "You were two weeks late in April. And four months ago you were almost three weeks late."

"Don't worry about it."

"How the hell—what do you mean don't worry about it?"

"I'll probably still come around. Always was the irregular sort, you know."

"I'd better call off the freighter," I said half-heartedly; I simply did not believe she was pregnant.

"No, you've got all your plans made. I know I'm going to get it."

"The thing is, there's not another ship for a month or more."

"I know—that's why you should take it."

"Maybe you'd better come with me."

"No money. And Daddy's coming down. Besides, I'll have it before you leave, you'll see."

But she didn't. And I left on schedule. And both of us cried.

In my own defense I can only say weakly that I was convinced that she was not really pregnant, that Gertrude could do something if she were, that if we ignored the whole thing it would go away. I also urged her to take a proper pregnancy test and wire me the results; I would somehow get the money for her fare to the States, though I wasn't sure what course we would take once there. But also deep inside I was terrified of the threat of a pregnant Betty; it represented marriage, responsibility, a confining, noncreative job, maybe even commuting and diapers and strollers and playpens and supermarkets and all manner of shackling institutions that I didn't want at this period of my life. There are different kinds of bravery, and apparently the courage of the bull ring was not necessarily applicable to life outside the arena. In this moment of truth I was a failure.

When I got to New York I found a letter waiting for me from Betty. Just a cheerful note. There was no mention of her condition so I assumed all was well. I put it out of my mind with relief. Just a close call.

I had my novel almost finished and I showed it to George Wiswell. He handed it back to me some days later, saying succinctly, "Run it through the typewriter again." He also introduced me to an attractive young lady named Marcella Powers, who was an agent.

"She used to be Sinclair Lewis' mistress," George said. "From the time she was about eighteen, for about ten years. She's leaving him to get married to a nice young guy."

Marcella, at twenty-seven, was dark-haired, petite, pert and intelligent. She read my novel and said, "Rewrite it." But she saw enough merit in it to take me on as a client. She also had some good ideas for articles.

Since I had no money and the rewrite of my book would take many months, I went to stay with my parents. They had moved from San Francisco to Santa Barbara when my father's health had declined. They lived near the beautiful old Spanish mission in a rambling sunny house. At the end of the garden there was a gardener's shack which I fixed up into a studio and I set to work diligently, every day, all day. Several afternoons a week I taught Spanish at the nearby prep school, Cate.

I had one letter from Betty, full of the gossip of Lima and bullfighting news and things she knew I would want to hear. Then a month later I had a letter from my cousin Gertrude:

Betty would murder me if she knew I was telling you this but it seems to me that you should know. Last week I took her to a doctor and she had an abortion. She was almost three month's pregnant. She was so brave—even went back to work the next day. But I know she suffered physically and mentally. She is still despondent—they say abortion depressions and guilts are worse than post-partum blues and I can believe it. So do anything you can to cheer her up—though I don't know what you can do at that distance. And don't let on that you know. Hunt doesn't even know. Nor, of course, her father, who is here now.

May I ask a silly question? How in the world could you have left that wonderful girl in that condition? Betty defends you, but I say you are a big shit. I love you but you are a big shit. There, that's the first time I've ever used that word. I trust I haven't used it in vain.

It was not used in vain.

I could not work on my book for a long time. I wrote Betty nearly every day but it was difficult, not being able to say what was on my mind. After a while her letters dwindled off. Several months later I heard that she was having an affair with a Peruvian architect, a married man with two children. He wanted to divorce his wife and marry her, I was told.

One day I picked up the newspaper and saw that Sinclair Lewis was in Santa Barbara for a six-week stay and had rented a house on Anacapa Street, not far from my parents. The mere fact that the famous novelist was in the same town and nearby made me attack the typewriter with renewed inspiration.

He was interviewed by the press constantly and I was intrigued by his impudent and powerful replies. His novel *Kingsblood Royal* was soon to be published by Random House and no book that he had written in years had stirred up such controversy. A daring approach, at that time, it told the story of an average successful small-town banker who was reviled and ostracized when it was disclosed that he had a small amount of "Negro blood" in his background. Lewis used this rather far-fetched plot to get in a great deal of highly researched information about the history of the Negro, and impassioned pleas for understanding of the race. In 1947, this created more advance furor than any of his books since *Main Street*.

I kept hoping that one of these days during his stay I would meet Sinclair Lewis. The newspaper had given the address of the house he was renting and I used to detour and drive by there on my way to teach school, in hopes of at least catching a glimpse of him. But I never did.

In a note from Marcella Powers, she said, "Red Lewis is out your way—give him a call." But I didn't.

One morning I read in the newspaper that he was leaving Santa Barbara sooner than expected to go to Hollywood for discussions of the film they were making of his novel, *Cass*

Timberlane. This spurred me to summon up my courage and write a note to him.

Dear Mr. Lewis:

I am an embryonic writer. I would like to meet you for no other purpose than to meet you. I realize how busy you are but if there were a free moment before you leave, I would consider it a rare privilege to be able to drop over.

I debated whether or not to mention that his ex-mistress was my agent. I decided not to, not knowing how he felt about her at this point. I dropped the letter off in his mailbox.

That noon his Negro chauffeur and factotum, Joseph Hardrick, stopped by the house. "Mr. Lewis would like you to come to tea at five o'clock," he said, and departed as quickly as he had arrived.

The house was a medium-sized dwelling that George F. Babbitt might have called "well-appointed." The rotund Joseph ushered me in to the living room at exactly five o'clock, saying, "He'll be with you shortly."

I sat down. There was a black binder on the cocktail table that looked terribly fat and interesting. On a strip of white adhesive on the cover was written "Ebenezer." Next to it was Plato's *Republic*.

Suddenly I heard a Midwestern voice say, "How d'ye do!"

I turned and rose to see Mr. Lewis coming into the room, his head back, his skeletal hand extended and held high. He was an awesome and startling sight. At sixty-two, he was tall and fiercely ugly, quite the ugliest person I had ever seen. I recoiled from the haunted eyes sunk in his scarlet face which was ravaged and scarred, pocked and cratered from countless operations for skin cancer. His once blazing red hair was now thin and orangy-white.

Yet I swear that ten minutes after I met him—when he started to talk and ramble—I no longer thought him ugly. He was kind and rapacious and charming and witty and factual and fanciful and reverent and irreverent and gossipy and profound, and one no longer was aware of a face but only of a powerful personality and a towering imagination and great boyish enthusiasm. We talked of all manner of things. I learned later that this was a talking period for him, a lonely period. Subsequently, I would know his long silent times; both were equally compulsive.

He fumbled a cigarette from a crumpled package and put it in his mouth. The words spilled from him: "So you're a writer, eh? I remember way back when I was at Yale— dreadful place—and I said to Professor Tinker—y'know, the great Tink—that I wanted to be a writer and nothing but a writer and he said 'But you'll starve,' and I said 'Don't care if I do,' and he said 'Then you'll succeed!' "

He was a great mimic, a remarkable imitator of infinite accents and dialects, and he reproduced Professor Tinker's refined intonations to perfection.

"You write every day? Work on a schedule? That's what you have to do, none of this bunk about waiting around for the muse to strike. I always say the art of writing is the art of applying the seat of your pants to the seat of your chair. Can't just sit around talking about writing. Gave a lecture once at Columbia and I started out by saying to the students 'How many of you here are *really* serious about being writers?' and they all raised their hands and I said, 'Well why the hell aren't you all home writing!'—and sat down. Only two ways you can learn to write, by reading and writing, and lately I'm not even so sure about the former."

I had the feeling I was in a Creative Writing Workshop

for one, but he was so enthusiastic and enjoying himself so much that I felt very privileged to be the audience.

"Keep notes? You have to keep notes, every writer has to keep notes. I wouldn't be without old Ebenezer here."

He picked up the notebook and handed it to me. I leafed through it as he talked. Terribly neat and orderly, it had such headings as "Dutch-American Names," "French-American Names," "Mannerisms," "Peculiarities of Dress," and so forth. Under "Titles," I got a little thrill when I saw such literary landmarks as *Main Street, Elmer Gantry, Dodsworth, Arrowsmith, It Can't Happen Here, Babbitt,* with a line drawn through them and the word "used" next to them.

When the tea arrived, he said, "You'd probably like a drink but I'm on the tea wagon. Haven't had a drink in eight years." (Not a totally accurate statement I was to learn.) "Can't stand that two-fisted romantic drunk writer pose!" he snarled. For the first time I caught a glimpse of that omnipresent, incipient temper. "The O'Haras and the Fitzgeralds and the Hemingways!"

He calmed himself instantly.

"So Marcella's your agent, eh? Tell me . . . how . . ." he hesitated tenderly, "how does she look? I taught her, you know—taught her everything, taught her well. I even named her! She was called Peggie before."

He looked off in space. Then he said: "Met her husband?" He snorted. "She'll leave him so quick he won't know what hit him! He won't be able to keep her mind—that agile, wonderful little mind—he won't be able to keep it interested. Then she'll come back to me. You'll see! Haven't changed a single thing in her room at Thorvale." The anger grew in his voice. "How can that young guy keep her happy? She'll be back! I'll take her back, any time—and she knows it. You're

.goddamn right she knows it and I give that young man and his marriage one year—one goddamned year!"

I noticed he put an enormous amount of sugar in his tea and his hand shook so that he could hardly get the cup to his lips. He slurped it noisily and brooded in silence. Then he suddenly said, pleasantly, "So you're working on a novel! What's it about?"

When I said it was a love story he snorted, "Hell, every novel's a love story—what's it about? I'd like to see it. How about some dinner? We'll pick up, say, the first seventy-five pages of your book on the way to the restaurant."

When we stopped at the house he said he would like to meet my parents. Since my mother is of a literary and musical bent, she was delighted to meet and talk with Mr. Lewis, who couldn't have been more charming. My father was less impressed, since he read little apart from O'Henry, Kipling and the collected works of his best friend, Stewart Edward White. My father could barely walk now, forced to shuffle along with a cane, and I noticed Mr. Lewis studying him.

When we left he said, "What's the matter with your father?"

"The doctors aren't sure," I said. "He had a blow on the head . . ."

"I know what it is," said Lewis offhandedly. "Paresis."

"What's that?" I asked.

"Syphilis of the brain," he said.

(An autopsy after my father's death ten years later did not substantiate this diagnosis.)

"I had to learn a lot about medicine for *Arrowsmith*," he went on. "I should have been a doctor. Wish I'd been a doctor. I was the only male in my family not good enough to be a doctor. My father thought I was a total failure. Oh, I suppose my brother Claude reads my books. Parts of them, anyway. But my family doesn't see what all the fuss is about. They still don't think I've done a lick of work in my life." He held up the part of my manuscript I'd given him. "But you know how much blood and sweat this little sheaf of papers cost you, and so do I!"

At dinner at the Casa de Sevilla he told stories about the old days when he used to sell short-story plots to Jack London for five dollars apiece. He imitated London's speech and his own as a callow youth. He also told me anecdotes about his ex-wife, Dorothy Thompson, even imitating her voice expertly.

"One day she came home from Washington, and I said, 'Dorothy, you should have heard Roosevelt on the radio tonight—he made the most magnificent speech!' 'I know,' she replied casually, 'I wrote it!' She was a grand girl. But then one day she disappeared into the RCA Building and I never saw her again." I had the distinct feeling of *déjà lu*, of having read or heard some of his anecdotes before, that he was trotting out "some good Red Lewis stuff for the kid." But no matter. He did Red Lewis better than anyone.

He was amazingly open to someone he had just met, someone who was thirty-seven years his junior. But somehow it all seemed perfectly natural.

"Everyone over twenty-five is the same age," he remarked sometime during the evening.

He smoked incessantly. The moment he'd take a cigarette out of the package it would assume a special character. He'd stick it in his mouth—already so bent one wondered how the thin paper stood the strain—strike a match and keep talking without lighting the cigarette until the match burned his fingers. He'd shake out the match and put the other end of the now soggy cigarette in his mouth. Then he'd light another match and repeat the performance. Ashes were a problem too. He'd get on a subject, and the cigarette in his skeletal fingers would get ashier and ashier and sometimes drop in his plate. A cup of coffee had to be exchanged because of the high content of ash.

He talked about everyone in the old days—all his friends from Robert Benchley to Edna St. Vincent Millay to H. L. Mencken to George Bernard Shaw. But he also talked about the present and the future. He was very excited about *Kingsblood Royal*.

"It's unquestionably my best book," he stated. "The critics lambasted my last couple of novels—*Cass Timberlane* and *Gideon Planish* and the one about Marcella, *Bethel Merriday*. But they can't deny me this one. Doesn't come out till next month, officially, but I'll smuggle you a copy. Maybe they were right; maybe those other books weren't so hot. But this one! If only one of my books were to exist I would want this to be the one."

When the check came, he got out his pencil and carefully checked the addition twice before paying. I found this a little odd for a multi-millionaire.

"A writer has to learn to be a tightwad," he said, as though reading my thoughts. "Otherwise he'll find himself broke and be driven to writing junk. A writer never should be driven by creditors and deadlines. Dickens was always two jumps ahead of his creditors and often had to turn out drivel to keep their hot breath off his neck. All right for Babbitt. Hell, he's just a money-making machine. But not a creative person. When your novel's a big success, don't go out and buy a Cadillac. Cadillacs are nice, but take a bus. And don't, for God's sake, get ensnared by that alluring tinsel, the long-term

Hollywood contract. Hollywood is the jumping-off place, the end of everything, finis. Nothing that goes on between paper and typewriter in that city has any relation to writing." He laughed at himself— "So saying, he trundles off to Hollywood on Saturday!"

The next morning I stayed close to the phone, but he didn't call. It couldn't take that long to read just seventy-five pages! Finally at four, I gathered up my courage and called him.

"Mr. Lewis, excuse me for bothering you, but have you by any chance had time to read those seventy-five pages?"

"Well, Barny," he said, "yes, I've read them."

There was a silence. Finally I said, "And?"

"I would be inclined," he said, and he said it not unkindly, "my inclination, that is, my first reaction . . . would be to throw away the first seventy-three or four."

"Words?"

"Pages."

I couldn't find my voice for awhile. "Throw . . . away . . . "

"Sure. Just toss 'em out."

"Not rewrite—rework—revise—?"

"Hell," he said, conspiratorially, "let's just get rid of them!"

"But—" I croaked, "why?"

"Barny," he said, "do you know what every story has in common, from *Little Miss Muffet* to *Moby Dick?*"

I hesitated, and he boomed back over the phone, "Conflict! Supposing the spider had been a nice little spider and hadn't frightened her? No story. Supposing instead of always trying to elude Ahab, Moby had spouted and said 'Hey, Cap'n, flensing-time, I'm over here—come get me!' No cross-purposes, no conflict, no story. Ennui."

"But I had to set the scene," I protested.

"For seventy-five goddamn pages? Look, when I want to read about the Azores, I'll buy the *National Geographic!* Set the scene in and around the conflict of the characters."

"I thought there was some fairly interesting information about—"

"Hogwash!" he interrupted. "People don't read novels for information! They read for an emotional kick! And you can't get an emotional kick without having people in conflict with other people or in conflict with nature or their environment or themselves or whatever. Sure you can feed the reader information: look at all the medicine and science I dished out to the reader in *Arrowsmith*. Plenty of it. They learned about how doctors and researchers work and lots more. But they got it by osmosis. I did it within the framework of the story of this young doctor's struggles against all sorts of adversities. Now, Barny, don't get discouraged. Remember, books aren't written, they're rewritten. You just have to learn to start your story faster. I remember when Saki was writing a story once and a wind from an open window blew away the first five pages of the story he was working on. He said he not only didn't miss them, it helped his story. A wind just should have blown away the first seventy-three pages of your book. But there's some good stuff and promise of things to come on those last two pages. Give me seventy-five more. I'll send Joseph over to pick them up."

He hung up.

I was sunk. All those beautiful, lyrical pages I had reworked and polished and lavished so much time on!

When Joseph came over after dinner, he brought a typewritten page:

B.—

You might profit by refreshing your memory by perusing those pretty good, familiar story beginnings. Course, a novel theoretically doesn't have to start as fast as a magazine article where the reader can just flip the page if you don't grab his interest quickly—with a novel he's either gone to the trouble of taking it out of the library or paid several dollars for it so he's going to give you a little longer to get started before he chucks it in the wastepaper basket. But why not start a novel fast? Never forget seeing a man on a ship going to Europe pick up an early book of mine, glance at the beginning and drop it over the side! Made quite an impression. The beginning obviously wasn't good enough. Doesn't always have to be a wham-doozler like the Ambrose Bierce quote below, of course, but it should be interesting and promise the reader 'stick with me, kid, I've got a whale of a story to tell you.' (Especially if your name is Melville!)

S.L.

None of them knew the colour of the sky.

The Open Boat by Stephen Crane

They threw me off the hay truck about noon.

The Postman Always Rings Twice, by James M. Cain

Please, God, let him telephone me now.

Dorothy Parker

Early one June morning, in 1872, I murdered my father—an act that made a deep impression on me at the time.

An Imperfect Conflagration by Ambrose Bierce

Happy families are all alike; every unhappy family is unhappy in its own way.

Anna Karenina

One dollar and eighty-seven cents. That was all. And sixty cents of it was in pennies.

Gift of the Magi by O. Henry

Elmer Gantry was drunk.

S. Lewis

I gave Joseph the next seventy-five pages. I had a stiff drink of Scotch for my flagging spirits and went to bed.

At two in the morning the phone rang. I stumbled out of bed and answered it. There was no salutation. Just an enthusiastic voice.

"Now she's moving!" exulted Mr. Lewis. "Yessirree, at last it's going! That girl is a honey and I care what's going to happen to her and to him and you don't need to save anything in those first seventy-three pages at all!"

My heart leapt.

"Sure, there are some things that could stand improving. You gravitate toward clichés like lint to blue serge—the way anyone does the first time around. But then when you rewrite you should catch them, come up with something original. You say things like: the old man was 'wrinkled and brown as a berry.' Jesus God, that doesn't do a thing for anyone's mental picture! Probably way back when Chaucer said somebody was 'brown as is the berye' it conjured up an image. Now we've heard it so darned often that it doesn't do a thing for us—like saying 'drunk as a Lord' or 'dead as a doornail.' Why not say the old man's face was as webbed and brown and seamed as the earth on the rain-creased hills where he lived—something like that—that way you get a double-header: you get the person's face and something about his environment. I'm not trying to write it for you, but you just can't get away with 'brown as a berry.' Lazy writing!"

All this at two in the morning.

"And of course your protagonist needs working on. Characters make your story—that and CONFLICT are the two most important things I can teach you. If you're going to be a writer you have to learn your craft. Funny, nobody would hang out a shingle before studying law or medicine or real estate or plumbing, but for some reason every sonovabitch in the world thinks he could write a book if 'he just had time!' They say only one American in a thousand reads a book a year, but three out of every thousand are trying to write one. And without knowing what the hell they're doing.

"Well, I'll let you get back to bed. Say, I had a good idea today: Do you know how to play chess?"

I said I didn't.

"Well," he said, "you take some lessons and then come East as my secretary. Forty-five dollars a week and expenses. I'll send you the ticket tomorrow before I leave."

I didn't get much sleep that night. What would my job consist of? I didn't know it then, but the next day Mr. Lewis would define my duties in a letter to Marcella Powers (as reprinted in Mark Schorer's monumental biography, *Sinclair Lewis*):

And thanks to you, Barnaby Conrad came to see me—extremely nice youngster, highly talented—in fact just the sort of chap for whom I was vaguely looking as a secretary-fellow-loafer for Thorvale, and I have asked him to spend the summer there, and he has accepted with fervor—will be along about May 15 . . . He will really have no duties except an occasional bit of research, and he can spend all day writing, and be around for a walk now and then . . . and chess. Yes, he is . . . learning it(?)

CHAPTER 15

ON THE WAY TO MASSACHUSETTS I spent a night in New York. I saw Marcella for lunch at Sardi's. Dressed in a bright green gabardine suit, "Mark," as she was called, was more vivacious and prettier than I had remembered her. She seemed radiantly happy and eager to talk of her marriage and the plans she and her husband, a successful young writer, had.

"Children, house on Long Island, all that corny, wonderful, normal stuff that I used to make fun of," she said.

She showed me a touching letter she had received from Sinclair Lewis after her marriage the previous month:

I send you every most affectionate, admiring and earnest hope for your great happiness, and my strong feeling that Mike and you will find it. You are a great person, both wise and amiably mad; to have known you has been the one distinguished event of my life . . .

"I always loved Red," she said. "Always will. Never 'in love,' you understand—just plain love."

Later I had a date with a wonderful girl whom I had met through Marcella. Her name was Jane White, whose father was Walter White, the erudite head of the NAACP. He was light-skinned, blue-eyed, and could easily have "passed." But he chose to be a Negro, to marry a black woman, to live as a black man and to help his race. (He wrote about his unusual life in *A Man Called White*.)

Jane, unlike her father, was very dark-skinned and could never have "passed." She was a delightful girl. Formerly a student at Smith, she was now striving to be an actress. She had visited Marcella and Sinclair Lewis at Thorvale and so she was able to answer some of the many questions I had about my forthcoming life. We met Dick Young (who was getting around well on his wooden leg plus canes) and his new wife and George Wiswell in the Algonquin lobby for cocktails. Someone said, "Where shall we have dinner," and to show my extreme sophistication (having been taken there once), I answered, "Where else but '21'?"

"Wonderful," said Jane.

As we got in a cab, a chill came over me. I had forgotten that Jane was a Negro. It would be awful if there were an embarrassing scene; remember, this was way back in 1947. But it was too late now—we would just have to muddle through. When we arrived at the intimidating entrance of the elegant restaurant, I marched stoutly up to the man at the velvet rope and waved, not too subtly, a five-dollar bill. "Table for five, please," I said as imperiously as I could, "and make it downstairs."

The man cast a baleful look over me, my bill and my group and said coldly, "I'm sorry, sir, there is nothing available downstairs or . . . "

Suddenly he saw Jane. "Miss White! I'm so sorry. I didn't see you! Right this way, please."

The rope came down, we went in and I learned a lesson.

I was met at the train by Mr. Lewis. (People who knew him intimately called him "Hal." People who knew him well called him "Red." People who knew him slightly called him "Sinclair." I called him "Mr. Lewis.") I was excited and a little apprehensive, but he was in an expansive mood and put me at my ease immediately.

"Y'know, Hemingway once described someone to me as the kind of finicky bastard who always got to the railroad station an hour before he needed to." He chortled. "I didn't have the nerve to tell him that I'm the kind of a finicky bastard who gets there *two* hours before train time!"

He turned to the chunky, stolid, dignified Negro driver. "You remember Joseph."

"Certainly," I said.

Mr. Lewis clapped him on the shoulder a little too heartily. "Joseph is without doubt the most versatile and adept human being I know. With the chimes he's sublime, with food he is an Escoffier and he's the Di Maggio of the croquet court, but can he learn to play good chess? No, the answer must be a resounding no."

Joseph smiled and said, "A regrettable lack of character prevents me from making a worthy opponent for Mr. Lewis."

His employer grinned appreciatively. "Let's get home now and find out how Barny here does against the old Red Master."

As Joseph drove us in the convertible Buick sedan through the attractive town and the campus of Williams College (which was so perfect that it looked like a Hollywood concept of what an Eastern college should look like), Mr. Lewis pumped me for information about Marcella.

"Does she seem happy? Happy with that Boy Scout?"

I said, "Yes, very," and saw a look of wistful pain cross his face.

"They're always happy in the beginning," he muttered. "But you wait. Hell, if you can't be happy the first month, you're in trouble. Funny, I left my first wife when I was forty-two. Left my second when I was fifty-two. And now this ungrateful girl ups and leaves me when I'm sixty-two for one of the Rover Boys!"

He snapped out of his melancholy as quickly as he'd gone into it. "And you, you punk kid, you're only twenty-five and going to be a hell of a writer, eh? Got to get right to work on the rewrite of that book tomorrow."

"Mr. Lewis," I asked, "just what are my duties? I'm not really qualified to be a secretary."

"Your duties," he said, "are to get up every morning at 5:30 and work on that goddamn book of yours!"

"For that I get paid?"

"Oh, no, we'll find some other things to keep you busy. Won't we, Joseph."

"Yes, sir," said Joseph.

Four-and-a-half miles in back of Williamstown on Oblong Road, the 750 acres of field and mountain and woods of Thorvale Farm began. Mr. Lewis showed me around proudly. It was the most beautiful estate I had ever seen, complete with a trout stream, a purposefully rustic swimming pool set in a birch glen, guest houses, barns and a tennis court. The handsome manor house had a fine view of Mt. Greylock, seven bedrooms, five baths and was beautifully furnished. Bookcases were everywhere, even running up the stairs.

Where there weren't books, there were valuable impression-istic paintings by Childe Hassam.

It looked as though he had been in this house always, would stay forever and pass it on to his son, Michael. (His oldest son, H. G. Wells Lewis, had been killed in the war.) But in fact, he had been in the place little more than a year. And, though he had announced that he had finally found nirvana and backed up that statement by doing $70,000 worth of improvements to the estate, the restless Mr. Lewis would put the house up for sale a year later and would resume his lonely journey in search of a happiness he would never find.

Mr. Lewis showed me his workroom upstairs off his bed-room, saying, "Here's the factory."

It was incredibly neat, with an almost sterilized feeling about it. A dozen freshly sharpened pencils were in an earthen pot on the L-shaped custom-built desk. Neat stacks of typed pages and notes on yellow legal paper were the only hints of the great activity that took place at that desk. Framed on the wall was a large detailed map of Lewis' mythical Mid-western town, the locale of so many of his books, with such labels as "Carol's house" or "Doc's place." There were half a dozen photos of Marcella, one of his son Michael and one of Wells in uniform.

My room was down the hall at the other end of the house. "Marcella's room," he said. "And keep it neat. She'll be using it again before long, you'll see."

My "studio" was the little library off the living room. It was filled with nothing but Sinclair Lewis novels in their many editions and foreign-language versions.

That night I played chess with Mr. Lewis before dinner. I had studied chess for only a few weeks and had little talent

Sinclair Lewis

for the game, but I managed to maneuver his king into a bad position fairly soon. I left to go to the bathroom, and when I returned I could swear the pieces had been moved to my disadvantage. But I didn't say anything and I managed to win anyway. He seemed upset.

"Luck," he snarled, "sheer luck!"

Then I remembered Marcella's admonition: "You mustn't win at chess—not too often, anyway. It's the most important thing in his day."

He was a trifle sullen at dinner, I thought, frowning over the fine leg of lamb that Joseph had cooked and served. For a fastidious man, he had infantile table manners; he liked to swirl his mashed potatoes and peas and meat and a butter ball and bits of bread all together in a Charybdis-like concentric swirl. Then, most frequently, he would send back the plate to the kitchen, the food half eaten and covered with a film of cigarette ashes like some meal interrupted at the time of the Pompeian disaster. He had barely eaten half his dessert when he said, "Now my friend, we'll see how much beginner's luck was involved in that first game!"

I followed him out to the living room and waited while he fortified himself by eating several chocolates. (There was always a box of Whitman's Samplers in every room, most of the contents ruined for other people by Mr. Lewis' inquiring forefinger.) He sat down at the chess table and rubbed his hands with anticipation. He immediately set out to lure me into a Fool's Mate—to beat me in a minimum of moves. Though it was one of the first maneuvers my instructor had showed me how to avoid, I let myself fall into the trap.

"Ah hah!" he exulted. "That will show you!"

He was delighted and ate three chocolates in celebration. In a euphoric mood he bid me goodnight.

"Welcome to Thorvale—see you bright and early!" he said, as he went up the stairs, breaking wind triumphantly with every step.

I woke up the next morning before the alarm went off at five-thirty. It was still dark as I dressed and went downstairs. He was up ahead of me. I saw him—Ichabod Crane—sitting in the dining room in a faded brown bathrobe, hunched over a cup of coffee. His three false front teeth were out, which did not enhance his appearance. He wore a green eye shade, like a small-town newspaper editor, and his orangy hair shot out from the sides of his head like horns. He pointed with a trembling finger at a thermos and a cup at the other end of the table. I sat down and poured a cup of coffee. It was quiet for a while except for Mr. Lewis' slurping of coffee and the keening of the quail outside. Smoking steadily, he stared off into space as though fascinated by a moving picture visible to his eyes alone. I finished my coffee and he still hadn't spoken. I noticed he had Band-Aids on his index fingers, which meant he was working, for he was a hunt-and-peck typist and had sensitive fingers. The backs of his skeletal hands were foxed like an antique manuscript.

Finally he said, "I'm intolerable in the morning. I get bearable around noon and around six o'clock I'm quite a splendid chap. You can go to work any time you want. I generally sit here for an hour telling myself what a capital fellow I am before going up to the factory. Give me some more pages of your book."

I went into my study and brought back fifty pages of the novel. I had some qualms about that part of the manuscript.

"Mr. Lewis, there are certain things in these pages which . . . "

"The pages have to speak for themselves," he interrupted. "Jowett said, 'Never apologize, never explain.'"

I noticed his breath smelled like photographic negatives.

I went back to my studio and worked until I heard the breakfast chimes at eight-thirty. Joseph was playing inventively on the six-toned instrument in the hallway. Mr. Lewis came down the stairs, clutching my manuscript. He never merely held anything; it was always clutched.

"Excellent, Joseph, excellent!" he said pleasantly. "Even better than yesterday—positively Wagnerian! Oh, if Damrosch could only hear you! We'll have to set up an audition soon."

Joseph grinned at the standing joke and retreated to the kitchen. We had breakfast on the screened porch, and Mr. Lewis went over the two pages of the notes he had made on my manuscript, smoking incessantly in between bites of scrambled eggs and sausages.

"Now here you go again!" he said sternly. "Wandering away from the story! Don't put down one line that doesn't either advance the plot or develop the characters or help the reader to envision the scene.

"Touch! Feel! Smell! See! You should write those words down on some adhesive tape and paste them across the front of your typewriter. Imagine yourself being the reader—try never to bore him. We writers are the only people who can bore people even long after we're dead. So let's try earnestly never to bore in print on purpose.

"You keep *telling* me that your heroine is brave; telling, telling—but you never *show* me! You must *show* her doing something brave before I'll really believe it. Even if minor characters in dialogue say how brave she is, that is better, more convincing, than when you, the author, tell me. And if you have a villain in your story don't *tell* me he's villainous, have him come on the scene and kick a dog or break an old lady's glasses or, let's hope, some more sophisticated refinement of villainy. Minor characters can help bring your main characters to life. Remember *The Iliad?* You never really see the beautiful Helen, over whom the Greeks and the Trojans have been fighting for ten long years, but you overhear a couple of weary soldiers talking about how they'd like to go home to their families and why the hell are they here in the first place—fighting for the possession of some silly female? And then, suddenly, Helen, in all her radiant beauty, walks by and the soldiers say, 'Wow, is she gorgeous! Where's my spear, let's get back to the fight, who cares about going home, we have to win back that woman!' Incidentally, that war, the Trojan War, is the only war in all history where both sides knew exactly what they were fighting for.

"And here you've written: 'his eyes crinkled as he smiled.' Jesus God, liberate me from crinkling eyes! Sure, I suppose that's what eyes do, but it doesn't conjure up any sharp picture. How about, 'when he smiled the corners of his eyes went as wrinkled as—' " He glanced around the table, saw the torn-open package of cigarettes and tossed them in front of me. " '—as wrinkled as the tinfoil on the package of the French cigarettes he smoked.' That's hardly a deathless simile, but you get the idea.

"You are too interested in action. Reaction—reaction by the characters to the action is more important."

After breakfast we both went back to our studies. When the mail arrived at eleven, Mr. Lewis came into my studio and handed me several fan letters and requests for autographs.

"Here," he said, "play Sinclair Lewis and answer these. Say anything you want and sign my signature to them." Then he tore open and read another letter.

"Look what this sonovabitch wants!"

He handed it to me. It was from an attorney and it read:

Dear Lewis:

Have read some of your works and would like to ask a few favors. Please send me a list of your stories, your autograph, your picture and a letter describing your life. How many children you have and their names.

Thanking you, I am,

Yours truly,
James J. Sneath

"I think I'll answer this bastard myself," said Mr. Lewis and the gleam of battle was in his pale eyes. "Barny, take a letter!"

Though I knew no shorthand, I managed to keep up with his exaggeratedly polite tone as he dictated as though conversing pleasantly to his new pen pal:

My dear Jimmy:

There was only one thing about your letter that I didn't like. It was so sort of formal. True, we have never met, and somehow I feel we are not likely to, but isn't this a democratic country? So let me call you Jim, and you call me Skinny or any other friendly name. No, Jim, I haven't got a photograph of me here, but I'll run right down and have one taken. I'm preparing a letter about my life for you, but it's been a pretty long one and a pretty bad one. That'll take me several weeks. Meantime, Jimmy, I'm interested in lawyers. Kindly send me your photo, pictures of your home, your office, a list of your assets and liabilities, average income, and the books you've read since 1930, if any. Kindly inform me whether you've ever defended a bootlegger or an author, and why. How do you get along with your wife? Kindly explain the sex part in detail.

Yours affectionately,
Sinclair Lewis.

There were many such letters over the next months. I remember one day Mr. Lewis received a letter from a former secretary of his whom he hadn't seen for years. It was a very high-handed letter—breezy, fresh and ultimately asking for a large loan as though it were Mr. Lewis' obligation to maintain him. He told me about him; how once when motoring across the desert, this man had told him that he had tipped over in a canoe when he was at college and the girl had drowned. "I could have tried to save her," the man had said, "but I thought it more important to concentrate on saving myself, for after all, I was almost a Ph.D. and she was a little nobody."

Mr. Lewis dictated an answering letter to me that went:

Dear Bill:

Fifteen years ago this September you and I were motoring together. At one point you got out of the car to look at the tires. At that moment, I was seized with a desire to drive off and leave you to die in the desert. However, I fought down the urge, an action I have since come to regret deeply.

Sincerely,
Sinclair Lewis

Another letter to someone began so wonderfully: "Dear John: How unwise of you to hate me . . . " I had great fun becoming Sinclair Lewis for two hours or so a day, answering the fan mail—the standard requests, the admirers, the cranks, the proposals of marriage from unknown women, the pleas for money and, always, the offer of someone's life story. "I'll tell it to you; you write it; and we'll split fifty-fifty!"

He would enjoy reading my replies and would chuckle over some. "God, I write a good letter!" he'd say sometimes. I would be very pleased. Often he would correct or add to them, and I learned from it. Then I would sign them, imitating his signature. I got so good at the forgery that I would sign his name to my pay check and the bank never noticed the discrepancy. Mr. Lewis enjoyed the deception.

Every few days I would drive down to the bank to deposit ten or fifteen pages of his new novel, *The God Seeker*, in a vault. It struck me as odd in the beginning, until I realized that if a fire destroyed all the copies of a Sinclair Lewis manuscript it would be like touching a match to a pile of at least one hundred and fifty thousand dollar bills.

But my actual secretarial duties were few. I used to cut the vast lawns with a power mower after lunch and go trout fishing in the stream (though Mr. Lewis disapproved of fishing and would always frown at me as he saw me going out with my rod). Sometimes I would go pick up books for Mr. Lewis at the library and meet visitors at the train. Nearly every weekend we had such distinguished writers as Carl Van Doren and Robert Nathan and George Jean Nathan and John Gunther come to visit.

I was rather nervous one day when Joseph was off and I had to drive Mr. Lewis and John Gunther around the countryside. "Think of my responsibility," I said. "I have this week's number one non-fiction title on *The Times'* list in the front seat and in the back I have the number one fiction title!"

The artist Norman Rockwell came one Sunday for a fried chicken picnic in the beautiful glen down by the pool, as did the distinguished Negro writer, Horace Cayton, grandson of the first Negro senator, and several other people from nearby Williams College. Mr. Lewis chose that day to break out a bow and arrow set, complete with a huge virginal target.

"A new one I bought for Marcella—best Abercrombie had. She hasn't come back yet to use it. She will, though. I want it to be kept in perfect shape, used and appreciated."

No one expressed any interest in shooting it. But Mr. Lewis had paid for it and was determined to see it in action.

"Come on, Barny," he said, handing the bow to me. "Let's see if you can do as well as Marcella."

I hadn't shot a bow and arrow since I was a child, and the circled target seemed much too pristine and professional to be violated by me. I looked around for something else to shoot at. Seventy feet across the pool I saw a huge toad.

"See that toad?" I said, in mock Robin Hood tones.

The guests laughed at the futility of the boast and kept eating their chicken. I drew back the notched arrow as far back as I could, trying to remember how the counselor had said to do it at summer camp when I was twelve. I wanted to get the string back to my cheek as I knew one was supposed to, but I couldn't, so I just released the arrow any which way.

To my utter amazement the arrow flew across the pool and struck the toad between the eyes. The poor creature gave a great "orkkk," spasmed out its legs and died a surprised death. The guests and Mr. Lewis turned to me in awe. I closed my gaping mouth, put down the bow and tried to collect myself, pretending I could do that anytime I wanted to.

"My goodness," said Horace Cayton, "I haven't seen a shot like that since the great Howard Hill!"

I tried to look properly modest. Suddenly I saw Mr. Lewis' face, which had worn an admiring look a moment ago, go bandana red.

"Do you *always* have to be wantonly killing something?" he snarled. "First trout and now this poor beast!"

The guests fell silent in embarrassment.

"We eat the trout—" I began, coloring.

"Isn't there enough cruelty in the world already?" he said,

slamming his drumstick down so hard on the plate that it broke.

"I didn't really think there was a chance—"

"Don't you think fish and frogs have feelings, too?" he raged. His face was almost purple. "Who in God's name do you think you are to kill other creatures? I guess you think you're pretty brave to have killed a poor little toad!"

"Mr. Lewis," I interrupted, "I really never thought I could hit it, but now that I did I'm not going to worry about it too much." I daringly picked up the drumstick off of his broken plate. "How about this poor little chicken? He was running around alive and happy yesterday." I imitated: "Buck, buck, bri'awk!"

Fuming, Mr. Lewis stared first at me and then at the chicken leg, his mouth working silently. Then he spun on his heel and walked away from the pool and his guests.

That was a silly way to lose a great job, I accused myself. He's gone to get my final pay check.

But an hour later, as some of the guests were leaving, he reappeared as though nothing had happened. When he had said good-by to them, he turned to me and said, "Barny, that was a capital idea! You're right—we've all been hypocrites!"

"What idea, sir?" I said.

"From now on we are all vegetarians here at Thorvale," he said. "I have just so informed Joseph."

Poor Joseph, who took pride in his culinary skill, was hard pressed to come up with attractive vegetarian dishes for the next few days. And it made no difference that the house-guests did not wish to eliminate fish and meat and eggs from their diets. They protested politely, then submissively ate vegetables and salads. And they left a day early.

The third day at breakfast, Mr. Lewis looked with great

distaste at the bowl of Rice Krispies that Joseph placed in front of him. He splashed on some cream, then poked his spoon about listlessly. "They're so goddamn noisy," he muttered. Then he ruminated: "You know, eggs aren't *really* meat."

By this time I would have given ten dollars for a single egg. But I had come to know how to handle Mr. Lewis at crises like this.

"I don't know, sir," I said, shaking my head dubiously. "I don't know about that—they sure turn into chickens and hence they're potentially fowl and hence flesh."

"Ah hah!" said Mr. Lewis. "There's the key word! Potentially! You put your finger on it . . . *potential*, yet not actual! Semantics—very important to pay strict attention to meanings of words—the difference between the right word and the almost right word is the difference between lightning and the lightning bug. Now! Eggs don't *have* to turn into chickens, do they! Joseph, two orders of fried eggs!"

At lunch Joseph sneaked a few sardines into the salad, and Mr. Lewis chose to ignore—though eat—them. At dinner, if one looked really closely, slim strips of rare beef, looking almost identical to the slices of julienne beets, could be detected in the chef's salad. But I certainly wasn't going to point them out, and Mr. Lewis joined me in a second helping of "beets."

The next morning barely detectable bits of ham could be discerned in the scrambled eggs, and when Mr. Lewis ate them, the era of vegetarianism was over. It was never mentioned again. Not even a week later when Joseph served him one of the nice trout I had caught in the stream.

The strange part of his make-up was that I don't think he had any idea that he was a "character."

I asked him once if he was a friend of Tom Wolfe's. "No," he said. Later I read about "Lloyd McHarg" in *You Can't Go Home Again*, an extremely detailed account of the alcoholic and horrendous weeks the two men had spent in England together.

"I thought you said you weren't a friend of Wolfe's?" I accused him.

"You couldn't be a friend of Tom's," he answered, "any more than you could be a friend of a hurricane."

He didn't think that portrait in *You Can't Go Home Again* was anything like him at all. I think he was hurt by the emphasis on his ugliness and therefore didn't like to discuss it. He was very shy about his face. "That's the way I'd like to look," he once said, holding up the theatrical touched-up photo of himself on the jacket of *Kingsblood Royal*. "Now there's a serious, fine, upstanding young author. He'll go far, that chap. Except for that sister of his—the one who runs the bordello and smokes cigars, y'know. If she has her way she'll have him take that position in the casket company and give up this damn foolishness. Why, only last week as she was taking her heroin she . . . "

How he loved to spin stories out of nothing! We'd be driving down the street and Mr. Lewis would suddenly clutch my arm. "See that little old woman going into the drugstore?" he'd say dramatically. "Looks like an ordinary package under her arm, doesn't it? Hah! You know what's *really* in there? Well, that's Grandma Fruitwood and she's carrying a . . . " and out would come a complete story with a beginning, middle and usually an O. Henry type ending.

"Lord," I'd say, always impressed, "you should write that!"

He would laugh and shrug it off.

The next week he asked me, out of the blue, to call him "Red"—"the way all my friends do." I was flattered, but it was hard to do. Despite the beautiful surroundings and the usually congenial atmosphere, Mr. Lewis—Red—was like a Roman candle that could go off at any time. The servants and I never quite relaxed. I say "servants" because besides Joseph, there was an attractive Negro couple, the Perkins, and their infant daughter, who lived in the guest cottage near the tennis court. Alma did the laundry, helped with the cooking, and Wilson took care of the grounds. I would play cards with them several times a week in their cottage, though Red seemed to resent it whenever I went over there. It wasn't necessarily that I preferred their company to his; it was just that one could truly be at ease in their pleasant company whereas Mr. Lewis' personality, brilliance and temperament were just too relentlessly in evidence at all times. I think he also resented the fact that here he was, the big expert on the Negro, yet he had no real Negro friends, whereas I did.

I wondered how Marcella had managed to stick out her role as mother-wife-and-mistress for so long, but apparently she had done a wonderful job as he spoke of her constantly and with touching affection. He played the "Grand Canyon Suite" all the time because that was her favorite. He would put on a symphony every night, Beethoven being his favorite, and would then work at listening to it for a while before going back to Ferde Grofé. I don't think he really enjoyed music; he just thought he should. "I never can recognize anything without sneaking a peek at the cover of the album," he confessed one night. He rarely played the radio.

"When I sit down to write I have to constantly remind myself that most Americans live by the radio, actually tell time most of the day and night by what programs are on! I also have to remember that most other Americans attend baseball games, like to go dancing, follow the football news, get excited about the Derby, keep up hunting and fishing gear and do other normal things completely incomprehensible and alien to me."

Once he turned the radio on to hear Dorothy Thompson speak (he was amazed at her frequent religious references) and once to hear *Dodsworth* done (he got bored and snapped it off almost immediately).

He always spoke well of Dorothy and his first wife, Grace, as well as Marcella. That is why I was amazed that among his very last writings before his death a poem was found which began:

Here, strengthened by their scholarly care,
I ponder on the Heavenly sphere
Where once, most miserable of lives,
I thought of my three horrible wives.

My first wife longed for social place
She thrashed about with scarlet face
To get a chance to meet a prince.
My second made me shake and wince
By violence, by blasts and blares,
As she managed other folks' affairs.
My third was winsome, playful, kind,
But often difficult to find,
For it was hard to keep in mind
In what man's bed she now reclined . . .

He was fascinated by acting and the theater. When the actor Jean Hersholt was coming for his first visit, Red had me make a sign, "Paul Christian, M.D.," the name of the doctor Hersholt played on the popular radio series. He was very excited about his little joke. He treasured small adventures and had me work very hard on it. I had to call all the radio stations around before I could find out Dr. Christian's Christian name. I had to make the sign in gold paint on a black background, like a professional's, and then we tacked it to the right of the main door. The result was that the Hersholts arrived, saw the sign, exclaimed at the remarkable coincidence and drove back to Williamstown almost five miles away to find out where their directions had gone wrong. They finally made it, but they were an hour late for lunch and Mr. Lewis was fuming.

He didn't enjoy practical jokes, but he did love the *idea* of practical jokes. For instance, for some reason I never knew, he decided not to like Phinney Baxter, the head of Williams College, though I don't believe he'd ever met him. (He often preconceived colossal hatreds which were immediately dispelled upon contact with the object of his wrath.) He spent a great deal of time thinking up splendid ways he could "do in" the unsuspecting Mr. Baxter. Once he called his friend Rex Falls of the Pittsfield *Eagle*, starting the conversation with "Rex, you know there is simply no truth in the fact that Phinney Baxter was found drunk in a brothel in Buffalo this morning at 7:53." He urged him to tell all his friends the story, but when Rex pretended to go along with the gag, Mr. Lewis hastily cautioned him against it "for fear some damn fool would believe it."

I once pulled out a book from his library entitled *Hike and the Aeroplane*. In the fly leaf was written, "To Sinclair Lewis, my altered ego, my closest friend and greatest admirer [signed] Tom Graham." I asked Red about this and he threw back his head and laughed like a schoolboy who has gotten away with a splendid practical joke. Tom Graham was a nom de plume and that was his first book.

His and my class reunions, '07 and '44 respectively, came that summer and Mr. Lewis decided to go down to New Haven for it. He deliciously dreaded the affair and talked of it constantly. Twice he decided to call it off.

"God, a bunch of Babbitts showing pictures to each other of the little woman and the grandchildren!"

But finally we went. I drove him in the Buick convertible sedan, and twice on the way down to New Haven he had me stop, park the car and wait while he took a forty-five-minute nap. On the way we passed a kennel that advertised Boston bulls. Mr. Lewis had been talking of buying one for some time, so we went in. He found a nice little female, but the woman was asking a hundred and twenty, which Mr. Lewis said was too much. He wrestled with the problem for a while and then said he would have to think about it. On the rest of the way to New Haven he argued mightily with himself. He was very tight about small money transactions. But Millicent Pancake, as he'd already named her, was very attractive; she reminded him of a dog he'd had when he was young; and he had all but decided to pick her up on the way home. At Yale I deposited Mr. Lewis at the "college" he was staying at and went off with Jim Kleeman, my ex-roommate who was still at Yale studying medicine. I told him about Mr. Lewis' dog dilemma and Jim, who raised Brittany spaniels in Ohio, said that he had a splendid hunting dog which he would give Red. After the weekend (which Mr. Lewis enjoyed heartily, until he began thinking about it and finding reasons why he shouldn't have enjoyed it—"Those bastards made me feel about as welcome as feces in the punch bowl!"), I told him about the new dog offer. This presented a terrible problem. Should he put up the large sum for Millicent Pancake, a dog he dearly wanted, or should he accept this bargain of a free unknown dog? His Sauk Center frugality triumphed by a slim margin, but he was very angry at himself for permitting it to; the poor spaniel was doomed before it even arrived. It came the next Saturday and, as I was away in New York that weekend, I didn't see it until Sunday. I came in the kitchen way and asked Joseph how the dog was. "Oh, it's a fine dog," said Joseph. Then his eyes rolled heavenward in exasperation; "But . . . "

I went into the living room and Mr. Lewis was there reading, the brown and white spaniel asleep on the floor. "How's the dog turned out?" I asked.

Mr. Lewis kept reading, too intensely. Then he looked up and said quietly, though savoring the dramatic impact of the words, "We are going to kill that dog."

Having learned a lot about handling Mr. Lewis by this time, I said cheerfully, "All right. Do you want me to do it, or shall I take it down to the vet's?"

This wasn't quite the reception he'd hoped for his little bombshell, but he mumbled, "Sure, take it down to the vet's."

I didn't say anything but leafed casually through a magazine, knowing he couldn't keep his grievance to himself very long. Finally he burst out.

"See that goddamn beast?" he cried, pointing a bony finger at the bewildered animal, "it barked at my luncheon guests yesterday!"

I found a good home for the dog with one of the painters who was working on the place and that ended the incident. William Makepeace Thackeray Shakespeare, the cat, as arrogant, unaffectionate and ungiving as any feline who ever ruled a household, continued to be his only pet at Thorvale, mainly, I believe, because it used to belong to Marcella.

Although I was Mr. Lewis' favorite punching bag and considered that as part of my job, no one was immune from that sudden and frightening temper. Carl Van Doren, the gentle historian, spent a lot of time at Thorvale and was probably Mr. Lewis' best friend; that's what made the following incident so terrible. There was a mathematics expert living in Williamstown whom Mr. Lewis enjoyed seeing once a week or so. Since he and Van Doren were both ornithologists by avocation, Mr. Lewis decided to get the two of them together. He prepared them both by saying, "I have a wonderful friend I want you to meet with whom you can really pour your heart out about these birds of yours."

He had them to dinner—just the four of us—and he was right; they got along famously. Before and during most of the dinner they talked excitedly about birds. Mr. Lewis sat there in ominous silence, not eating. Suddenly, just before dessert, he brought down his hand on the table with such violence that he broke a dish.

"Now listen, you two bastards," he said, his face even redder than usual and his voice trembling. "This is my house, I invited you into it, you're eating my food, so I think you might have the common decency not to be *completely* rude to me!"

Van Doren, who also knew Mr. Lewis well enough to know how to handle him, said, "You're absolutely right, Red. "I'm sorry we've been so inconsiderate. Let's talk about something general."

But the party was over. The math expert went home, and the fact that Red called him the next day to beg his pardon didn't quite make things the way they were before. Mr. Lewis always managed to hurt the people he liked most— deliberately, it seemed. (A touching document found among his papers after his death was a partial list of the good friends he had alienated during his life. It was a very long list.)

Part of the reason for his temperament at this time was not only the loss of Marcella, but the reception that *Kingsblood Royal* was getting. While it was a commercially successful—a best selling book—the reviews that were coming in were not what he had hoped for at all. When they would arrive in the mail from a clipping service, he would spill them out of the envelope contemptuously and pretend not to be interested in them.

"Joseph Conrad and I agreed that we might consent to *measure* reviews," he said haughtily, "but never to read them!" Yet he did read them—every line—and he would rage at the reviewers.

"What a hell of a profession we've chosen, eh, Barny? What other job is there in the entire world where any unqualified, ignorant, talentless, jealous, stupid sonovabitch who wants to, has every chance to tear your work to shreds? Listen to what this boob writes!"

Nearly all the reviews lauded Lewis' intentions, praised his research, but derided the far-fetched plot, the archaic language and the thinly drawn characters. Nearly all of them said that the book fell far short of the several powerful novels he had written in the past. For every bad review he had a particular reason why that reviewer would want to write a bad report of any book of his.

"What do you EXPECT a Luce publication to say!" he'd snarl. "That messianic crook has been out to get me for decades! I make him nervous."

And of another publication's review: "They're notoriously anti-Negro—naturally they aren't going to like it. Always remember this: abuse from certain sources is a compliment."

But one day a review came that was written by his long-time friend, Clifton Fadiman, a man he admired greatly. "Ah-hah!" said Lewis, as he tenderly held the clipping in his trembling fingers. "Let's see what old Kip has to say! His literary opinions are worth all the rest put together."

He read the first sentences and beamed. "Well, I'm delighted *somebody's* glad I'm 'still in the arena and still punching,' " he said. "Good old Kip! And you're damned right I did a lot of research on this book."

Then he read on, and he began to scowl. Soon the scowl twisted his red face and he began to talk back to the piece of paper, oblivious of my presence.

"What do you mean the characters don't live!" he muttered. "Why, they dance all over the pages!" And then, his eyes skipping down to the next paragraph, "Preposterous? Of course you'd think it was preposterous, Fadiman, what the hell do you know about the Negro? What do you know of the way he's treated, the way he lives? What the hell do you know about life, when you get right down to it—stashed away in your ivory cocoon!"

By the time he had ended the long and thoughtful review, the paper was twisted and torn. He started to crumple it up. Then, mechanically, he smoothed it out and gently placed it on the low table in front of him. He sat there looking at it in silence for a moment. Finally, he gave a low moan-like sigh. "Maybe," he murmured, "maybe it *is* . . . a bad novel."

He dropped his face in his hands, and I took that moment to quietly leave the room.

CHAPTER 16

I NEVER HEARD HIM MENTION THE BOOK AGAIN.
And he appeared, at least outwardly, to recover from
this most recent and devastating blow to his ego.

All his energy centered around his new novel, *The God
Seeker*, and he spoke of it as enthusiastically as though
Kingsblood Royal had never happened.

Certainly he was his old self the next evening. I had been
invited (for one hundred dollars) to speak at Williams College by an undergraduate group on the subject of bullfighting.
It was my first lecture and I was nervous. The big auditorium
was almost filled. I started off shakily and was further un-
nerved when I looked down from the podium to see my
famous employer sitting in the first row of the auditorium—
especially since he had been vitriolic in expressing his ab-
horrence of bullfighting many times. However, everything
went along fine for about forty-five minutes. Then, in the
course of my speech, I explained that a bull is not overly

intelligent, that his brain is very small—about the size of a baseball. Mr. Lewis could not resist:

"And just how big is a bullfighter's brain?" His voice rang through the hall and the lecture broke up.

Yet in spite of his distaste for the subject, he complimented me on the talk and urged me to see a lecture agent when next I went to New York. He even presented me with an unsolicited written blurb: "This lecture is terrific—truly sensational."

Though outwardly his same feisty self, I seemed to note a change in him; he became more introspective, more introverted. I hesitate to say more spiritual. One morning at breakfast, after a blistering attack on the standard concept of a heaven, he mused: "My God, supposing after they throw the last spadeful of dirt on us, we find out it's all true?"

He spoke of religion all that week very knowledgeably, though he constantly referred to himself as an atheist. We went to church that Sunday in Williamstown, his first time in more than a decade.

"I just want to see if it has improved any," he said.

Apparently it hadn't, for he slept and snored through most of it. But he invited the earnest minister for lunch afterward and they argued theology, though it was difficult for the younger man to discuss anything when Mr. Lewis kept referring to "the Christ myth." I remember his saying to the shaken preacher: "Good Lord, what a concept Christianity's God is! Here is this supreme egotist sitting up there who fashions creatures and puts them on earth for, we are told, the sole purpose of worshipping Him, the one who created them. Then if they do that well all their lives, He snatches them up closer to Him where they can adore Him better and recite how wonderful He and His whole family is and mouth 'Holy, Holy, Holy' throughout all eternity!" He seemed to be thinking about death a great deal. The imminence of his own caducity hung over him and his choice of reading matter and conversation reflected this. Some days we used to drive for miles to see some cemetery, particularly the old ones. We went to Plymouth not to see the Rock, but for the old graveyard. Mr. Lewis used to make notes when he found an especially interesting tombstone or name, notes that would be entered in his notebook Ebenezer.

Though I was often Mr. Lewis' punching bag and a day seldom went by during which he didn't find some way to berate me painfully, I never wanted to leave. I never found him boring or repetitive—except when he recited *Kubla Khan*. The only poem he knew by heart, or so I assumed, he would recite it in its entirety with or without encouragement, proudly, but yet ridiculing himself the while. He was also inordinately proud of his German and would spout it to people who didn't understand a word of it. The joke pleased him enormously and he tended to belabor it, protesting that he was "very short in this country from Bremen and couldn't speak no English." We had Italian lessons twice a week, and he took great enjoyment in these. Even in Italian he made up stories. One of the characters in our traditionally dull grammar book was "*poverina Caterina*" ("the mushroom of poor Caterina is on the table," etc.). She was "*molto stupida*," and to the consternation of the hapless little Italian teacher, Mr. Lewis would depart from the text and, in his bad but fluent Italian, would lead *poverina Caterina* through the damnedest and most scandalous escapades. The teacher was humorless and didn't understand, so Mr. Lewis was always gentle with him, as he was with all gentle people. While he often humiliated and excoriated me, he was never consciously rough with his Negro servants who were in no position to fight back or quit.

Mr. Lewis was never contemptuous of any lack of knowledge, as long as there was no presumption or pomposity. A farm girl who worked at Thorvale used to bring her pedestrian poems to him, and he was extremely patient as he worked with her, spending hours of his carefully husbanded time. But when she began to feel she knew it all and became dogmatic, he had nothing more to do with her. I never saw him refuse to read a young author's manuscript, though he dreaded the task. Yet generally he would write a detailed critique of the many manuscripts and poems he received from aesthetic Williams' students or elderly crackpots. And though I heard him growl and call the popular novelist Robert Nathan "a damned fool" for wasting his time answering fan mail, I never saw him fail to answer any sincere letter. Either that, or have me answer it.

One morning, he said thoughtfully, "Man is the only animal that laughs and weeps, for he is the only animal that is struck with the difference between what things are and what they ought to be." He paused and wrinkled his forehead. "Now, did I write that? Or did Montaigne or Hazlitt? I get us all confused sometimes."

Another time he mused, "Hemingway must be the most illiterate great writer who ever lived. I wonder if he's ever read a serious book and if so, which one."

One morning I went down to Washburne's book shop— with Mr. Lewis' admonition, "Be sure you're here for lunch at twelve sharp!" ringing in my ears. Behind the counter was a very attractive young lady of about twenty-six. We got to talking about books and movies and fishing and Sinclair Lewis and other things. Her name was Ida Kay and she was tan and pretty, and as we chatted it was brought home to me in a rush what a monastic life I had been leading the past few months. It was great for my youthful ego to be the center of attention for a change. Suddenly I looked at my watch and realized I only had eight minutes to get home for lunch. Blurting out "See you tomorrow!" I dashed out of the store and with the vision of Ida's bright black eyes still before me I jumped into the parked car. But for some reason neither of the keys would go into the ignition. I tried every way to force them in, to no avail. Finally in desperation, I took off the hand brake and let the car coast down the inclined main street until I came to a garage. I explained I was in a great hurry, that something was wrong with the ignition lock, and then went to phone Joseph to tell Mr. Lewis that I would be unavoidably delayed. When I returned, a mechanic was on his back on the car floor working away on the ignition with his tools.

"Say, whose car is this anyway?" he asked as he hammered.

"Sinclair Lewis'," I said.

The man stopped working. "This isn't Mr. Lewis' car," he said. "He has a Buick."

And indeed it wasn't. In my foggy state I had picked someone else's vehicle. I took the time to phone the police that if anyone reported a missing car it was in this garage. Then I abashedly apologized to the garageman, ran back up the street, collected the correct automobile and sped home.

I quelled some of Mr. Lewis' wrath at my tardiness by telling him about the lovely girl at the book store.

"Ask her to lunch tomorrow," he said unexpectedly. "She sounds like Marcella."

Ida came—that day and many subsequent ones—and Mr. Lewis was delighted with her. Unfortunately, so was I, and when I would go walking by the stream with her or would take her to a college play or the movies, we would find Mr. Lewis waiting up for us and scowling like an overly protective father. Mark Schorer wrote:

He was indebted to Barnaby Conrad, too, for introducing him to another companion who was to be of real comfort to him before he abandoned Williamstown—a young woman named Ida Kay who clerked in the college bookstore—pretty, sprightly, literate, free to be called upon at any time, full of chatter and gossip and sufficient deference to the mighty to prove highly satisfactory.

After I left, and I'm not sure Ida's appearance didn't hasten my departure, he was to see her frequently and even ask her to marry him, despite the vast difference in their ages. She declined the offer despite the many blandishments offered.

One morning, over our 5:30 thermos of coffee, Mr. Lewis mused, "Y'know, he really didn't die in that barn in Virginia at all."

"Who?" I asked, blinking. It was awfully early in the morning.

"Booth," he replied, his eyes fixed on his private motion picture. Then he began to ramble: "Boston Corbett claimed he shot him after they set fire to the barn. But that isn't what happened. Oh no, not at all! When Booth first took refuge in the barn he found a Union soldier sleeping there. Booth killed him with the man's own pistol and changed clothes with him, fearing that the soldier would turn him in for the reward for Lincoln's assassin. Then where did he go? Where would you go if you were Booth?"

I found myself caught up in his enthusiasm and said, "Not North, certainly."

"Exactly! They'd lynch him in the North. So he headed

right straight for the one man he counted on to treat him as
a great hero, to give him the rewards he had risked his life
for. He slipped out of the barn before Boston Corbett and
his men even got there and limped off directly to Robert E.
Lee. 'I've come, my General!' Booth exulted to Lee, 'I've
come to help you rally the armies—the war's not over yet!'
'Who are you, my poor friend,' said Lee. 'The war is virtually
over and we have lost.' 'I am the man who killed Lincoln!'
Booth said. 'Make me a general and together we'll defeat
the North!' "

Mr. Lewis was so wound up now that he was imitating the
Southern flowery accent of the actor. And then switching
expertly to the weary tones of the defeated general: " 'You
—you did that?' Lee was horrified. 'You infamous madman,
you've killed the best friend the South could have at this
tragic time. Get out of my sight before I shoot you myself!'
So in a state of disillusionment and shock, Booth reels from
Lee's headquarters and starts his lonely hegira west. He comes
across the funeral train slowly carrying Lincoln's body to
Illinois. He sees the thousands upon thousands of people
weeping as they watch and the enormity of the crime begins
to become clear to him. He goes out to the Midwest and
settles in a little town. He lives a recluse's life on a little
farm with a girl he has taken on as a wife. He becomes
stranger and stranger, brooding, gaunt, and he grows a
Lincolnesque beard. One day the town council comes to
him and asks him to play in their annual Fourth of July
pageant. They have heard his wife boast of her husband's
beautiful recitation of poems and because of his beard and
gauntness they want him to play the lead part—that of
Abraham Lincoln. At first he demurs, saying he is not fit to
play the great man, but finally he agrees. An unreconstructed
Southerner, the town drunk, threatens to kill anyone who

plays the part of the President, but Booth goes into the makeshift theater anyway. He is on the stage reciting 'Four score and seven years ago,' when a shot rings out. Booth topples from the stage and dies, murmuring '*Sic Semper tyrannis.*' "

It was impressive; he told the story almost as though he were reading it in finished form. He would make up as good a story as that at least once a day.

"You should write that," I said.

"I've got a better idea," he said. "You write it. Aren't you almost through with your novel? We'll write this one together."

At lunch he produced a contract that he'd written; we would write *Thus Ever to Tyrants* together, he would get twenty percent of any profit, I would get eighty. We signed in high spirits; both of us bursting with gimmicks and touches to improve the story.

"We'll tell Bennett Cerf about it," Mr. Lewis said. "My publisher—he's coming up this weekend. And we'll also show him your book."

I started to work on *Thus Ever to Tyrants* that afternoon. But after the first flush of enthusiasm had worn off, it was heavy going. For one thing it wasn't my story, I didn't really feel it. Another thing was that I didn't really know enough about Booth and that period of the Civil War to write convincingly about it. Then too, Mr. Lewis was adamant that the plot be expanded into a novel. I felt that because of its anecdotal quality it would do better as a short story of the type that then ran in the *Saturday Evening Post*. The next day after writing a few pages, I decided I'd better study at least the last volume of Carl Sandburg's *Abraham Lincoln*; and I put the manuscript aside with relief.

Mr. Lewis asked me every day about how much I had done

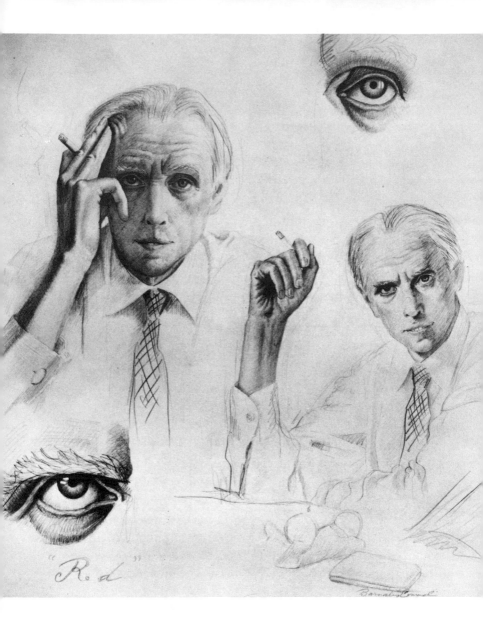

Sketches for the oil of Sinclair Lewis

on "our novel" and was irritated by my lack of progress. But I had the excuse that I had to polish my own novel for Bennett Cerf.

I was also working on a portrait of Mr. Lewis. This side effort did not please him either. "Never posed for a picture and am not about to start with you," he growled. I had to work furtively and usually caught him when he was too engrossed in a book to notice my sketching. The portrait was eventually finished, but with little help from him. (It now hangs in the University of Texas at Austin.)

The Cerfs arrived on Friday morning and Mr. Lewis was very pleased to Have his renowned publisher there. Bennett and Phyllis were as friendly and attractive a couple as I had ever met. Pretty and youthful, she reminded me of Ginger Rogers, and I wasn't surprised when I learned that she was Ginger's first cousin. Bennett's charm was infectious—he was exuberant and boyish and full of jokes with which he could seduce any audience, especially since he himself found them so entertaining.

Mr. Lewis talked happily with them for a while, telling Bennett about my novel and hoping that he would be able to read it over the weekend. Then they talked of Mr. Lewis' new novel, *The God Seeker*, which Random House would be publishing during the next year. Bennett stretched out on the chaise lounge on the porch, happy and relaxed in the sun.

But they hadn't been there for twenty minutes before Mr. Lewis announced that it was "Tennis time!"

"But Red!" Bennett protested. He explained that he was tired and wanted only to relax and unwind from his big city fatigue.

"Tennis!" Mr. Lewis commanded. "I want to watch."

The real reason was that Mr. Lewis had had the tennis

court resurfaced some months before, no one had used it all summer, and his small-town frugality demanded all the benefits from his expensive estate. Bennett tried protesting again but realized it was useless. He and Phyllis went dutifully upstairs and changed their clothes and came down with their rackets.

"Very nice court," Bennett said as he and Phyllis warmed up. Mr. Lewis, watching from the bench, beamed.

Five minutes later as Phyllis was about to serve the first ball of the first game, Mr. Lewis slapped his knees and got up.

"Splendid, splendid," he said. "Well, come along, time for the walk."

"Walk!" exclaimed Bennett. "We're just starting to play!"

"Enough tennis," said Mr. Lewis. "Walk time."

While Bennett hadn't wanted to play in the first place, now that he'd gone to all the trouble of getting out there he damned well was going to play. But I noticed they played only two very quick games before putting down the rackets and following Mr. Lewis on his walk; that famous temper had caused him to change publishers in a flash before.

Mr. Lewis gave Bennett my manuscript of *Christmas in July* that evening. No mention of it was made over the next two days. Mr. Lewis seemed as nervous about it as though the publishing fate of *Babbitt* were in balance. The next evening when the Cerfs came down for dinner, Mr. Lewis put on a recording of "The Moldau" and asked, as casually as he could, "How's the book strike you, Bennett?"

"Book?" he said. "Oh, yes. I'm enjoying it. Exciting—the bullfight." Then cocking his head to the music, he said, "Ah, dear Smetana—now there's a man who knew what side his bride was bartered on!" Then he laughed that infectious laugh and went outside to play croquet.

The next day, the Cerfs' last day there, we were sitting in

the living room when Mr. Lewis burst out with, "Well what about it?"

"About—?"

"The book—the book," said Mr. Lewis.

"Bennett," said Phyllis, "this poor kid would like to know about his novel!"

"Are you or aren't you going to publish it?" Mr. Lewis demanded.

Bennett looked around us in mock astonishment. "Oh *that* book. I thought I'd told you all that I liked it?"

"But is Random House going to publish it?" Mr. Lewis pursued.

"Why, naturally," Bennett grinned. "I always publish things that I like."

"Whoopee!" said Mr. Lewis, and it struck me that while I had read that word, I had never actually heard it said before. He jumped up and shook my hand and put his hand on my shoulder, a remarkable display of affection for him. Though I was enormously excited that my book had been accepted, I think I was equally pleased by Mr. Lewis' pleasure.

"Let's wire Marcella!" said Mr. Lewis. "This calls for a drink! Whoopee!"

This was the most astounding thing of all since no guest had ever received a drink in the house without asking—nay begging—for it first. (His own gargantuan thirst temporarily curbed, Mr. Lewis chose to forget that many people in the world could use alcohol in moderation without disappearing on week-long benders, without insulting people and without wrecking whole rooms full of furniture.) Over the drink Bennett discussed the book and had several good suggestions for improving it. He also said that we had to find a new title

since a motion picture had recently been announced called
"Christmas in July."

"Let's see," Mr. Lewis mused, "What's the name of the
house where the boy and girl live?"

"La villa Inocenta," I replied.

"What about that?" said Mr. Lewis. "*The Innocent Villa.*
Especially since it's so uninnocent."

"Not bad," said Bennett.

I had painted a picture of a beautiful Spanish girl, part
Betty, part Chelo, for the dust jacket and I showed it to
Bennett.

"At last," he said, "I'll have an author who won't com-
plain about the jacket of his book!"

Instead of taking money for the art work, I elected to
receive payment in the form of the complete Modern
Library, more than two hundred volumes even in those days.
They arrived a week after the Cerfs departed, but I didn't
unpack them. I had a distinct feeling that I was not going
to be at Thorvale much longer. Mr. Lewis seemed increasingly restless, pacing like a caged cougar. He spoke constantly of going to Europe, and while he had always said,
when "we" go to Europe, it was now "I." He also wanted
to go to Minneapolis, he said, to do some sort of research
on his book, *The God Seeker.* He was tired of Thorvale,
tired of being the country squire and tired of me. Now that
he had "made an author" of me, the project, interesting while
it had lasted, was over.

Though always irascible and hard to please, he now began
to find more and more fault with me. Because he was compulsively fastidious and I was compulsively sloppy, this was
not hard to do. If I left the lid up on the piano after playing
it, he would berate me—often in front of guests—growing

empurpled as he ranted. He was furious that I had not progressed more on *Thus Ever To Tyrants*, even though I was researching the period and also trying to make the many extensive changes that Bennett and his editors suggested for my novel.

"You'll never make a writer," he bellowed once. "If you don't write that Booth story you'll never make a writer!"

Mark Schorer gives an accurate impression of the time in his biography of Lewis:

Conrad, with his boyishness, his eagerness, the naïveté of his ambitions, pleased Lewis at first, and the arrangement worked out well for both of them. Conrad did finish his novel during that summer, and Lewis had his chess and his company and the satisfaction, important to him now, of knowing that he was working *with* someone rather than over someone.

Yet it was not very long before Conrad began to irritate him. His lack of interest in a rigid discipline and routine, his *dégagé* quality, probably his whole flavor of a leisure-class background, proved irksome, and very soon in the engagement books appears the stern rebuke, "Barny rm order," several times repeated. It is not hard to see him, as rigid in his ways now as a spinster and as fixed as his father in his notion of what was proper to his household, peering into his new tenant's bedroom, a young man's litter of rumpled bed and opened books turned face down on the floor, of castoff shirts and socks and sneakers and even the horror of a sweaty jock strap tossed on what should have been a taut and pristine candlewick spread. How often did he have to tell him that there was a fixed arrangement for the poolside chairs and that one was not to be casual in such matters! Barnaby Conrad's successor would be a more earnest person.

(I believe my successor lasted some three days. I think I held the record, with my predecessor, John Hersey, qualifying as runner-up.)

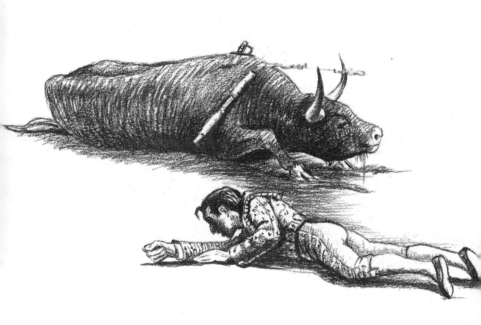

Manolete and Islero

On August 29 he told me that he would be leaving for the Midwest in five days, would be closing the house and that he would hire a successor out there if he found he needed one. That same day a cablegram arrived from Spain. Joseph brought it to me as we were having lunch on the porch. It was from Luis Morales in the American consulate in Málaga:

TERRIBLE NEWS. MANOLETE KILLED YESTERDAY BY MIURA. DETAILS FOLLOW.

I was stunned. Other matadors, yes—but Manolete? It couldn't be true. I handed it to Mr. Lewis.

"Some bullfighting chap?" asked Mr. Lewis.

"Yes," I said mechanically, taking the cablegram back. "Some bullfighting chap."

"Saw a bullfight once," he said. "Rooted for the bull."

The New York Times carried the story on the front page; how Manolete had emerged from retirement to accept the challenge of the young matador Dominguin, how he'd been bested by the youngster on his first miura bull but came back on his second to show the crowd in Linares what great bullfighting was. At "the moment of truth" he had elected to kill the dangerous bull honestly instead of simply dispatching it safely. He ran straight at the bull, plunged the sword in and he and the animal annihilated each other simultaneously.

When I could think about it straight I saw that tragically, Manolete had written his own plot, his own third act. Again it occurred to me that there was a great novel in the story of this man. I could even see a parallel between Sinclair Lewis and Manolete; tall ugly loners who had been *El Número Uno* of their fields and who didn't know how—

or were unable—to step down. Manolete's story was less of a tragedy, since he had gone out at the peak of his powers, demonstrating for the last time that he was indeed the once and future king, showing indelibly why his honor and his prowess would always be a yardstick for perfection.

As for the Sinclair Lewis of this twilight time—America's erstwhile "Angry Man" was clinging and clutching to the grandeur that had been and was no longer, afraid to admit even to himself that he could not turn out the kind of novels he had written in the twenties.

He accompanied me to the station. Red—I could bring myself to call him by that undignified nickname now that I was no longer in his employ—was warm and lavish with great predictions for *The Innocent Villa* and full of fatherly admonitions. As we said good-by he awkwardly handed me a first edition of *Cass Timberlane*. It was inscribed: "To Barny Conrad, whom a summer at Thorvale has proved the most amiable man living."

It made up for a lot. I was sad as the train pulled out and I saw his pathetic silhouette standing hunched and alone on the platform.

CHAPTER 17

I WENT BACK TO SANTA BARBARA, NOT ONLY because I had free room and board with my parents, but also because I have always found it a pleasant place to live and work. Some of my roots are in the sleepy city, my paternal grandparents lived and are buried there (next to matinee idol Ronald Colman), and I know a lot of people there. But I didn't look up many of my old friends—I was primarily interested in being with writers and talking shop.

Now that I was almost an author, I met several genuine authors, among them Ken Millar—the versatile writer who raised the detective story to new heights under the name of Ross Macdonald—and his wife Margaret, who has written some twenty successful books (not one of which contains a line to top the beginning of her poem written at the age of eleven: "Oh what is death but an end to idle breathing . . .").

"How I envy the Millars!" I remember Sinclair Lewis

saying once about the stimulating young couple. "How jealous I am!"

"Their talent?" I asked.

"No," he said poignantly, "their marriage."

Through the venerable Pulitzer poet Leonard Bacon, I met the English legend, Alfred Noyes. Incredibly, the author or *The Highwayman*, which we all had to memorize in grammar school, was still very much alive. I went swimming with him and his family often, and though over eighty, he would swim way out beyond the breakers. Since he was nearly blind he would say, "Dear boy, *do* keep an eye on me—I lose m'direction, get twisted about, and might veddy easily end up on Catalina!"

Another couple whose company I needed and valued was Guy Gilpatric and his wife, Louise. After my long day at the revisional typewriter, I would put aside *The Innocent Villa* at five o'clock and head for their house up on "the Riviera," that section of Santa Barbara above the stately old Mission, for my medicinal cocktail and, even more medicinal, stimulating conversation. Guy was the epitome of the professional short-story writer of that era; he had peddled his first story to *Collier's* when he was fifteen and had sold every story he wrote thereafter, including some seventy-five stories to the *Saturday Evening Post* about that scurvy but irresistible poltroon, Colin Glencannon. The wild escapades of that first mate of the Inchcliff Castle still delight readers of the anthologies around the world.

I took time off from my novel to write a short story about a cowardly veteran matador who tries and succeeds in making a combat to win back his girl. I showed it to Guy. He said some good things about it but the ending bothered him.

"All the way through you have your hero a coward because he's afraid of the wind, since it once blew the cape and

caused him a goring. The gimmick is so well planted, why not
have the wind become his friend in that last fight when he's
tossed—it blows the cape but distracts the bull away from
the fallen man and saves him from a goring."

He was right. It made a better story. I called it "Cayetano
the Perfect," sent it off to Marcella and, after a month, forgot
about it.

Guy taught me a lot about writing. He and Louise were
closer than any man and wife I've ever known, and their end
was shocking. One afternoon he took Louise to a doctor for
a routine check-up. The doctor found evidence of cancer and
told Guy in private. Guy and Louise drove back home; what
was said is not known. When she went into the bedroom he
took a pistol from his desk, shot her in back of the head and
then killed himself.

I felt honored, some years later, when I was invited to
write the foreword to the final anthology of his last stories
published by Dodd Mead.

I had several letters from Sinclair Lewis, some warm and
encouraging, others cold and cutting, depending upon his
mood, all asking for news of Marcella. One merely said:

I take it that, this winter, you have decided that you are not
going to be a writer—not at all. Your decision, or at least hanker-
ing, to flee off to the bogus paradises of Paris and Naples after a
winter devoted to aimless idleness, is the old story. That your
decision is unconscious probably makes it only the more final.

Ever,
S.L.

Yet one letter I received from Ida Kay said:

But Barnaby it would warm your heart—never does he get away
from the subject of you, your writing and your book! He attacks
you mercilessly, then immediately comes to your rescue before

he beats you to a pulp— He criticizes you severely and then immediately praises you to the skies. I'm usually very perceptive about the meaning of people's actions but I'll be damned if I can quite make the pieces fit in this Lewis-Conrad relationship— You would be amazed if you could just sit in the background and listen. He eggs me on trying to make me say things I don't really want to say, then jumps on me—if I praise, I'm wrong; if I mildly analyze one Barnaby-Barnaby (very impersonally) I'm being too hard!— I have yet to be up there for one evening, but at least one half hour is spent on a certain, former secretary, his faults, his virtues, his many and varied abilities, his destiny, his failings, his writing career or lack of one—ad infinitum— Ho-hum.

Meanwhile, I finished *The Innocent Villa's* revisions and the day of publication approached. The exciting moment came when the folded, sinuous strips of galley proofs arrived; the last chance for corrections and improvements. How different one's words looked and read in print. Not long after came the miracle of the bound book, replete with dust jacket, photo on the back and a flowery summary of the book's plot on the flap. To make me feel even more like an author, Random House scheduled autographing parties for me in Santa Barbara and San Francisco.

Publishing day came and I couldn't understand all those people walking along the sidewalks going about their business just as though it were some ordinary day. A letter from Sinclair Lewis had arrived:

THE book has come, handsomely autographed, and it looks extremely good—including your jacket picture . . . You're probably right in saying that I am too hard on you as an active conscientious objector to writing— I am likely to go on being so because of your peculiar peril of being highly versatile and talented—two of the worse crosses any young writer can bear.

I am doing nothing whatever but work—though I suppose that I must, without noticing it, occasionally sleep and eat.

Friends and relatives bought copies of the book and some even said nice things and wrote letters. But it was the professional critics one wanted to hear from. The first one I saw, unfortunately, was from *The New Yorker*. After a brief and routine summary of the plot, the paragraph concluded: "According to his publishers, Mr. Conrad once overcame a bull in a Spanish ring himself and was awarded his opponent's ears by the crowd for his trouble. He is hardly in a position to be granted a comparable tribute by the readers of his first novel."

Marcella was quick to soothe my bleats of pain by saying that this was to be expected from the supercritical *New Yorker* and she forwarded two favorable clippings from the *Washington Star* and the *Cleveland News* which concluded by saying that "the author deserves both ears for this exciting effort."

My ego was somewhat restored, until a lengthy critique from the *Brooklyn Daily Eagle* arrived. Written by one Professor F. Cordasco, it started out: "Out of the limbo of lost novelists has come Barnaby Conrad whose *The Innocent Villa* is his passport to literary perdition."

After that comparatively laudatory beginning, Professor Cordasco then rolled up his sleeves, broke out the scalpels and set to work with a will. He warmed to his work—"puppets . . . shabby . . . patently false . . . irritating . . . sad tribute to the Consular Service of the United States."

It seemed perfectly rational for me to scream at the clipping: "What do you mean phony characters, Cordasco? They were real people, I knew those people, lived with them. What the hell do you know about Spain, you damned Italian . . ."

As I bellowed at the scrap of paper, I suddenly thought, Good God, Conrad, you're behaving just as irrationally as Sinclair Lewis had so many months before.

The review ended with this last indictment: "The publishers tell us that Mr. Conrad was conceded the ears of the dead bull for one of his performances in the ring . . . for this novel Mr. Conrad will be conceded only the ugly cries of an obstetrical monstrosity that should never have seen the light."

Herb Gold, the novelist, recently said to me enviously, "Oh, to have written a book which could inspire such a review!" But I'm afraid at the time I had no objectivity about it and when, sometime later, the *Brooklyn Daily Eagle* folded, I was glad, *glad*.

Many of the reviews compared me to Hemingway; they kept saying how much better Hemingway was! But Marcella soon sent me *The New York Times* review which was somewhat of a balm for the wounds. In it, Charles Poore, after reviewing the plot—"a treatment, shall we say, of the Madam Butterfly theme . . . "—wrote: "His hero, Lance Peters, is a strayed reveler from the American coteries that used to breeze happily through Pamplona and Madrid with copies of *The Sun Also Rises* under their arms and an interest in bullfights and manzanilla . . . What happens to him is in the cinematic tradition, complete with a last-minute troublesome love affair. If you don't take it all too seriously, you can have quite a lot of fun out of the book."

Marcella thought we should be thankful for such a review from the revered pages of the austere *Times*. When the *Chicago Tribune*'s review came out by Victor P. Haas, we had a pretty good idea what most of the critics would say:

Take generous portions of illicit love and bullfighting, add a gorgeous Spanish girl, a handsome American diplomat, a happily mad Irish-Peruvian, a sexy old dragon of a diplomat's wife, a heaping tablespoon of local color and just a dash of tragedy, mix thoroughly, and you have *The Innocent Villa*.

It's unimportant, it's frequently too glib, it will set no literary bonfires but, believe me, it's fun! I read it at one sitting, not because there was any need for haste but because it winds up with a bullfight so exciting that I could no more have gone to bed without finishing it than I could have written it.

Mark Twain spoke for all writers when he said that he was always embarrassed when people complimented him because they never said enough.

The better reviews were all more or less like that, and the really bad ones—well, there were none quite as bad as the professor's. The book had a fair sale for a first novel, around 8000 I believe, which at least made its costs back for the publisher, but little more for me than the advance I had received: $500.

Perusing the book now, it seems to me that I got off lucky in every way. But then, after the first flush of having a book published, came the inevitable letdown. Magazine editors seemed no more kindly disposed toward my short stories and articles than before. I couldn't sell either my fiction or my articles anywhere, and I had no burning plot ideas for another novel. I vacillated, sometimes feeling "damn them all," and moments later feeling that Sinclair Lewis was right: I would never finish *Thus Ever To Tyrants*, I would not persevere, I would never write another book, I simply was not a writer.

"The world is filled with one-book authors," Sinclair Lewis had sneered once.

Welcome to the club.

My brother Hunt had returned from Peru and was working in San Francisco. He was living in a quaint little brown cottage nestled in the trees on Telegraph Hill, with floors so sloping that it resembled one of those mystery houses at amusement parks where water appears to run up hill. I moved in with him.

Purposeless, I used to hang around a nondescript bar called Twelve Adler Place, on Columbus near the Old Barbary Coast district. Other writers and painters manqués used to frequent the place for its informal sawdust atmosphere and pretend they were in McSoreley's Wonderful Saloon in New York. One day I took a wrong door in back and found myself in another bar with a separate entrance. I asked about it and the owner explained that it was part of the same building but run by an old Italian for his friends. It was a nicely shaped room and had a fine old mahogany back bar. It seemed to me it could be made into a very attractive place. I had always been attracted to bars principally because I wanted to do the murals and decorate one. I spoke to the owner. He shrugged.

"You fix him up good, we splitta the money."

The only trouble was I figured that it would cost about $1500 for paint, fixtures, chairs, tables, glassware, plates, et cetera. And I didn't have a dime. I was selling my blood to a blood bank as often as possible for four dollars a shot. I was about to take a job as a busboy in a Foster Cafeteria for seven dollars per day and meals, and was actually on my way out the door of our cottage to report for work when the mailman arrived with a letter from Marcella. It said that the short story I had written months before called "Cayetano the Perfect" had been accepted by *Collier's Magazine* for $750. I canceled my busboy job and returned to the typewriter with renewed enthusiasm for the first time in a long while. A week later, a telegram arrived from Marcella saying that

"Cayetano" had won the *Collier's* Story Prize for an additional thousand dollars. (It subsequently was included in the 1949 O. Henry *Prize Stories* collection.)

I left the typewriter, took the money and started to work on the bar. First of all it needed a thorough cleaning job; it was filthy. Once clean, I then set about making the square room look like a round bullfight arena, with a *barrera* fence all around and *burladero* shields with big circles on them in the corners. Then I did a trompe l'oeil mural on one wall of the bull ring stands and the *plaza de toros* arches. When the fence was painted red and sawdust was put on the floor in lieu of sand, one did get the feeling of being in a bull ring. On another wall I painted a nocturnal Spanish street scene. My friend, Budd Boetticher, who directed the technical scenes for *Blood and Sand*, contributed the taxidermed head of Maromero, the magnificent bull which Tyrone Power was supposed to have fought in that film. It glowered down from a red curtain-draped wall. I smothered the walls of the entranceway to the main room from the bar with photos of the greats in action on one side and Goya's tauromaquia etchings on the other. In the outer bar I had posters and paintings of corridas. Checkered tablecloths and candles completed the job. Someone said, "You've got to invent some special drink, very chic." I poured some tequila and brandy and anis into the blender with some ice. And then, to impart a deathly green color, I added some creme de menthe. It was nauseating, but the first "Death in the Afternoon" drink was created. Two shots of tequila made it an "Adiós Amigo."

I hired a waiter, a bartender and a chef to cook steak sandwiches and we were ready to open. I had sent out five hundred announcements, hoping for a hundred customers, including my immediate family. But I hadn't reckoned on the tremendous power Herb Caen wields in San Francisco. Just about everyone in the Bay area starts the day reading his combination of gossip, gags and irreverence. Herb was amused by the concept of the Café Goya and casually mentioned its premiere in his column.

Opening night was a shambles. The place normally would hold sixty-five people. At least 1100 people crowded through the place before the curfew came at two in the morning and the customers—socialites, show people and the just plain curious—actually overflowed out on to the sidewalk. Everything went wrong. The mustachioed Italian bartender, Francesco, was overwhelmed by the hordes of people, but he was determined not to cut down on quality; his concept of a classy place was one where they put a shot of grenadine in the drinks. All drinks. He was even sending the martinis to the tables with a rosy glow. I stopped that, but the customers still complained about the martinis.

"Are you sure you're making them six to one?" I asked Francesco. "They've got to be six to one at least."

He swore he was making them six to one. "You justa watch!"

I watched him make the next batch and he proved it to me: six shots of vermouth to one shot of gin!

Then there were the waiters. One arrived dead drunk. He plunked himself down at a table with a socially prominent grande dame, kissed her low on her cleavage and then put his head on the table and went to sleep. The other one, the fat one with the thin face, was very efficient and worked industriously, but strange sounds came from him. I swore I heard Mario positively gurgle when he hurried by me to attend to the guests. Also, very little money was ending up in the till. Halfway through the evening the bartender pointed out to me that the ratio between the small amount of money in the register and the large number of tables that Mario had served did not exactly work out right. Not even remotely. When Mario next approached the bar an alarming thing took place: Francesco took the bar knife and suddenly lashed out at the waiter's opulent stomach. There was a horrible sound— something like "glorp." Instantly the obesity left Mario's left side and his shirt and coat were stained with a liquid I took to be blood. But who had brown blood? Then Francesco ripped open Mario's shirt and the mystery was revealed: there from the waiter's neck on the left side hung a slashed douche bag. On his right side hung a full one. The tubes ran down his arms under his shirt and the ends barely protruded from his cuffs. He had Scotch in one and bourbon in the other. He would pick up ice-filled glasses from the end of the bar with water or soda in them, fill out the order on the way to the table by pressing a release on the tube running down one arm or the other, and bypass the bartender and the cash register completely except for mixed or gin or vodka drinks. Francesco made him give up a pocketful of bills and siphon the rest of the bourbon back into a bottle before throwing him out. For the rest of the evening I was the waiter.

For some months the saloon was fun. It seemed that every writer, journalist, actor and actress who came to San Francisco used to end up at the Café Goya. I met many interesting people and rather fancied the place as a counterpart to the marvelous bar depicted by William Saroyan in *The Time of Your Life*. Somewhere Doctor Sam'l Johnson says something about a good publick house being one of the noblest works of God, and I felt I was filling a need in the nocturnal life of San Francisco. Yet running a saloon left little time for any other pursuits, namely, writing. Quite possibly that was the underlying motive.

But the talented, intelligent visitors were, naturally, in the minority and I found myself becoming a solitary drinker—an effort to avoid death via boredom. The bartenders were stealing whatever profit the place made, but I had little stomach and less talent for policing them. ("If you can find an honest bartender," Mike Romanoff once advised me, "breed him!")

I was going nowhere very fast. My contemporaries, it seemed, were all progressing in their careers as lawyers, doctors or businessmen. They also were married and raising families. It seemed to me that I was a very odd duck to be still a bachelor with no real profession at twenty-six. I found myself thinking of Betty more and more. Was she still in Peru? Had she ever married? Would she ever marry me and if so could I support her?

Then I met Dale. We didn't "meet cute" as they say around the Hollywood story conference table. ("There's a bargain sale, see—and she grabs the top of the pajamas and he grabs the bottoms and so they start to talk—") We met at a wedding reception, and I reminded her that we had gone to school together as children, and she recalled my having been sent home for sliding down the mud bank. I remembered her as a beautiful solemn eight-year-old. Now at twenty-three she looked like a Dresden doll, petite and shy, with a blond beauty that was reminiscent of Prince Valiant's Aleta. When I asked her to have dinner with me that night, she declined because she said she had some reading she wanted to do. She had just graduated in pre-med from Stanford and was doing some research for her own pleasure. I escorted her to her car, a beat-up old Chevy, and noticed that on the seat she had a copy of *Coming of Age in Samoa*, *Calculus Is Fun!*, *The Life of Freud* and *Scientific American*. I was intrigued. I called her the next day and made a date. After a performance of *La Bohème* we went to the Café Goya. Apart from her physical charms, I liked her straightforward manner, total honesty and lack of "side." I liked the fact that she liked children and dogs and painted and played the piano and read. I felt an instant impulse to take care of her (or was it the other way around?). Later that week she invited me to a swimming party at her family's home in Hillsborough, twenty miles south of San Francisco. I was astounded by the setup: the house, on many beautifully gardened acres, seemed just a little smaller than Balmoral Castle—the tangible results, I learned, of Dale's grandfather's oil and lumber empire. Her parents made me feel at home instantly and said they hoped I would come again.

The next day Dale telephoned to say that there was an opening for a columnist on the Women's Page of the *San Francisco News*. Would I help her write some sample columns? We spent a week collecting items and then writing them up in front of the fire in my little cottage. We tried to make them sprightly and informative and apparently we succeeded; Dale got the column "Buttons and Bows" the next week. We saw each other every day after that.

And, to lapse into Jane Austenese: Reader, I married her.

CHAPTER 18

I REMEMBER A *NEW YORKER* CARTOON SHOW-
ing a man bending the ear of a bartender: "When we
were first married we were very happy," he is saying
lachrymosely. "But then as we were leaving the church . . . "

Dale and I did not begin to quarrel at the church. As a
matter of fact we were married at her home before some
seventy-five people. But we did have our first altercation at the
reception: I wanted to stay and enjoy the fine party with my
friends and family, she wanted to leave right away. It was a
pattern that would continue through our married life. I was
always ready for a party, she was introspective, studious, shy,
and preferred to keep people at arms' length. But she made
a beautiful bride.

Dale's grandfather attended the wedding but disapproved
of it, and he somehow reduced her to tears before stalking off
to his own mansion which was only two acres away. Her

father, on the other hand, presented us with a staggering check for five thousand dollars.

"However," he announced, "there is a string to it. It cannot be hoarded away or invested the way Dale would like to do—it must be spent in frivolity, high living and travel."

We took a freighter bound for Spain. In Torremolinos, near Málaga, we stayed at the wonderful sprawling old hotel called La Pensión Santa Clara. It was owned and run by friends of mine, Edie and Fred Saunders, and I had done the murals in the hotel's bar three years before. He was an Englishman who had the unenviable distinction of having been crucified by the Turks while fighting with Lawrence of Arabia (he was cut down from the cross by Lawrence's men at the last minute). Edie was an attractive and capable Danish woman.

"We want to go to Copenhagen for a vacation," said Fred. "Run this here place for us and you can have everything free."

And so we did for six weeks. The old whitewashed buildings were on a promontory overlooking a lovely beach used mainly by fishermen. It was one of only two hotels between there and Gibraltar, which is hard to believe today inasmuch as the area now looks like Miami Beach due to the building boom of the last few years. The hotel could accommodate thirty people and we had such disparate guests as Sharman Douglas, the daughter of the American ambassador to London, the English novelist Rose Macauley and the matador Antonio Bienvenida.

I took Dale to the bullfights and tried to get her interested in them, but though she valiantly attended some thirty corridas in an attempt to learn to appreciate the *fiesta brava*, the virus never took. She did not like Spain, the starkness of it, the beggars in the streets and restaurants—the general harshness of the country in those years. The food cooked in olive oil made her ill, the mattresses and pillows were hard and there were never enough hangers for the clothes disgorged from her thirteen pieces of luggage. She was delighted when the Saunders returned after two months and we could go to Paris.

We acquired a nice apartment on the Left Bank, I attended the Julien Academie of Painting and Dale went to the Cordon Bleu to improve her cooking. She was now writing a weekly cooking column called "A Cook's Tour" for the *San Francisco News* about the various restaurants we encountered on our travels.

We met a delightful couple, Jack and Lee Leggett, who were very much in our position—newly wed, living on the Left Bank, he finishing up a novel and she attending the Cordon Bleu. She had gone to school with Dale and we saw a great deal of them.

One day on the Champs Elysées we bumped into Betty Lane (the Vassar one), who had also gone to Saint Timothy's School with Dale. She was getting married that Saturday and we *must* be her attendants. She was glowing and even though I was on my honeymoon, she brought back memories of the other Betty, the real Betty, wherever she might be.

I knew that Sinclair Lewis was in Paris and I called him. He insisted that we have dinner with him. We picked him up in our Citroën at his hotel. He'd only been in Paris a day, but he seemed jubilant—frenetically so. He was stimulated by the city he'd come to know during his early triumphs.

"First time I've really been in Paris for twenty years," he said. "I'm going to take you to a marvelous little place on the

Left Bank where we all used to go. You'll love it—gay, stimulating—all the good artists, writers go there, the top newspapermen, the thinkers."

We crossed the river and, after asking a few people, arrived at the address. It was a miserable and dirty little café with only one customer, a student who was studying a book by the light of a candle in a bottle.

"This can't be the place!" Red exclaimed.

Dale checked the address and the name, and it was correct.

"But where is Madame Blanc?" he asked of the bored looking waiter.

"Dead," yawned the man, "these fifteen years."

"Sixteen," said the student, who might have been Madame Blanc's grandson.

We sat down at a table and Red ordered a drink. I had never seen him drink before. It was astonishing to watch him down a brandy: it disappeared in a single sucking sound. He had three to our one and kept looking around the dusty café, frowning.

"This is simply not the place," he repeated irritably, "that's all there is to it. The other place was far bigger— brightly lit, music, full of people. Not it at all."

As we ate our depressing meal, the waiter routinely brought an old ledger that served as a guest book. It was full of names of the past. On almost the first yellowed page I saw the signatures: John Dos Passos, Dorothy Thompson, Sinclair Lewis. I tried to show the page to Red but he wouldn't look at it.

"Matter of fact," he said as he motioned the waiter for another brandy, "I remember now—wasn't even on this street. Different part of town."

Somehow we got into a discussion with the student. Red invited him over and asked him a great many questions about his life and studies. The student didn't introduce himself and neither did we. He spoke English well but with a thick accent. He was a literature major and was very serious behind his thick glasses.

"And what American writers do you read?" Red asked, too casually.

The student thought for a moment, then said, "My favorites are Fitzgerald, Hemingway, Steinbeck and Sinclair . . ."

Red's face lit up pathetically. "Ah—Sinclair—"

"Upton Sinclair," continued the youth.

Red frowned and cleared his throat uncomfortably. "Any others?"

The youth shrugged. "I've read them all. But those are the ones I most admire."

We left. In the taxi Red mimicked the student's accent and manner to perfection: "My fahvoreets ahr Feetzgerohl, Emeenwhy, Stynabecque, an' "—here he departed slightly from the original—"An' thees Seenclair, thees Seenclair Loowees."

I found it hard to believe that he had actually convinced himself that the youth had listed his name among his favorites. Yet when we joined Red's brother, Claude, at the Café du Dome later that evening, Red recounted the story, the accent honed and the story embellished. ("My fahvoreet nohvell off thees Seenclair Loowees ees how-you-call-heem, Ahrohsmeet.")

He had several more brandies. I looked around the café at the interesting characters. "Isn't this where you and Fitzgerald and Joyce and Hemingway used to come?" I asked.

"We all used to come here," he snorted. "But I was always at a different table. Never belonged in their group, never belonged to any group. Never belonged to anybody." He put his arm around Dale awkwardly. "Now if I'd only had a beautiful little sweet wife like this, the whole story'd be different. I might have been a great writer."

We helped Claude get him home, helped him up the stairs to the lobby of the hotel.

"If he keeps drinking like this he'll be dead in a year," said Claude mournfully as we said good night at the elevator.

We had a date for dinner with them the next night, but upon arriving at their hotel at six o'clock, we found that Red was in a drunken stupor. He left Paris for Italy soon after and we never saw him again. Claude did not miss by much in his sad prediction, for Sinclair Lewis died in Rome of alcoholism. (I heard of a final macabre irony: a friend of mine went into the United States Embassy at Rome and saw a consular official down on her knees with a broom and pan. "What are you doing?" he asked her. "Sweeping up Sinclair Lewis," was the answer. Red's ashes had been put in a safe pending final disposal and the urn had fallen out, its contents spilled.)

After eight months of traveling, our money began to run out. We decided to return to San Francisco. There we found a nice little flat for eighty-five dollars a month on Arguello Boulevard across from the Temple Emanuel, and began to fix it up. Our only possessions were three fine Dufy oils that we'd bought in Paris remarkably cheaply and a bed. I painted trompe l'oeil furniture all around the apartment—a phony bureau here, a magnificent curtained window with a Mediterranean view there. Another possession, a live one, was Garance, a Gibbon ape that we'd acquired in our travels.

Garance was black with a white fringe around her face and she was gentle and affectionate. Dale desperately wanted children, but a series of miscarriages seemed to indicate that Garance might have to act as a substitute.

Because Dale's grandfather disapproved of the marriage she received no allowance. But her grandmother, a sprightly eighty-five-year-old, would weekly come to San Francisco from Burlingame in her chauffeur-driven Cadillac filled with a welcome roast beef or turkey and canned goods. Four nights a week I taught painting and creative writing at an adult education program and made a hundred and eighty dollars a month. During the day I worked hard on my new book. It was called *La Fiesta Brava* and I felt it would be the definitive book on bullfighting. Besides offering a well-researched history of the spectacle, it gave a step-by-step description of the seven acts that make up the modern corrida. The photographs were the best ever taken. For years I had gone to the top taurine photographers, riffled through thousands of pictures, chosen their best shots and bought the rights. I guarded these pictures with my life because most Spanish photographers didn't bother to file their negatives and in many cases only had one print of each picture.

Besides the photos I did dozens of drawings and diagrams to help explain the different maneuvers and cape passes. After six months the book was finished. Marcella wrote that she had a prominent publisher who was interested in seeing it. Because of the original drawings and the irreplaceable photos, I would have preferred to have delivered the manuscript by hand, but at this time I simply didn't have enough money for the fare to New York nor, for that matter, even enough money to have photographic copies made. So I insured and registered the book and mailed it off. I was

Garance

greatly relieved when Marcella wired that it had arrived safely. She also said that "it looks great and should sell well." Dale and I earnestly hoped so, for we were tired of being poor. We watched the mails daily for the big check that was sure to come from the publisher.

No check came. But a letter did. It seems Marcella gave the publisher the manuscript over lunch at the Algonquin, and that on the way back to his office he left it in the taxi. It was never seen again. Six months of my life went with that taxi.

Marcella hired a lawyer who was pessimistic about our chances of recovering anything, since manuscripts are submitted at the author's risk. We settled out of court for three hundred dollars, of which Marcella got thirty, the lawyer one hundred and fifty and I, one hundred and twenty.

To distract me from my depression, Dale, with some extra money she had made decorating, bought an aquarium and a sea horse to go in it. Sea horses were hard to come by in those days and this was a fine big male of about ten inches. Citation hovered around his tank in serene majesty, his fins going like rotors. Then he would moor himself to a piece of coral with his tail and stare out as us regally.

The next day I was watching Citation when a strange thing happened. He suddenly bent forward at the waist and reared back in a convulsive jerk. And miraculously, in the water with him was a tiny sea horse, no bigger than a dime, but an exact replica of Citation. Then the bigger sea horse repeated its convulsion and there was another baby in the tank. I called Dale, and by the time she got there, there were five. In half an hour there were sixty. By the end of the morning there were one hundred and eighty-five.

"How much did you pay for Citation?" I asked Dale.

"Ten dollars," she said.

We looked in awe at the herd of sea horses. "We're rich," I said. The Great Ichthyologist in the sky had chosen a new and profitable profession for me.

I went down to a tropical fish store and bought a larger tank and a book on sea horses. The first thing I learned is that the female deposits her eggs in a pouch in the front of the male and he carries them until they are ready to be expelled. The next thing I learned was that it is not easy to raise sea horses. First one must raise tiny brine shrimp with which to feed the critters. That required a separate tank where brine shrimp eggs were hatched under a light bulb. When the tiny shrimp would hatch and wiggle toward the light, I would scoop them up in a net and feed them to the baby sea horses. After two weeks of constant care the sea horses had grown to the size of a quarter. A wholesaler offered a dollar apiece for them and we took it.

Then I graduated to raising angelfish, quite a feat since the water and plant conditions had to be absolutely perfect before the exotic creatures would deign to lay. More and more tanks were added to the flat. What with the Gibbon ape, two cockateels, a parrot, and a mynah bird flying around loose, the flying squirrels, Orville and Wilbur, and the tanks, our home was more menagerie than ménage. But how satisfying it was to raise the fish—far less complicated and soul bruising than writing stories and books for people to reject or lose. For the next year I went from species to species.

Finally there was l'affaire Grande Berthe.

I had bred sea horses successfully. I had bred Siamese fighting fish, where the male makes a nest of bubbles with his mouth and then guards the contents after the female lays, catching any that fall and returning them to the nest. I had

raised Egyptian mouth breeders, where the female keeps the eggs in her mouth until they hatch and continues to offer her oral cavity as a sanctuary to the fry until they are independent.

What was now left for me in the piscatorial world? Of course, I could always teach the ichthyology I had learned,* but some pioneering spirit in me cried out, Go on, go on! Something inside of me said, Sure, you might be the king of the freshies, but how about salt? Progress to salinity, man!

One day I saw an ad in the paper advertising the sale of some aquaria, "including the famous Big Bertha." I called on the owner-maker, a T-shirted ex-sailor named Sut, who was renowned for his custom-built tanks. His arms were so covered with tattoos that bare skin was not visible; the designs and legends all ran together unintelligibly, preceding psychedelic posters by fifteen years.

In Sut's basement were several fine tanks, all several gallons larger than my largest, which was thirty gallons. But then we came to one huge one, the largest tank by far that I'd ever seen out of a real aquarium. It was just a bit smaller than a billiard table tipped on edge.

"There she is," said Sut proudly. "Big Bertha! Took a year to build her—two hundred gallons. Absolute steal at seventy bucks."

It was beautiful. Stainless steel, thick glass—and so big!

---

* I can't help thinking of the time in 1965 when John Steinbeck swung through San Francisco on his automobile odyssey with his famous poodle. Sitting in Enrico's sidewalk café, he said to the brilliant advertising man, Howard Gossage: "Look at my dog Charlie there: yesterday in Muir Woods he lifted his leg on a tree that was fifty feet across, a hundred feet high and a thousand years old. I ask you, what's left in life for the poor dog after that supreme moment?" Gossage thought for a moment and then replied with his attractive stammer: "W-w-well—he could always t-t-teach."

"How come it's empty?"

"Basically designed for salt water," he said. "I'm too lazy to fill her."

"But is it safe?" I asked. "Will it stand all that pressure when it's filled?"

Sut looked hurt. "Bertha's never blowed out. Filled six weeks with fresh water, never has blew yet." Then he lowered his voice and said conspiratorially, "You know what you could do in Bertha?"

I shook my head.

"You could—" he whispered it "—you could breed yellow surgeons in her!"

"You're kidding," I said. "Yellow surgeons? Really?"

He closed his eyes and nodded solemnly at the enormity of his pronouncement.

"Yellow surgeons."

"Wow," I said. "I'll take her."

On the way out I asked myself, What the hell are yellow surgeons?

It took the sale of my camera and three strong men to effect Bertha's transfer from Sut's ownership to our flat. It was installed on its stand in the little room off of our bedroom that I used as a studio. Dale was impressed with Bertha, as how could anyone not be since it dominated a quarter of the room, but she did have a comment or two on the diversion of our meager funds and hockable possessions toward more practical items, such as that mundane and relentless thing called food.

"But we could breed yellow surgeons in it!" I said in rebuttal.

She wasn't entirely convinced, adding with a discernible tinge of sarcasm some remark about the scarcity of Chinese doctors in the world.

The next day we went to Steinhart Aquarium and asked to see a yellow surgeon. In the special Matson tank we were shown the only one in California. It was the most beautiful fish we'd ever seen. Designed by a master architect, its symmetrical and graceful body was no larger than a salad plate and not much thicker. Its color was the most remarkable iridescent yellow, more brilliant than Quimper china, deeper than cadmium. All of the creature was the same shade, as though it had been held by the tail and dipped into a bucket of some enchanted paint. Only an obsidian eye, as shiny black as the end of a hat pin, marred its superb yellowness. I arranged an interview with the head of the Aquarium and discussed surgeons. They came from the South Pacific, were extremely hard to come by, cost around fifty dollars apiece and, yes, it would be quite a feat if someone were to breed them successfully in captivity.

The gauntlet was down.

I prepared Big Bertha by driving down in my old convertible to the Marina beach with four five-gallon water bottles, filling them and then emptying them into the great aquarium. It took ten trips and I nearly incurred a hernia. But filled, Bertha was even more prismatic and dazzling, especially when Dale arranged some rocks, coral and sand decoratively around the bottom. A filter, thermometer and a salinity gauge made the tank perfect for surgeons. But who could afford them, even if there were any on the market?

Bertha's splendor, however, demanded an occupant. One day I saw an archer for sale in a tropical fish store. I had read about this remarkable fish in *Believe it or Not;* it was said that he could squirt a stream of water and knock insects into his range. He was seven dollars and irresistible.

Since he was only six inches long, Archie's black and white striped body presented a lonely and not very glamorous figure in the vast briny reaches of Bertha. But he performed splendidly and on cue: when a dab of wiggling brine shrimp was put on a stick and held over the tank, Archie would poke his long snout out of the water, let fly with a stream of water pellets at least a foot long and rarely miss his target. It was the more remarkable since his eyes were under water and allowance for the refraction had to be made. Sometimes he performed without cue. Once Veaudeen, the female cockateel, a bird full of curiosity, flew over and lit on the edge of the tank. Archie, attracted by the glitter of the bird's bright eye, quietly headed for the surface, upped periscope, fired and drenched the head of the most startled bird in the animal kingdom. Another time, when Dale's uncle was looking at the tank, Archie surfaced and, attracted by the glow of the cigarette in the man's mouth, shot a long stream and neatly extinguished it. Until one has actually seen an archerfish perform, one is inclined not to believe it. Once seen, however, it seems perfectly natural and practical, and one wonders why no other species of fish has learned the trick.

But even Archie could not extinguish the memories of the yellow surgeon, and I yearned for one. One day, out of the blue, the head of Steinhart Aquarium called me, said he had acquired another surgeon and since I had the perfect tank and wanted to try to breed them he would sell them to me. But I didn't have a hundred dollars and was forced to decline.

Two days later came a jubilant letter from Marcella saying I had sold a story. It was about a mousy man who murders his wife and thinks he has created the perfect crime when he gets rid of the corpus delicti by putting it down the disposal bit by bit. (But he has given her diamond ring to his mistress and in his absence she loses it down the disposal when doing the dishes. She calls a plumber who arrives while a detective is on the premises and the jig is up, the man being nailed for the right crime for the wrong reason.) It was imitative of Roald Dahl and John Collier, and Argosy gave me five hundred splendid dollars for it.

The yellow surgeons were in Bertha that same afternoon. They were stunning as they made their nervous flutterings and dartings about the tank. How beautiful they were, how happy they seemed in Bertha, how productive they soon would be! The following week many people came to observe and admire the surgeons, some of whom were total strangers. Sut came to advise on the best food and temperature for encouraging them to breed and was as excited as I at the possibility.

"They'll give you a whole article in Kelp 'n Coral if you pull it off," he said. "Then we'll try breeding Moorish idols."

We would at once be advancing science and getting rich. Let's see—there'd probably be about two hundred baby yellow surgeons and at fifty dollars apiece that would be. . . .

Then it came. It happened the night of February 18, at exactly five-thirteen in the morning.

Dale, a perennial burglar-listener, heard it first.

"What was that!" she whispered with dread, sitting up in bed.

"Nothing," I mumbled, "go back to . . ."

Then I heard it. I heard the noise—an unearthly, eerie, chilling sound. No words out of the typewriter could possibly describe it, but it was sort of like Whooooooomffffshhh-brackshhhhhh—the combination of cracking glass and gushing water, gallons and gallons of water exploding to freedom. To my horror I realized that Big Bertha had blowed out, and blowed out real good. We turned on the lights to a terrible sight. Bertha's front panel was a jagged hole. On the floor flopped one hundred and seven dollars in the form of three fish. I splashed across the floor, scooped them up and put them back in the shattered tank which still contained enough water in the bottom to keep them alive. Dale was wailing. I was cursing Sut, the piscine gods and myself as we splashed around the flat trying to get the water up in pails and with mops. The dawn came and we were still at it. Noon arrived before we could call a halt and collapse back to bed.

The carpet went to the Salvation Army, the surgeons went back to the Steinhart Aquarium, Bertha went back to Sut and I went back to work writing, abandoning my brief career as a breeder of fish.

I'm not sure exactly how it happened. For several years, ever since the first day that I met Manolete in Madrid, there had been a book germinating in my mind. I had thought of it again in Peru when I had seen him wanting to extract himself from his dangerous position as the top matador in the world. Then when he was killed in 1947 I saw how the story could end. But why it all suddenly came to a head inside me and demanded to be put down on paper I don't know. All I know is that one morning, almost as though compelled by some outside force, I put a sheet of paper in the typewriter and began to write: "A novel starting in the morning and ending at the end of the bullfight—just seven hours—no flashbacks, just every single thing that happens in that day, everything that happens in the fight, the character to be like Manolete, a loner, ugly, over the hill but unable to step down from being *El Número Uno*. Not a bad title . . ."

But I called it *A Day of Fear*, and I started to outline the chapters that day and once launched I could not stop writing. It was hard for me to sleep at night, the ideas tumbling from my brain, and many times I would awaken poor Dale, who was now very pregnant, by turning on the light and scribbling some phrase or detail. At the first sign of light I would get up and go into my studio and stay there all day.

For some reason the writing process was different than it had ever been. I seemed to have caught fire, a feverish compulsion that I'd never really felt before. When I sat at the typewriter I didn't ask myself "How would Hemingway phrase this or Fitzgerald or Sinclair Lewis?" but only what was the true and accurate and graphic way to say what I wanted to say. Day after day this exhilarating process went on.

In eight weeks the book was finished. I was exhausted, not so much from the labor as from having lived that terrible day so totally alone with my protagonist. I did not know how good a book it was, but I certainly felt that it was the best thing I had written. Dale thought it was, too. Confidently I sent it off to Marcella, who sent it on to Random House. The following week a wire came from the editor, Robert Linscott. I tore it open excitedly and read: VERY SORRY, NOT QUITE ENTHUSIASTIC ENOUGH ABOUT A DAY OF FEAR TO PUBLISH. RETURNING MANUSCRIPT.

This was the end.

The publishing house which had published my first novel and to whom I was under contract did not think enough of the work even to publish it. Then the disquieting and demeaning thought occurred to me: maybe they had published the first book only as a favor to their best-selling author, Sinclair Lewis.

Maybe Day of Fear was terrible, too terrible to be published as a hard-cover book. I had heard of a second-rate paperback firm that was looking for novels and might pay five hundred or even eight hundred dollars for mine. Of course that would be it—no further royalties. I was going to send it off, but Dale believed the book was better than that. "Why not get Jack's opinion?" she said.

Jack Leggett was the attractive man of my age whom we had met in Paris. He had tried writing a novel, disliked it, and returned to New York and into the Houghton Mifflin publishing house. I sent the manuscript to him, but with no real hope. A week later a wire came from the head of Houghton Mifflin, Paul Brooks: ABSOLUTELY DELIGHTED WITH YOUR NOVEL DAY OF FEAR. HOPE YOU WILL ALSO ILLUSTRATE IT. HOWEVER WITH YOUR PERMISSION WE WOULD LIKE TO CHANGE THE TITLE TO MATADOR. PLAN TO PUBLISH SOONEST. ONE THOUSAND DOLLARS ADVANCE ON ITS WAY TO YOU.

We were jubilant. The first thing I did was to buy a lot of licorice. I've always liked licorice and to be able to walk into the elegant Blum's candy emporium on Polk Street and say "a pound of that and a pound of that and two pounds of that" was a luxury beyond belief. A week later we were ecstatic and in the following weeks we were stunned with the miraculous wires that seemed to be never-ending. I have them framed on my wall in the order they arrived in:

READER'S DIGEST CONDENSED BOOKS OFFERS TWENTY THOUSAND DOLLARS ADVANCE FOR MATADOR. HOORAY—AND IT'S ONLY THE BEGINNING.

BOOK-OF-THE-MONTH-CLUB TAKES MATADOR—YOUR SHARE TWENTY-FIVE THOUSAND ADVANCE. IF YOU AIN'T A MAJOR WRITER YOU'LL DO TILL ONE COMES ALONG. THE BOOK IS TO BE FEATURED ON THE FRONT PAGE OF THE NEW YORK TIMES BOOK REVIEW AS WELL AS THE SATURDAY REVIEW. TIME MAGAZINE

GIVING IT TWO PAGES. CHARLES POORE IN DAILY NEW YORK TIMES GIVES ALL OUT RAVE, QUOTE STRIKINGLY EFFECTIVE . . . ONE OF THE NOTABLE BOOKS OF THE SEASON ETCETERA. VICTOR HASS CHICAGO TRIBUNE SAYS QUOTE WHAT A STORY THIS IS! IT IS MORE THAN A NOVEL ABOUT THE MAN—IT IS THE MAN . . . LIKE SOMETHING BY GOYA . . . OLÉ.

DELL PUBLISHING OFFERS YOU TWENTY-TWO THOUSAND DOL-LARS FOR PAPERBACK RIGHTS TO MATADOR. SINCE THIS IS THE HIGHEST PRICE EVER PAID FOR REPRINT RIGHTS YOUR PERIOD OF HESITATION SHOULD BE BRIEF.

MATADOR NOW NUMBER ONE BEST SELLER IN NATION. WE'RE ALSO SELLING RIGHTS IN ENGLAND, FRANCE, ITALY, GERMANY, ARGENTINA, HOLLAND AND SCANDANAVIA. ISN'T THIS A LOVELY BUSINESS—ONE KEEPS SELLING THE SAME PRODUCT OVER AND OVER YET YOU CONTINUE TO OWN IT!

And finally from José Ferrer:

JOHN HUSTON AND MY POSITION VERY SIMPLE. WE WISH TO BUY AND MAKE MATADOR INTO A FINE MOTION PICTURE WITH YOU DOING THE SCREENPLAY. WILL PAY ANY REASONABLE PRICE. CAN YOU COME TO HOLLYWOOD TO DISCUSS?

Success had come to little Barny Conrad, aged thirty, and all was unbelievably rosy. He had read in F. Scott Fitzgerald that success was something that nothing fails like.

But he didn't believe it. Not really.

The dust-jacket painting for Matador

CHAPTER 19

THE FIRST THING TO GO WAS THE MARriage. It all happened with incredible rapidity, all in the space of five or six weeks, a snowballing of events.

While I had been so busy playing the role of the big novelist, Dale had quietly put out a first edition of her own, a ten pound boy, B. C. III. I was elated but too full of myself and the extraordinary things that happen to one in America —and only in America—when one writes a best seller to give Dale and the event the proper attention. I would eventually become an attentive and appreciative father to four children, but right now my head was too filled with Big Ideas.

Tennessee Williams observed somewhere that when a marriage goes on the rocks the rocks can usually be found under the mattress. This wasn't the case with us. We were simply pulling and tugging in different directions. And of

Dale and B.C.III

course Dale's main shortcoming was that she stubbornly and willfully refused to turn magically into Betty Layne. Now more and more my thoughts returned to Betty. Where was she and how was she? A Christmas card I had surreptitiously sent her the previous year came back from Peru marked address unknown, but a mutual friend said he'd heard she was someplace in Southern California.

Dale's and my marriage had been shaky for some time. Both of us had tempers. And we hadn't learned the little marriage-saving catch phrases: "You may be right," in the midst of an argument; or "I love you but," to precede a criticism.

We were too quick to use those marriage-destroying words "never" and "always." ("You're *always* late" and "You *never* do anything to help.")

The baby and the home were all-important to Dale. She didn't need or want the excitement of people and the hullabaloo that *Matador* had stirred up in my life. She was grateful for the money that was pouring in, pleased with the new house we rented, but resentful of my having to be away so much, of the constant telephone calls from all sorts of strange types at strange hours and the unknown people who would suddenly appear at the door to get a book autographed or want me to lecture at such and such a luncheon. Even my friends at the drugstore and cleaners and market now treated me differently when I came in, with a stilted deference that made me uncomfortable. ("Well—you sure have become *quite* the celebrity!") At restaurants people who never before would have spoken to me now seemed under some compulsion to come over and do so. Usually they said nice things but sometimes they would merely say, "I've read your book" —no opinion either way—or "We've got your book," and just leave the statement lying there for me to answer while the food grew cold.

One day *Look* magazine moved into the house with a barrage of lights and cameras to do a big story on the happy home life of the author of the number one on the best-seller list. But before they could complete the story Dale had moved out and down to her parents' home with the baby after sad and angry scenes that I'm sure are indigenous, with very little variation in dialogue, to every domestic sundering.

"It never fails," sighed the editor assigned to write the article as they scrapped the project. "Fourth time it's happened to us."

Now I was free, loose of foot and far more shaken by the separation than I would realize for a long time. My first act was to purchase that time-honored badge of success in America, The Car. I knew little about automobiles, but I chose a secondhand custom built Mark IV Jaguar—gaudy, rare and frightfully expensive. On the way down to Hollywood to see John Huston I stopped at Santa Barbara and showed my new acquisition to my parents. My father studied the outsized headlights, the leather upholstery and the fruit wood paneling and its many gadgets. He shook his head.

"Looks like something designed over the telephone by Al Capone for his mistress," he said dryly.

He was impressed by writing as a career for the first time now when he saw the financial statements from my publishers, and he endorsed it still further when my mother, doing a *New York Times* crossword puzzle, suddenly exclaimed like a woman of Chaillot, "Sixty-three across—sixty-three across!" —brandishing the paper triumphantly. "Sixty-three across" required my name in the squares in answer to the text: "Author of *Matador*."

With me on the hegira to the south was Niels Mortensen, a fellow writer. We had met in the Café Goya three years before and with music (he played nine different instruments), books and tropical fish in common we had soon become great friends. Though Danish and brought up in Denmark, he had trained both as an engineer at M.I.T. and a writer-reporter on various American publications, newspapers and radio. I was relying heavily on his good judgment to help me through the Hollywood labyrinth, for I had read of many writers' fates in Lotusland and I was determined it wouldn't happen to me.

Niels and I checked in at The Garden of Allah, that fabled cottage hotel on Sunset Boulevard where Parker quipped, Benchley quenched, Flynn wenched and Fitzgerald expired. After a swim we went to TBA, the movie agents with whom I had signed a contract. They were housed in Beverly Hills in a pretentious building which tried desperately to resemble Tara. My particular agent was Ted Sheinbaum, who turned out to be a tweedy, pipe-smoking friendly fellow. When we were ushered into his thickly carpeted, book-lined, leathery office he got up from his desk, took Niels' hand in both of his and said "This is one of the great moments of my life."

"Er," said Niels gesturing to me, "*he* wrote the book."

With no loss of poise Sheinbaum revolved to me, took my hand and repeated the statement with embellishments.

"Never—I swear to you—never have I read such a book. *Such* a book! My wife would have to call me from the pool—'Ted, dinner! Dinner Ted!' 'Just a minute,' I'd say, 'just one more page, please one more page!' " He shook his head at the enormity of my achievement and looked deeply and sincerely into my eyes, still holding my hand. "And you wrote this book, this great book."

His hands were moist.

"A great work of art," he added solemnly. "*The Brave Bulls* should go into The Modern Library collection, a classic."

"*The Brave Bulls?*" I echoed.

Sheinbaum let go of my hand and struck his forehead with his fist.

"I mean *Matador!* I was just saying to someone how much better it was than *The Brave Bulls*, that's why I made such a stupid mistake."

He gestured to a chair and installed himself behind his desk.

"Now, let's talk a little business. This is the greatest property of the decade and we intend to see that you get a great big old pee-pot full of money for it. So—who do we sell it to?"

I looked startled. "I told you on the phone about John Huston and José Ferrer's telegram."

"Chicken feed," said Sheinbaum. He had a strange mannerism of seeming to take snuff—the index finger and thumb in conjunction going purposelessly to each nostril in turn at metronome intervals. "We've got some *real* offers!"

He rattled off some names of some big stars and directors who had been bidding for my book, all of them impressive but all of them totally wrong for the film in my opinion. The best team for the project, concluded Sheinbaum, was a popular matinee idol noted for his white teeth and inability to register or elicit any emotion whatsoever, a director whose films were slanted toward teen-agers and an aging ingenue whose bust measurement must have been a higher cipher than her I.Q. I'll call them Stolid Mann, Lazlo Puttee and Charlean Balloons, since they're all still around and doing their thing.

"I'm sorry, but I don't see them at all," I said. "Ferrer and Huston would be perfect."

"Sure they've got a big hit in *Moulin Rouge*," conceded Sheinbaum. "But Ferrer's really no sure draw in films and Huston's a wild Indian. You never know what he'll come up with. And he'll probably want to put that French actress in it and she's from nowhere. Now with Stolid and Charlean you've got great talent and great box office at the same time."

"But they can't act," I said. "I want to see a good film made more than I want a lot of money."

"Do you think I'm only interested in money?" Sheinbaum looked hurt. "Didn't you see *Fast Draw at Big Bend?*"

I had to admit I hadn't.

"Stolid was nominated for that one," he said, "and Charlean got raves. She's just never had the right vehicle—I swear she'll get an Oscar for *Matador*."

He talked for an hour about the virtues of his three favorites for *Matador* and he seemed so sure and so sincere in his admiration that he had me virtually won over by the time we left his office. After all, what did I know about the picture industry? We left full of brotherly love and with a date to meet the next morning with the stars and the director. Niels hadn't said anything in the office, not a word, but I noticed he was frowning as we drove back to the Garden of Allah.

"Maybe I was wrong about Ferrer and Huston," I said. "What do you think?"

"I think," he said slowly, "I think you are getting royally screwed."

"What—?"

"I can't put my finger on what or how or especially why,

but I know I wouldn't trust that guy as far as I could punt him."

"But why would he pull anything? He wants me to get the best deal possible—after all he receives ten percent of everything I get."

"I don't know. I just don't know."

Back at the hotel I ordered a couple of double Scotches as Niels nervously paced up and down.

"There's got to be a reason," he kept saying. Suddenly he snapped his fingers. He got the telephone and dialed my agents. Then "Hello, I'm calling for Dore Schary, that's right, over at MGM. Mr. Schary's planning a big picture for next year and he's wondering if you still handle Stolid Mann, Lazlo Puttee and Charlean Balloons. You do? Thank you— he'll contact you soon."

Niels hung up. "There's the answer! Simple—they don't handle Ferrer and Huston, but they do handle this other package. And they probably get much more than ten percent for their actors and directors, so to hell with their novelists."

"What do I do now? I'm under contract to them!"

"You've got to be protected from them."

"Fine thing—from my own agent I need protection."

"If we only knew a lawyer!"

I suddenly thought of Lou Blau, the air attaché I'd known in the Lima Embassy. I remembered he'd left Lima to return to his law practice in Beverly Hills. I looked him up in the telephone book and to my relief he was listed. He remembered me and congratulated me on the success of *Matador*. We reminisced for a while and he asked us for dinner at his house that night. After catching up on mutual friends, I explained my predicament.

"First thing is to get you away from your agents," he said.

"But I signed a contract," I said.

"Standard contract?"

"Yes."

"I know that contract pretty well and I'll break it in five minutes," Lou said, adding with a chuckle, "I drew it up for them five years ago. Next thing is to get you together with Huston and Ferrer."

Huston and Ferrer flew in from Paris that day, and Lou set up an appointment at Huston's Bel Air Hotel cottage for the next day. I was anxious about the meeting and had several drinks that evening to try to relax enough to go to sleep. I still had to take two sleeping pills and felt nervous and tired the next morning. To get myself aroused for the appointment I had a tall Scotch and soda and was a little startled to find myself putting my hangover Alka Seltzer into the drink.

"Let's do the drinking afterwards," said Niels. "Never celebrate before the deed."

"Just upholding literary tradition," I said. "Name me one great American writer from Edgar Allen Poe to Faulkner who didn't drink too much."

"Mary Baker Eddy," said Niels, taking the glass out of my hand.

We picked Blau up at his office and drove out Sunset toward the hotel. At a stoplight I saw a girl in a yellow cardigan and tweed skirt crossing the street. I couldn't see her face too well but there was something unique about the figure, the long legs, the bearing, the set of her shoulders ("only thing I ever won at school was the posture prize"). The brown hair was not so streaked with blond nor so long as I'd remembered it four years before, but there was no doubt that it was she. It was incredible. I stood up and yelled: "Betty!"

She turned but looked the wrong way. The light had changed and the cars behind me were honking.

"Garden of Allah!" I was able to yell before having to move on. I couldn't see whether she heard me or not.

"We've got to go around the block and catch her!" I said.

"No time for dalliance," Lou said. "We're late now."

But I drove around anyway. She had disappeared and I began to wonder if she were a figment of my hangover. So many incredible things had been happening in my life lately that it didn't seem too unreasonable that Betty should re-enter my life.

Huston's cottage was already full of people when we got there at ten o'clock. Actors, lawyers, agents. A bar was being operated briskly in one corner by Huston's constant companion, Jockey Billey Pearson, the subsequent winner of the "$64,000 Question" and the "$164,000 Challenge." A glamorous French actress was appropriately draped across the chaise lounge next to a jeroboam of champagne. Soon a tall man, a brown cigarette jutting from his big tan face and dressed in a Paisley dressing gown, emerged from a bedroom.

"I'm John Huston," he said with a great smile, "and I hope to hell you sell us that fine book of yours."

Huston's charm has been written of many times and none of the writings have exaggerated it. We drank and talked for several hours, not of terms ("Let the lawyers handle it—there'll be no problems"), but of how we would translate my novel into the film medium. The only point we differed on was that Huston thought we should start with the protagonist in the arena and flash back to the events of the day ("After all it's Greek tragedy you've written"). I felt that we would lose some suspense since there is some doubt throughout the first part of the story as to whether he'll even get to the arena. But John was reasonable, articulate and skilled, and I enjoyed our meeting immensely. José Ferrer joined us after lunch; he, too, was charming and a pleasure to deal with. They invited me to the premiere of *Moulin Rouge* that night and set a date for the next day for more talk. The liquor did not stop flowing all day but no one appeared to be particularly affected by it.

When Niels and I got back to the hotel Betty was in the lobby. We didn't kiss or even speak. We just held hands and looked at each other. Then she crumpled in my arms in tears. When she could speak she said, "I heard you got married."

"Yes," I said.

"You know," she said, taking my handkerchief and blowing her nose, "one of these days you're just going to go too far."

The next day after another long and rather hectic session with Huston and Ferrer, Betty and I went to a real-estate office in Malibu and rented a little cottage isolated from the rest of the houses. Niels had to go back to San Francisco the next week so I decided to drive up with him and pick up some of my belongings. Also I wanted to get a brief respite from the pressures. Too much had happened all at once. I found I could get no sleep at all unless I took vast quantities of alcohol and then to quiet my nerves the next day I took more alcohol and pills. Soon I found I was getting dizzy spells and could get no sleep no matter what I took. Betty was worried about me and agreed that I should get away from Hollywood for a few days. My brother Hunt had married a fine girl whom we'd grown up with in Burlingame, and he and his wife had a ranch three hours from San Francisco. I invited myself there for the weekend; their little house on the river at Knight's Ferry was just what I needed, I was sure. But still I was so wound up I kept up the drinking and pill taking.

After I'd been there one day I started to crack up. Hunt was up at the barn when this awful sensation started coming over me. I moved from the kitchen to the living room as a murky numbness came over me.

"Something terrible is happening to me," I muttered to my brother's wife, Marion.

"What is it?" she asked, after a look at the weird expression on my face.

"I feel—I feel as though I were going down a drain," I said. "I feel unless I break something I'll go crazy. Can't help it . . ."

I picked up a phonograph record, broke it with my fist and felt temporarily better. I broke several records as Marion looked at me in terror. When the records ran out I started breaking the windows.

"I'm sorry," I remember saying as calmly as I could. "I'll replace all the records and the windows—but I'll go mad otherwise."

She fled out the door to get my brother while I broke every window in the house with my fist. I cut myself on the last pane and that seemed to bring me to my senses. Just then Hunt charged in the door.

"You bastard, you've wrecked my house!" he said and knocked me down.

I apologized and tried to explain as best I could what had been happening to me. I suddenly felt infinitely better. After a long cold shower I dressed, made arrangements with a glazier to repair the windows and returned to San Francisco where I spent the night with Niels and his wife. I was convinced that if I could just get one good night's sleep I would be all right. But again I tossed and turned in spite—or probably because of—several glasses of Scotch and a sleeping pill. I took endless cold showers but nothing helped. Around five in the morning I felt it coming on me again—that horrible maelstrom whirling me around at an ever-increasing speed, a sickening vortex threatening to suck me down a giant drain. I dressed and without waking the Mortensens I drove toward the nearest hospital. I knew I was going mad, knew I had to get help and get it very fast. Yet it was similar to when you have to go to the bathroom very urgently: you don't dare run too quickly. I had to keep myself under strict control, just hold out till I got there—I didn't dare drive too fast. As calmly as I could I walked up the hospital steps, holding myself rigidly. The only doctor I knew in the place was Dale's pediatrician and luckily I bumped into him in the lobby.

"Dr. Marsh," I said in measured tones, "I am very very sick. I am losing my mind. I need to sleep desperately."

He smiled reassuringly and ushered me to an elevator. That's the last I remember. I was told later I went beserk, was giving a massive hypo and was taken in a strait jacket to a sanitarium thirty miles from San Francisco. There I spent a week manacled to a bed and raving while the doctors argued about what to do with me.

The distinguished neurologist that my brother and mother engaged recommended that I be given shock treatments immediately. But Dale, as my legal wife, had to give her consent. She had her psychiatrist examine me. Afterward he said he was against the shock treatments.

"He needs deep analysis," he reported to my brother.

"How can you analyze somebody who's so far gone he doesn't even know who he is or where he is?"

"The last case I saw like this," the analyst said gloomily,

"sat in a darkened room for two years playing with himself. Analysis brought him around."

Of course I was unaware of the conflict going on about my condition. On some days I had some brief, fluttering moments of lucidity when I wondered where I was and why I was manacled to the bed. But then I would drift off into the milky void and hallucinations of the insane. When the male nurses would unshackle me to feed me, I would accuse them of trying to poison me and throw the food at them.

Finally the neurologist threatened to pull off the case.

"It's a clear-cut case of alcohol and barbiturate poisoning," he said, "and shock will get him out of it."

Dale gave her consent at last. I was wheeled into the treatment area, the cathodes were attached to my head and the current turned on. I went into the room a maniac and half an hour later came out rational, asking the conventional "Where am I?" and "How'd I get here?" I stayed two more weeks in the sanitarium, then returned to Malibu and Betty in good shape. But it would be more than three years before I could take a drink and I have never taken a pill since. It must have been a more ghastly experience than I am able to convey now, but time has conveniently drawn a film over most of it for me.

I found that while I'd been on my hallucinatory voyage the real world had gone on quite satisfactorily without me. The contracts for the film, with me to do the screenplay, were ready to be signed: *Matador* had gone into five more languages (making sixteen); Houghton Mifflin wanted to send me to Spain to regather the bullfighting photos and rewrite *La Fiesta Brava*, which had been lost in the taxi, and several magazines wanted articles. And there was the crowning success of all: *Saturday Review* had asked a dozen distinguished writers to pick their favorite book of the previous year and John Steinbeck had picked *Matador*. I wrote him a letter, though I had never met him, to express my deep appreciation. He wrote back a long warm letter in which he said in part: "I like bullfights, because to me it is a lonely, formal, anguished microcosm of what happens to every man, sometimes even in an office strangled by the glue on envelopes. In the bull ring he survives for awhile—sometimes."

He concluded by saying that he and his wife were going to the Virgin Islands and "after Spain wouldn't you and your wife like to come join us for a few weeks?"

I took him up on the generous offer with unconscionable alacrity.

Betty's father was ill so she couldn't come to Spain with me for the three weeks of research, but we made plans to be married as soon as I returned and could conclude the divorce proceedings. I barely made Spain myself, since when I went to get a ticket the airlines said it was strictly on a standby basis.

"The Eucharistic Congress in Barcelona," explained the clerk.

I finally got on a plane but was only assured of passage as far as Lisbon. The plane was filled with priests. I sat down next to a plump cardinal.

"The Spanish refer to it as the Black Olympics," he said to me pleasantly. I recognized him as Cardinal Spellman. I introduced myself and we had a pleasant chat as we crossed the Atlantic. He said he had enjoyed my book and would send me a copy of his novel, *The Foundling* (which he subsequently did).

Even my eminent seatmate could not keep me from being

bounced off the plane when it stopped at Lisbon. But I thought it would be no problem to get to Spain.

"No space for four days," I was informed. Same with the trains and buses.

But I had to be in Madrid the next day as Belmonte and others had set up various appointments for me with newspaper editors, photographers and publishers. So, I jauntily strode out of the Lisbon airport with my suitcase, hailed the first cab I saw, an ancient, square, high affair several decades old, and got in. The car was sort of The African Queen of automobiles.

"Where to?" asked the chauffeur, who sported a guardsman's mustache above his rodential mouth. I savoured the moment.

"Madrid," I said.

How often does one have the delicious opportunity of telling a taxi driver in the capital city of one country to take you to the capital city of another country?

"Sim, Senhor," he replied brightly. Then the double take and his head swiveled around. "Madrid!" Did I know the trip would take fifteen hours? Did I know it would cost one hundred and fifty dollars? And did I know he would have to go home and ask his wife and get his passport?

We chugged off to his modest house and he went in. A few minutes later he emerged with a great hulk of a man. With his size and his golf cap he resembled Victor Maclaglen in The Informer.

"My wife says I can't go," said the chauffeur, "but Manoel, my brother-in-law, he will take you just as good as me."

Manoel smiled a big Lennie-like smile and installed himself behind the wheel of the car, clutching it as though it were the shoulders of someone he was about to shake violently.

He blew the old vehicle's horn—cayooooga—in farewell and we started off with a series of jerks. I had no reading matter, but I consoled myself that at least for the next fifteen hours I would be able to practice my Portuguese.

"*E um bonito dia,*" I started tentatively.

Manoel didn't answer.

I tried again louder. He didn't answer and he didn't turn around. I leaned forward and tapped him on the shoulder. He turned around with a big smile, nodding pleasantly; he was a deaf mute.

It would be a quiet ride for the next fifteen hours, though occasionally I would burst into song simply to hear a friendly voice. But it was a good time to think, something I had not done much of for some time.

"You should write more about other things than bull-fighting," Herb Caen, "Mr. San Francisco," had advised me.

"You should write more about Los Angeles," I snapped back. But he was right.

How about a novel about Sinclair Lewis? There was certainly a book in him. And what about a play? And a book on San Francisco. And there was Tahiti—a question mark in my life that I would dearly love to resolve. Maybe Betty and I should go live there for a couple of years after the Virgin Islands and I could write a book on it. What about creating a really attractive bistro with a good pianist, fancier than the Goya; could be called El Matador. There was the movie to look forward to (though little did I know that Mr. Huston would hold the rights for years and never make it. It still has not been filmed!).

The future looked good now. And so did the present as the beautiful Portuguese landscape and the colorfully dressed farmers swept by. But being driven by a deaf mute? How had he ever obtained a driver's license, if indeed he had one?

Suddenly we swung around a corner and there in front of us was a giant sow lying in the road suckling her offspring. Skillfully Manoel swung the wheel, applied the brakes and we screeched to a halt. Manoel cayooogaed several times and the pig ambled off the road dragging several of the hungrier piglets.

Manoel turned with his good toothy smile and made the "okay" sign with thumb and index finger. I made it back to him, and we lurched off again toward the land of Don Quixote de la Mancha. I settled back in the seat and closed my eyes: Manoel was a good driver and we would get to Madrid eventually and Betty was waiting back in California. And for the moment, everything was fine, just fine.

A LAST CHAPTER

FOR SOME REASON, THE RETURN TO MADRID seemed to mark the end of a period in my life, though I am not sure why. Perhaps the border I crossed was not only geographic, but also the one that marks the line between youth and beginning maturity.

"And then," says Malraux's priest friend after fifteen years of hearing confessions, "the fundamental fact is that there's no such thing as a grown-up person . . ."

There would be more, lots more, but it all somehow seems "another story," as Mr. Kipling was wont to say. I wouldn't have missed those years of adventure for anything, but I do not desire to go back or give up what I have now, which has other rewards.

Manoel and the taxi and I did wheeze into Madrid, finally, and in time for the press conference. How different Madrid was to me now than the day—was it almost ten years before?

—when I had arrived gaping at the exotic city and had nervously telephoned Sidney Franklin. Now things were changed. Now there was responsibility. I was forced to do other things than to simply follow my own private joys. Instead of my seeing Madrid it was as if it were the other way around. Although the great Belmonte attended the press gathering in my hotel, it seemed, rather embarrassingly, as if the reporters were more interested in what I, as the new spokesman for the *fiesta brava* of the non-Latin world, had to say about the present state of bullfighting and the new crop of toreros.

I got through the subsequent interviews and in two weeks completed my photograph gathering for the new book. After fighting in an exhibition fight with Belmonte, I returned home to Betty, waiting at the Malibu beach cottage in California. But Thomas Wolfe was right; we just couldn't seem to pick up where we had left off so long ago. I kept telling myself how lucky I was—not many men get second chances in their lives. But Betty and I had grown to be two different people than we had been as teen-agers or at the college age or in our year in Peru together. We didn't quarrel and there were no scenes, and we made love. But there was an unspoken thing, an excessive politeness, a tense feeling in the air. I kept seeing Dale's beautiful hurt face and hearing accusing voices; I wondered what the baby looked like after these many months and who it resembled. I kept asking myself: how hard *had* I worked at making the marriage work?

As I had done so many times before, I decided that a geographic change would solve things. I left Betty and joined John Steinbeck and his lovely wife Elaine in the Virgin Islands. It was a pleasant and privileged couple of weeks

Dale

in their stimulating company. But I was restless and troubled, and one day I just packed up and flew back to San Francisco and Dale. We second-honeymooned in Mexico.

During the next years, in addition to fathering a charming big-eyed girl whom we named Cayetana after Goya's Duchess of Alba, and another fine son, Winston, I tried to achieve some of the things I had resolved to do during that ridiculous taxi ride to Madrid. I would write from nine till noon, in my Telegraph Hill studio, and paint portraits or still lifes until six. And I also kept my projects. Some worked out, some didn't, a rather common formula with almost everyone, I have discovered, as I totter on the brink of maturity.

"If one project in ten that you attempt turns out as you hoped," Sinclair Lewis had remarked once, "count yourself a lucky man. Not recognizing this basic fact of life has led a lot of people to despondency and ultimate failure."

One project that worked out was El Matador. In 1953 my editor from Boston was visiting us in regard to *La Fiesta Brava* which I had just finished. After dinner he remarked that he'd like to go to "an attractive bar and listen to a good piano." I had to answer that there was no such thing in San Francisco. "Why don't you start one?" he said, half seriously.

I lay awake thinking about it that night. I personally found most bars and night clubs so garish and uninviting— why not a truly chic and comfortable one, a place where attractive and interesting people could congregate? The next day I took $35,000 from the money the novel had made, bought an old Mexican dance hall near the Barbary Coast district and Niels Mortensen and I set about to reconvert it into an elegant bar with a bullfighting motif. We put original Goya etchings and a Picasso drawing and beautiful bullfighting costumes and capes on the walls. We designed

Life-size oil of Manolete in El Matador

a fine piano bar—stools around a grand piano, surely the first in the West—and we set a large glass cage in the wall for four spectacular macaws. In six weeks the place was transformed and we were almost ready to open.

But something unforeseen happened: as I painted away in El Matador, desperately trying to finish the mural before our big opening, I was approached by a swarthy and furtive little man carrying a large box. He said he'd heard I liked unusual pets. He put the box on the bar, and when he slid the lid off out stepped what was unquestionably the most magnificent bird I had ever seen. It was an iridescent blue macaw, a giant creature—almost four feet long from its beak to the tip of its tail—with a round head and a mocking black eye encircled with bright yellow—a caricature of a bird.

"Hello there!" he said to me, with impeccable diction. "Macgregor here!" Gently he held out a claw for me to shake and I swear his great black beak smiled. It was love at first sight, the only bird I had ever seen that was a match in personality for the hapless Benito I had lost so many years before when I was at Yale.

"I've had Macgregor since he fell out of his nest at my feet in the Brazilian jungle," said the man, looking over his shoulder uneasily. "He's just like a brudder to me. He's the only hyacinthine macaw in America, wort' at least twelve hunnert, but I'll let you have him for eight hunnert 'n fifty."

Attributing the man's nervousness to his reluctance to part with his pet, I quickly wrote out a check before he could change his mind. The man patted his brudder a hasty good-by and departed. A few days later an official-looking man in a trench coat arrived at El Matador, ordered me down from the scaffold where I was painting and showed me his

FBI credentials. He pointed at Macgregor, happily swinging from a horn of the mounted bull's head, and explained the bird's true origin. It seemed I had dealt with Rodzima, the head of a gang of five which had smuggled in an incredible half-million dollars worth of parrots and macaws from South America the previous year. With the birds anesthetized in special compartments under the floor boards of trucks or in clever false trays under chicken crates, they got their wares past the guards along the Mexican border. Because of their beauty and rarity, the Brazilian government itself would not let the birds out of the country, so they had had to be smuggled twice over at least two borders. Once in the States, pet shops and zoos eagerly bought the rare birds. The FBI man assured me that Macgregor was indeed worth at least twelve-hundred dollars. Rodzima knew the FBI was closing in on him, so he had come to me rather than risk going to the more lucrative markets.

"It's legal to have parrots once they're in California," said the FBI man, "but not if we know how and where it was smuggled in. We marked your macaw with infrared ink before it even left Brazil and we've been on its trail ever since. Got to confiscate it."

I felt the same sick feeling in my stomach that I had felt when the Connecticut officials had taken Benito from me.

"Don't look so sad," he said, handing me a subpoena. "We'll let you keep the bird—if you show up in court in San Diego on the second of the month, turn state's evidence and identify Rodzima."

"But that's the day we open this place," I exclaimed. "There are a thousand invitations out, TV cameras, newspapers—"

"Then it's bye-bye birdie," he said, turning to leave.

"Wait—" I said, I'll be there!"

The life-size painting of Manolete was framed and up on the wall, but the thirty-by-thirteen foot mural of the Sevilla bull ring was only half finished, even though Niels was painting frantically on one side and I on the other. Nevertheless I was forced to abandon the work to fly with Macgregor to San Diego, six hundred miles away. The prosecution had me make a grand entrance past the jurors with the macaw on my shoulder so they could finally comprehend why people paid such prices for the birds and how the smugglers had turned their efforts into a half-million-a-year industry. Once on the stand, Macgregor created havoc by leaving me, flying to the judge's bench and, with the gavel in his beak, imitating the judge's pounding. Then when I was asked to identify Rodzima as the man who had sold me the bird I picked out an innocent witness for the State by mistake! There was a hubbub in the courtroom.

"Mr. Conrad forgot his glasses," said the lawyer, hastily handing me his and hissing, "The defendants are over there!"

I finally fingered the right man, the court saw that the smugglers got five years, the FBI gave me permanent custody of Macgregor and I flew back to San Francisco, arriving two hours before the opening of El Matador.

When the people started coming through the door the liquor hadn't even arrived and I was still up on a ladder finishing the mural, but El Matador was an instant hit. It was a far cry from the humble Café Goya. A New York columnist called it "the most attractive room in America" which sent droves of tourists to us.

In the beginning people came because it was a pleasant place to go before or after dinner, and then as it increased in popularity they came to look at the celebrities who came

there. One never was quite sure who would be in El Matador;
I remember one night we hosted the unlikely potpourri of
Noel Coward, Charles Addams, Henry Fonda, Marilyn
Monroe, Ronald Reagan and champion bronc rider Casey
Tibbs (none together). Another time it was Sinatra,
Hermione Gingold, Zsa Zsa Gabor and William Randolph
Hearst, Jr. Tyrone Power came in with Charlton Heston and
drank to the mounted bull's head which came from his film,
Blood and Sand. When I admired his handsome gold cuff
links, he took them off and gave them to me: people did
things like that in those days.

Then I used to look forward to going there in the evenings,
seeing old friends and meeting new ones. We had an excellent piano player, but I enjoyed relieving him, secure in the
knowledge that here, unlike Lima, no one could fire me.
Piano stars enjoyed stopping by and playing for fun—Fatha
Hines, Duke Ellington, Art Tatum, George Shearing, Andre
Previn—and I listened to them with awe. Niels took care of
the business and personnel problems during the day, while I
wrote and painted portraits. Over the next years I did hundreds of portraits and wrote several more books on bullfighting and bullfighters. I did a big profile on San Francisco
and plotted a novel based loosely on Sinclair Lewis.

One day in 1958 I was looking at some still photos of
Manolete taken in the arena a few seconds apart. An idea
came to me gradually. I looked again. I gathered together
some other photos, taken on another occasion, but of approximately the same maneuver. It suddenly occurred to
me that if one took a motion picture camera and moved the
camera across this series of stills, dissolving smoothly from
one to the other, one could not only give the illusion of
motion, but one might even create a separate art not strictly

belonging to either the world of still photography or of motion pictures. I found a group of audience shots to which we could cut away from the action. Now: supposing one added crowd noises and the band playing, as we panned across these faces—wouldn't these pictures come alive if we kept the camera always moving?

The afternoon Manolete was killed there was only one motion picture camera taking pictures and when the terrible goring occurred, the man knocked over the camera, it fell open and the film was ruined. Why couldn't I re-create the fatal day on film with the hundreds of stills I had and with this new technique I had in mind?

I talked to several people in the motion picture and television business. They laughed at the idea. Even Niels, usually enthusiastic about my projects, tried to visualize it but finally shook his head and said, "The essence of moving pictures is the fact that, as the name implies, they move. Why use movies to show a bunch of still pictures? It'll never work."

At that time *Omnibus* was unquestionably the most artistic, varied and esteemed show on television. With no real hope I telephoned Robert Saudek and Alistair Cooke in New York and discussed putting my idea on their program. I stammered in my eagerness to describe what no words could really convey.

"I don't quite understand what you plan to do," said Saudek finally, "but we'll take a chance if it's only going to cost us $1,000."

I gathered up eight hundred fine stills, put them in order to tell the whole story of Manolete's life and last fight, and wrote a narration for it. A San Francisco film maker, Dave Butler, saw instantly what I was trying to do, and together we shot the photos. We moved in on some, pulled back from others, dissolved, lap dissolved, cut, panned, zoomed, jiggled, vibrated and even spun some of the photos to get the effects we wanted, all to a carefully timed narration. We added a guitarist playing a score I wrote, plus sound effects, and after two months we had it perfected. *Omnibus* was delighted with the results. "I still can't figure out how it was done," said Alistair Cooke as he introduced it on the air. "But it is wonderful."

They ran it not once but three times during the next year. It was nominated for an Oscar, won awards in several film festivals abroad, and is still playing in theaters all over the world. Using the same technique I made short films on the San Francisco earthquake, the Wright brothers and the assassination of John F. Kennedy. It is a technique now seen everywhere, much abused by TV commercials, film titles and historical films. Oh, to have been able to patent the process!

I had always been intrigued with motion pictures. When I was thirteen a group of us borrowed a camera, begged some film and shot a ten-minute epic entitled *The End of Rasputin*, starring me in a horrendous red beard. Therefore I was very sympathetic when a twenty-two-year-old would-be film maker came to me and said he wanted to make a feature film version of Steinbeck's classic short story about a Mexican family near Monterey, *Flight*. I helped him get Steinbeck's permission and also tried to raise the $90,000 he said he needed to make the film. Although he had never made a complete motion picture, I saw some of his footage and he had great talent. I will call him Orson, for that is the way he thought of himself. I was pleased that he looked like a great director, a cross between Frankenheimer, Kazan and Kramer. It was an obsession with him to make this story. Finally,

Orson found a noted San Francisco financier who said he would not put up the first money but would double whatever was put up. Orson convinced me that if I put up nearly all the cash I had, $45,000, a week later I would have it back and would be the producer of this great film. Reader, I did it. And the great philanthropist reneged on his offer. Now I was stuck. We formed a little company and I raised the rest of the money from friends and gave it to Orson. The movie, he assured me, would be finished in less than three months. Secure in the knowledge that we were producing another *Citizen Kane*, and not wishing to interfere in the creative process, I wished him luck and left for the place I'd always dreamed of going to—Tahiti.

Somehow it wasn't quite the way I had imagined going to Tahiti when I was a youth. I didn't leap off the top of a schooner's mast as we came into the harbor and swim into the arms of a luscious *vahine* the way that Jon Hall did in the film, *The Hurricane*. The island didn't disappoint—it was even more beautiful than I expected—but I arrived sedately on board the luxury liner Monterey with Dale, the governess and our three children.

Tahiti was full of characters and full of joy. We spent our languorous days eating breadfruit and *poisson cru*, skin diving in the lagoon in front of our thatched house, teaching the children to swim at the base of a waterfall, sailing to Moorea with Sterling Hayden on the majestic schooner *Wanderer*, watching the endless parade on the road—including Gauguin's son—and going native, in general. There was no radio, no newspaper, no airport, no neon, no PTA, no crime and, seemingly, no problems. If it hadn't been for the movie we might never have left; Dale and I had never been so happy. Three months flew by and we left with tears and leis, vowing to our many new friends to return the next summer.

Gauguin's son, Emile

The very day we arrived in San Francisco I arranged to meet with Orson to see our film, *Flight*. We went to a screening room, the lights darkened and the film came on. Pepe, the young Mexican kid, had just knifed a brute in a bar in Monterey and in an effective moonlight scene he sobbingly told his mother about it in their little shack by the sea. "You must run to the mountains," she said. "Here, take your dead father's rifle." It was beautifully filmed and the faces were perfect. I had just settled back to enjoy the movie when the lights went on.

"Great," I said to Orson, "put on the next reel."

"That's it," he said.

"But that was only seven or eight minutes," I said. "A feature has to be at least eighty."

He explained to me that he'd had bad weather for months and had kept hoping the fog would lift to shoot the escape into the mountains, "the dark watchers," the posse, the wild animals the boy encounters and the rest. He also cleared his throat and said he'd run a bit over the budget—about $20,000 worth in credit, in equipment rentals, in film stock —and in my name. I understood, didn't I? The weather had recently cleared and they would now go great guns.

All I understood was that I was stuck for the additional money, that I didn't have it, and that I was in terrible trouble. We somehow raised some more money, but a month later Orson still hadn't produced much usable film. We now had about $130,000 sunk into a motion picture of which only about fifteen minutes had been shot. The little company of investor-friends I had lured into this dubious venture voted to oust Orson. I acquiesced reluctantly since the whole idea had been his originally, but finally we brought in a new director. Orson, his dream of creating a classic film masterpiece shattered, went a little wild, appropriated all the film that had been shot, plus all the scripts, threatened suicide and then went East to tell every magazine film critic who would listen how we had abused him and taken his baby away from him.

We now had no film, no script and huge rental obligations for cameras, sound equipment, horses, hawks, mountain lions and rattlesnakes. The stockholders were grumbling, people were demanding that bills be paid, and the director and crew were standing by in a very costly fashion on location below Monterey. We had to come up with a finished movie and fast. But we didn't even have a script. In my zeal to remain aloof from Orson's creative process I had not even read Steinbeck's original story. I found a copy of *The Long Valley*, the book it appears in, read it before breakfast, scribbled off a scene on the airplane to Monterey and handed it to the director at the airport. He shot it that afternoon. Five weeks and $100,000 later he had a finished picture; how good a picture we didn't know, but it was a picture. The great guitarist Laurindo Almeida did a beautiful score for it and we sent it off timidly to the Edinburgh Film Festival. To our surprise and joy they accepted it and designated it the official U.S. entry, beating out a Walt Disney candidate. We polished up the best print possible and I was selected to take it to Scotland. The day before I was scheduled to be at the festival, the lawyer for our company called a meeting and pointed to a small clause in our agreement with Steinbeck: the author had to approve of the film in writing before it could be shown anywhere.

In a panic we telephoned Steinbeck in Sag Harbor, Long Island. Could he possibly see the film the next day on my way through Manhattan to Scotland? No—he wasn't well enough to come in to New York, but there was a little theater in Sag Harbor if I would bring the film there. I arrived the next morning in New York, and since the only train had left for Sag Harbor, I took a hundred dollars worth of taxi ride to the theater where the bear-like Steinbeck and his wife awaited me. The three of us sat alone there as the theater went dark and the film began. For an hour he didn't say a word, only occasionally sighing as he watched the creatures of his imagination flit across the screen. I squirmed and kept sneaking looks at his goateed face, wondering what he was thinking, trying to gauge what the occasional frown or neck tugging portended. How childish my dialogue suddenly sounded, how amateurish the acting. Finally he spoke. As he watched a tight close-up of the wounded, fleeing, frightened Mexican boy creep slowly around the weather-beaten boards of a deserted shack, Steinbeck cleared his throat. He cleared it again. I tensed. He leaned over to me and I leaned toward him eagerly. He patted me on the arm.

"Good texture," he rasped, "good wood texture."

I sank back into my seat. I sweated out the final twenty minutes. The lights came on. We left the theater and drove in silence to the Steinbeck's rambling house. John immediately retired to his study.

"How did he like it?" I whispered to Elaine.

She shrugged sympathetically. "Who knows?"

A few moments later Steinbeck appeared and handed me a piece of paper. It read: "This film has tremendous quality, great simplicity of approach, and I found it moving—deeply moving." He broke out the champagne and we toasted happily to wood texture. The movie received fine reviews at Edinburgh as well as at the London and other film festivals, and Columbia agreed to distribute it. But for reasons not clear to me it has not gone into general release and has not made back any of its $248,000 cost. This was my first and last venture into film producing.

Perhaps wiser and certainly grayer, I went back to writing, was commissioned to do a book on Tahiti, and returned joyously with my family to that island for another few months. This time, besides the obvious blandishments of Tahiti, Bora Bora and Moorea, I had the pleasure of the added purpose of trying to learn the language and history of those glamorous islands. Back in San Francisco, besides the Tahiti book I managed to finish *Dangerfield*, the first novel I'd dared attempt since *Matador*. It dealt with a fading famous writer, not unlike Sinclair Lewis, and his mistress, and was later made into a Broadway play. (Duration: one night.)

Dale and I never got along better than during our times in Tahiti, perhaps because of the lack of outside pressures and people. But back in San Francisco in less exotic surroundings we didn't fare as well, what with my hectic work schedule, the nightly demands of El Matador and a lack of mutual friends. To add to our drawing apart, Dale plunged into the world of higher mathematics which I couldn't begin to share. Then it was horses. She developed a crush on horses the way a fourteen-year-old girl does, culminating in her finally moving to Woodside, an equine community thirty miles away from San Francisco where one can hardly hear oneself talking for the neighing. There she could be closer to her palomino jumper, ride to the hounds and only dismount long enough to go to a horse show.

One day I discovered Mary Nobles Slater on a tennis court. She was a tall, tawny, glamorous divorcee of twenty-seven with two children. After Dale and I were divorced in 1962, Mary and I were married. She is the kind of girl who goes

Mary

along with a man anywhere, and in the last seven years she has been to Mexico with me four times, multiple times to Spain, France, London and Bora Bora (including a wild expedition to Cannes sponsored by the man who invented Beethoven sweatshirts to secure Picasso's permission to reprint a drawing of his on a blouse!). Mary plays first class tennis and bridge, is a professional decorator, a conscientious mother, is unbelievably well-organized and is such a great cook that I have put on twenty pounds. She also likes bull-fights even more than I, and last summer in Spain, when after seeing twenty fights in a row I 'lowed as how maybe we should knock off a day, she threatened to go alone.

That same trip I achieved a giant step toward maturity. Since my days in Lima I had fought bulls only twice—once killing a bull at Arruza's ranch in Mexico in 1956, and once getting terribly gored in Spain in 1958. On this trip when invited to take part in an exhibition corrida with some other aging toreros, my heart leapt and I started to accept. Then I thought about it and finally declined. (Was it maturity or merely cowardice?) I have finally arrived at the point where I don't have to fight bulls, I don't feel driven to fight bulls, I don't want to fight bulls; I would rather watch my four year old daughter skate than fight a bull. While it lasted it was fine, but I have other toys now.

And I firmly believe that one of the secrets of feeling alive and young is to have toys. Whether the toys are pets, hi-fi sets, golf, Sunday painting, wood carving, water skiing, flying, skiing, acquiring a new language, gardening, surfing, or what-ever, they can be very important to the lives of us grownups. I have tried all the above activities at various times and many I keep up. But I'm always acquiring new toys. I discovered tennis at forty and am a fanatic—an inept one, but no less fanatic for that. My newest toy is Wardian cases. A Wardian case is a bottle garden named after a chap in England who discovered a hundred years ago that you can cork up a little garden in a big bottle, have it create its own atmosphere—its own clouds and rain storms—so that it doesn't have to be watered more than once a year or so. It is challenging and as maddening as constructing a ship in a bottle, but the results are satisfying and decorative. Our house is filled with these terrariums. I have many such toys to keep life amusing which, in my salad days, I might have scoffed at.

One is collecting last words, of which I have some 1300. (It's easy—you just go to a library, take down all the biographies and read the last chapter!) For example, did you know that the noted French grammarian Dominique Bouhours said upon his deathbed: "I am dying—or I am about to die—either expression is correct." Or that William Palmer, an English poisoner, upon being led to the gallows and told to step out on the trap, quavered: "D'you think it's safe?"

And Lady Mary Wortley Montague, just before she expired, remarked: "It's all been very interesting!" I can think of no more apt epitaph for the years I have lived nor a better wish for the years I have yet to live.

About the Author

BARNABY CONRAD was born in San Francisco in 1922. He attended the California School of Fine Arts, Cate, Taft, the University of North Carolina, the University of Mexico, the Académie Julien in Paris, and graduated from Yale. Since then he has worn an appalling number of hats: muralist, portrait painter, novelist, biographer, diplomat, filmmaker, journalist, bull fighter, teacher, lecturer, restaurateur, chess opponent and secretary to Sinclair Lewis, tropical fish breeder, playwright, and pianist in a Peruvian night club, to name a few. Although he has sold his famous night club, El Matador, in San Francisco, he maintains a studio nearby in the old Barbary Coast district, and lives not far away with his wife and children and pet fox in a hundred-year-old Victorian house. He has written for most of the magazines of America since his first sale to *Esquire* in 1945, has translated three books, and written twelve others. His novel *Matador* sold some two and a half million copies and has been translated into eighteen languages. His hobbies range from making miniature rooms to skin-diving.